ON THIN ICE

MICK FOWLER

ON THIN ICE

ALPINE CLIMBS IN THE AMERICAS
ASIA AND THE HIMALAYA

Foreword by
CHRIS BONINGTON

BÂTON WICKS · LONDON

Also by Mick Fowler
VERTICAL PLEASURE

On Thin Ice is published in Great Britain in 2005 by Bâton Wicks Publications, London
1 3 5 7 9 8 6 4 2

All trade enquiries in to: Cordee 3a De Montfort Street, Leicester LE1 7HD

British Library Cataloguing in Publication Data
ISBN 1-898573-58-1

Printed and bound in Great Britain by T.J.International, Padstow
Colour origination by MRM Graphics, Winslow

ACKNOWLEDGEMENTS Thanks and appreciation are due to: my family – Nicki, Tess and Alec Fowler; to the late Alan Rouse for his inspiration; to my climbing partners – Chris Watts, Pat Littlejohn, Steve Sustad, the late Brendan Murphy, Andy Cave, Simon Yates, Mark Garthwaite, Noel Craine, Mike Morrison, Jon Lincoln and Paul Ramsden; to others who made trips such good fun – Jerry Gore, Crag Jones, Siobhan Sheridan, Roger Payne, Julie-Ann Clyma, Dave Walker, Kenton Cool, Duncan Tunstall, Chris Pasteur, Paul Eastwood and Roger Gibbs; to film team friends – Richard Else, Brian Hall, John Whittle, Dave Cuthbertson, Keith Partridge; to US friends – Jack Tackle, the late Kurt Gloyer. The text from *Extreme Alpinism* in Chapter 15 is quoted by kind permission from Mark Twight © 1999 and The Mountaineers Books.
  In the preparation of this book I wish to thank Andrew Nurnberg Associates, my publisher, Ken Wilson, Graham Cook, Marilyn Clarke, Don Sargeant, Keith Allison, Lees Fell and the ever reliable Maggie Body for her editing assistance.

Contents

MAPS AND DIAGRAMS IN THE TEXT

All by Don Sargeant, in some cases based on preliminary visualisation of others

PHOTOGRAPHS IN THE TEXT

between pages 64 and 65

on page 111

between pages 192 and 193

all photos are by the author except

1, 5 Nicki Fowler;   10 Chris Watts;   18, 19, 20, 21 Pat Littlejohn;   22 Ken Wilson;
27, 32 Steve Sustad;   47 Michael Burgess;   63, 68 Paul Ramsden

Foreword

by Chris Bonington

In his second set of climbing memoirs Mick Fowler writes about a series of alpine and rock adventures that would be the envy of any ambitious mountaineer. The appellation 'The Mountaineers' Mountaineer', which he was given after a poll in *The Observer* in 1989, reflected climber approval of his highly original approach to his sport – explorations on chalk sea cliffs, alpine north faces, Scottish crags in winter and summer and his first major expeditions to greater ranges which resulted in superb climbs on Cerro Kishtwar, Taulliraju and Spantik. All of this was recorded in his first book, *Vertical Pleasure*.

Here was a totally modern mountaineer, rejecting the necessary, but by that time outdated, styles of my era (sieging, fixed ropes and camps, large parties) and the capsule compromises of the big wall era. Instead he embraced the complete commitment involved in a full alpine-style approach to major mountain problems. All sports evolve, and mountaineering is no exception. Better training, greatly improved equipment and cheaper travel have made much of this possible, but the perceptions of what might be possible have risen too, and Mick has been at the forefront of this new approach. His identification as the Mountaineers' Mountaineer was, like the election of a new politician, a vote of confidence for the future.

Well the electorate (which included me) must now be well pleased. If ever one person has confirmed his early reputation it must be Mick Fowler. During the last fifteen years he has pulled off a further series of wonderful climbs and has established a world-wide reputation. Short holidays and family commitments have restricted his activities to accessible peaks up to the 7000-metre level – no 8000-metre-peak-bagging here – but these have been amply balanced by the sheer sporting challenge of his chosen climbs: on Changabang the steep remorseless ice slopes, the sustained mixed climbing on Taweche, the tenuous route-finding on Arwa Tower, the spindrift battles on Mount Kennedy and the relentlessly steep technical ice work on Siguniang. This latter climb, which he made with the equally tenacious Paul Ramsden, was internationally admired as the epitome of the challenging alpine climb in the greater ranges. Not surprisingly it attracted awards from their peers in both the United States and Europe.

The reader should not underestimate the commitment of these climbs. Climbing is, at this level, an extreme activity. Yet this factor, as it has always done, concentrates the mind and brings out the finest skills and judgements from those who venture forth. The lure of the great line on the savage peak is as real now as when Balmat and Paccard first climbed Mont Blanc in 1786. Like the sailors who pit their skills against the great oceans of the world, the top mountaineers bring (usually with suitable humility and caution) their fitness, judgement, strength and skill to the great mountains. Mick Fowler and his friends are part of a New Golden Age of climbing that is now fully under way on the world's greatest peaks, an even more exciting saga than the one played out in the Alps in the nineteenth century.

Most leading climbers commit themselves fully to the sport, deriving a living either from guiding or from lectures, books and various sponsorships. Mick does not fit this mould and has retained a 'normal' nine-to-five job with the Inland Revenue since he left school. He now heads one of the teams that is responsible for assessing the share value of unquoted companies, a seemingly arcane field, but one that is of vital interest to Britain in retaining its national wealth and preventing it from being spirited away to distant tax havens. Just as in climbing he warms to the task of unravelling the problems of a great peak, so too, in his professional life he is envigorated by the endless chess game with corporate lawyers and accountants.

I have climbed with Mick for just one week of rock climbing on the island of Mingulay in the Outer Hebrides. He was not the athletic super star I had expected and indeed, even though far younger than me, I was delighted to find that his rock skills seemed reassuringly mainstream and we both shared a simple enjoyment of climbing. Yet here is one of our greatest mountaineers. Those who have partnered him on his big climbs speak respectfully of his all-round skills, stamina and coolness under pressure. It is also clear that his guile and judgement count for a lot. When these qualities are combined with a patient tenacity the most daunting mountain situations can be overcome. Readers will be able to assess this in his entertaining and exciting book which will surely take its place as one of the most important accounts of contemporary high-standard climbing.

Caldbeck, Cumbria, 2005

Preface

This book records a selection of my climbs of recent years that I have found rewarding and memorable. Chronologically there is some overlap with *Vertical Pleasure* (1995). The theme of both books is similar, though the pace may have quickened. Chapter 1 gives background information for those who have not read the earlier book.

In introducing *On Thin Ice* I should stress that climbing can be a dangerous activity. I hope my writing brings out the joy of adventurous climbing but please remember that I, and my companions, have made these climbs after serving long apprenticeships that have equipped us with the skills and experience to make a reasonable assessment of the risks involved. The Scottish cliffs in winter, and hard alpine climbs in winter and summer, provide the ideal training for anyone with aspirations to climb in the greater ranges.

In the text the use of christian names has been broken up with use of the more formal but more reader-friendly surnames. Heights and distances also prompted debate and it was decided to use imperial measures for horizontal distances and metric for the vertical, an uneasy combination that I hope will find approval. Technical climbing terms have been kept to a minimum and those used are now generally familiar.

I would like to pay tribute to: my wife Nicki and our children Tessa and Alec for putting up with my long absences; to my climbing partners for their skills and good humour, together with the others on our trips for injecting fun and camaraderie into proceedings; to my agent and publishing team; and to Chris Bonington, who has honoured me by writing the foreword.

Modern climbs could not be achieved without fine equipment and clothing. In this respect the North Face has given me unstinting support as long-term sponsors. I am also indebted to Black Diamond, Scarpa and Cascade designs for their products.

Finally I must pay tribute to the Mount Everest Foundation, the BMC and other funds (Nick Estcourt etc) for their financial support – contributing vital additions to expedition budgets of British climbers.

MICK FOWLER
Melbourne, Derbyshire, 2005

1

Background to it all

*Alan Rouse gives direction – my early climbing – the great alpine classics –
ice climbing trips to Scotland – early Himalayan ventures –
The Mountaineers' Mountaineer – photoshoot at Harrison's Rocks*

One day, back in 1981, at a drunken climbing party in Sheffield, a twenty-
five-year-old taxman found himself talking to Alan Rouse, then one of
Britain's most talented and forward-looking mountaineers.

I felt a little uncomfortable and awestruck. Al Rouse was very much
a leading light of his generation with achievements ranging from first
ascents in the Himalaya to reputedly drinking vomit from Noel Odell's
pre-war Everest boot at a Cambridge University Mountaineering Club
dinner. The London-based group that I was part of felt that such achievements were to be admired if not repeated. To me he was very much a
contemporary hero. I felt slightly honoured that he was talking to me and
listened awkwardly whilst he enthused about South America.

I was of course aware of various possibilities but my civil service job
came with a limited holiday entitlement and I was very wary of the time
commitment of greater range climbing trips and the health problems
posed by high altitude. That said, I had just climbed the North Face of
the Eiger and was close to completing my tick list of alpine classics. I was
ready to try somewhere new and exploratory. Al Rouse caught me at just
the right time. His enthusiasm for the potential for short trips to Peru was
infectious and led directly to Chris Watts and me making the first ascent
of the South Buttress of Taulliraju in 1982.

At that time I was obsessed. I tended to regard any day off work,
which was not spent climbing, as a day wasted. I often wonder whether
failure would have prompted me to drop the idea of greater range climbs
as an inefficient use of my limited holiday entitlement. But, as it turned
out, we had completed the climb and were ready to return home after just
two weeks away. A realisation of what could be achieved, whilst holding
down a full-time job, dawned on me. And success gave me my first taste
of an enduring sense of euphoria which, combined with the eye-opening,
mind-expanding experience of operating in the developing world, ensured
that I was hooked. A way of life had been born.

But, going back farther, it was my father George's fault really. I can thank him for introducing me to the pleasures of the outdoors, firstly via walking trips in North Wales and the Lakes and then to rock-climbing at the sandstone outcrops of the Weald – nearer our London home.

I would not pretend today that I was exactly enthusiasic about all of those early trips but they must have had some long-lasting effect. In fact, I now find myself repeating the process and introducing my own children Tess (thirteen) and Alec (ten), to the rigours of outdoor action. George had limited experience of the outdoors and to a certain extent we were learning together, progressing from hill-walking to scrambling and then on to rock climbs where we peaked at around the Very Difficult grade.

By 1969 I was thirteen, and George was now keen to get involved in alpine mountaineering. Up till then we had sort of just found our way – but George was more hesitant on the mountaineering front. Twenty years before he had accumulated some unwelcome experience of alpine crevasses and benightment. Such memories led him to book us in for a week's course run by the Austrian Alpine Club in the Tyrol's Stubai Alps. I was too young but he persuaded them to take me anyway.

The whole experience was something of an eye-opener. Not only were the mountains monstrously huge and spectacular compared to those back home, but dangers such as rockfall and gaping crevasses were memorably new experiences. At one point it was decided that the group should practise crevasse rescue and I have an enduring memory of an extremely refined young man called Ignatius smiling grimly whilst walking boldly over the edge of an open crevasse. The idea was that another member of the course would arrest his fall and Ignatius would then demonstrate self-rescue by prusiking up the rope. This somehow didn't happen and the rope-holder was soon skidding rapidly towards the edge. The guide was next on the rope but the bare ice of the nearly snow-free glacier gave no ready purchase. Ignatius fell heavily onto a convenient snow bridge whilst the guide stopped the second man two feet from the edge. This crevasse rescue business looked all very exciting. I have treated them with great respect ever since.

But George was not to be deterred. With the course completed he set about using our new found experience to the full. The next few summers were spent ticking off the easier routes up the 4000-metre peaks of Switzerland until, after a few years off (teenage revolt), I was suddenly motivated to tackle some of the famous alpine climbs I had seen.

By this stage I had been visiting the southern sandstone outcrops under my own steam for some years and the friends I made there were obvious climbing partners for a first foray onto harder alpine climbs. In 1976 Mike Morrison, John Stevenson, (two like-minded South Londoners) and I resigned from our jobs, squeezed into my 850cc minivan and headed out to Chamonix for two months.

The transition to harder alpine climbs went remarkably smoothly. All that experience gained with George on easier 4000-metre terrain stood me in good stead. Mike and John were more hesitant but by the time we returned home in September I had, together with Howard Crumpton, a more experienced climber from South London, managed an early ascent of the highly respected Cecchinel/Nominé route on the Eckpfeiler Buttress of Mont Blanc. A further two-month trip in 1977 led to regular seasons where I aimed primarily for the North Face classics, such as the Matterhorn and Eiger. These were first climbed back in the 1930s but were far from straightforward and provided Mike Morrison and me with plenty of fine epics and enduring memories. By and large I stuck to established routes in the Alps but I did manage a new line on the Eckpfeiler with the Cardiff climber Phill Thomas but, on a face already criss-crossed with routes, this felt uncomfortably like a series of variations. My first published article was about that climb, so I suppose it must have made a mark. In general though I steadily began to think that the most appealing mountaineering lines in the Alps had been climbed and that inspiring unclimbed objectives lay further afield.

My attitude in the UK was very different. Regular trips to southern sandstone were possible on public transport and this enabled Mike Morrison, John Stevenson and me to achieve a reasonable standard of ability and establish a fair number of new climbs, even before we acquired minivan transport in late 1975 – a development that marked a sea change in our activities. From that time we spent virtually every weekend away climbing. From London, it was just as easy to get to the sea cliffs of the South-West as the traditional areas of North Wales and the Lakes. The more we climbed the more we noticed unclimbed possibilities and set about attempting them. At one stage (1976/7) our enthusiasm for technical rock climbing was such that John Stevenson and I moved to Sheffield – heartland of the English rock climbing scene. John stayed but, after a year or so of climbing virtually non-stop on the gritstone and limestone outcrops of the Peak District, I tired of the intensely competitive, locally focused scene and moved back to London where, ironically, I found it much easier to find partners keen to drop everything and spend weekends exploring the climbing potential in the more remote parts of the UK.

Gradually, as our horizons broadened we became aware of huge unclimbed sea cliffs in Devon, Kent and Orkney to name just a few. The urge to have a go was irrepressible. The approaches to some of these cliffs were often serious in their own right and the rock we came across was varied to say the least. Sometimes, as on the chalk cliffs at Dover, it was soft enough to use ice-axes and crampons, whereas in other places, such as some of the big shale cliffs in Devon and Cornwall, we improvised by using pieces of angle iron as 'peg' runners. In retrospect I suppose accumulating all this experience at tackling unusual and challenging situations was to put me in good stead for greater range mountaineering trips. But I certainly never regarded adventure climbs in the UK as training exploits, they were simply exciting ways to break up five-day stints working as a tax collection manager in a London office.

Winter weekends became particularly rewarding. By the late seventies, road improvements had reduced the London to northern Scotland driving time to ten hours, making even the most distant places reachable in a weekend. Eleven weekends in a row remains my personal best at the time of writing. Shield Direct on Ben Nevis, climbed in March 1979, was a great start. An easily accessible, snaking ice line on Britain's most popular winter climbing mountain was something of an unexpected introductory bonus which opened our eyes to Scotland's vast potential. In the coldest conditions bizarre alternative venues closer to home were investigated for ice climbing potential, varying from coastal waterfalls in North Devon to frozen toilet overflows on St Pancras station.

By the early 1980s I was regularly practising all of these branches of climbing. The great classics had been ticked off and I was keen to act on Al Rouse's advice and start on the bigger challenges further afield.

After climbing in the Andes a trip to the Greater Himalaya was the next step. In 1984 my first efforts on Bojohagur Duanasir, in the Karakoram range of Pakistan, were pathetically ineffectual. We never actually tied onto the rope and were totally unable to cope with the rigours of altitude. But in 1987 success with Victor Saunders on the prestigious Golden Pillar of Spantik (7027m) overcame any lingering doubts cementing my enthusiasm for such ventures. This was more like it. Good ethnic action combined with Scottish-style mixed climbing, plus an icy Devon-style shale chimney thrown in for good measure. I always knew that North Devon ice climbing experience would come in useful!

The Spantik climb brought Victor and I into higher profile. This was a climb that combined an obviously challenging target with a small team approach to big scale mountaineering.

Since then there has been no turning back.

These objectives don't *have* to be mountaineering but they do have to be based in steep and varied parts of the world where uncertainty and challenge mean that plenty of memorable moments are likely to ensue.

Possibly as a result of Spantik and the Taulliraju climb in 1989 I was flattered to be voted 'Mountaineers' Mountaineer'. in *The Observer's*

Experts' Experts series. To this day I can't quite work out how it happened. Pleased as I was with my alpine and greater range ascents, they hardly compared with the monumental achievements of the likes of Reinhold Messner, Doug Scott or Chris Bonington. The key to this conundrum appeared to lie in the lack of any firm direction on the criteria to be applied by those required to vote. It may be that as these giants of the sport were seen to already be public property, climbers wished to opt for someone less well known – a representative of 'the underground' so to speak. But why should I worry? *The Observer* had decided that I was the Mountaineers' Mountaineer and a photographer had been sent to capture some suitably spectacular shots with which to illustrate the piece.

In retrospect I can confidently assert that the decision to go for a beer before posing for the photographs was an error. The freelance photographer employed by *The Observer* was not familiar with climbing and wanted to 'discuss the shoot first'. The Crown overlooking the green in the village of Groombridge is conveniently situated close to the much frequented sandstone outcrops in Kent. And an extremely fine pub it is, the sort where time just sort of slips by. I had only managed to give a very brief outline of what this climbing game was all about when our glasses were empty and refills were judged necessary.

Suitably refreshed, we strolled along the track towards Harrison's Rocks. The usual form on these sandstone outcrops is to rig up a top rope and climb stiff problems in complete safety. This did not fit in with the photographer's idea of action climbing fit for a Mountaineers' Mountaineer. Instead he searched for a position from which he could capture some spectacular solo climbing from a vantage point halfway up the cliff. A nondescript crack, I think it was the one known uninspiringly as Noisome Cleft Number 2, was deemed sufficiently difficult-looking and well positioned. Soon the photographer was in position and it was time to go.

'OK,' he shouted. 'Take it slowly.'

The climb was not hard and I was able to focus on holding hopefully photogenic positions and not worry too much about the difficulty. After two or three ascents the photographer was clearly nonplussed.

'Mmmmm, we can do better. Could you lean out more, please?'

By the third or fourth time I was getting better at understanding exactly what he was after. The idea seemed to be for me to look as worried as possible and make the climb look as hard as possible. I laybacked spectacularly, wondered vaguely whether a large hold that I missed out would feature in the photographs, grimaced in a suitably worried way and made a long stretch for a sloping edge.

Suddenly it was all going wrong. My hand slipped on the sandy hold and, before I could correct the situation, I was falling. As sod's law would have it this was one of the very few climbs at Harrison's with a nasty landing. With a suitable look of panic and concern I landed heavily on my side between two boulders. The click of the camera shutter continued for a few seconds, followed by silence.

'You OK?' he enquired, doubtless wondering if this sort of behaviour was normal.

The fall had been five metres or so and I lay quietly waiting for the immediate pain to subside. A small crowd gathered to marvel at the Mountaineers' Mountaineer in his unflattering posture. Helpful comments poured forth liberally:

'Did you slip?'

'Shall I call an ambulance?'

'I think there's a doctor farther down the crag.'

Things were not going well. I struggled to swivel round and sit up, whilst trying to give one of those disarming 'it's all OK really' smiles. A pain shot through my rib cage. In fact I had been fortunate in that I had landed on my side between the boulders, rather than directly on top of them. One though must have caught me a glancing blow in the ribs. It hurt – and while I managed to smile enough for the crowd of onlookers to disperse there was no way I was going to be able to continue performing as required.

I looked unhappy. So did the photographer. The discovery that he had set his camera incorrectly was the last straw. We sat grimly contemplating the situation.

'This is my first assignment for *The Observer*,' he confided, staring miserably around.'What do you think?'

I did feel sorry for him; but what I was beginning to think was a visit to hospital might be in order.

'Perhaps I could manage an abseil.'

It felt rather pathetic really. A caption reading 'Mountaineers' Mountaineer abseiling at Harrison's' didn't seem quite right somehow.

But there was nothing else for it. The abseil was excruciating with the resultant photo showing me grimacing and curled in pain, whilst fighting hard to keep a grip on the rope.

I visited casualty on the way home.

'Cracked ribs. Take it easy. You'll be OK.'

A couple of days later the photographer rang.

'They're not really very good,' he said sadly. 'I don't think they'll use me again.'

'Probably not me either,' I sympathised.

2

The Essential Components of Fun

*Visit to Petra – Christmas noodles in Wadi Araba – a meal with
the Jordanian border police – a wild taxi ride in the desert snow –
climbing at Wadi Rum*

'Jordan. I like the idea of Jordan.'

Nicki and I were still in the 'getting to know you better' stage of our relationship and her suggestion of a venue for our first holiday together rather caught me by surprise. Yet it seemed to fit in well with my 'steep and varied parts of the world' criteria. It also sharply focused my attention on the adventurous side of her personality, for when she said Jordan I already knew her well enough to know that she meant 'adventure' Jordan rather than tourist Jordan. We had a week over Christmas to spend together and I had visions of sun-baked rock climbing in the desert, exploring desert gorges, sub-aqua in the Red Sea and passionate middle eastern nights. It was by far the best suggestion that either of us had come up with. My enthusiasm was immediate.

The well-known British desert climber Tony Howard had published a book on desert climbs and treks in Jordan and one in particular caught our eye. It was the ten-mile gorge that connects the ancient red rock carved town of Petra to the broad expanse of the Wadi Araba, a vast arid plain straddling the Jordan/Israel border.

I was prepared to compromise my anti-tourist trip principles to the extent of visiting Petra, and so was Nicki who has a degree in archaeology. We were both stunned, as everyone is, by the spectacular approach. The valley narrows and becomes a deep slit called a *siq*, perhaps three metres wide and seventy high. It was quite dark at the bottom and the twisting and turning means that it is never possible to see very far. Suddenly on rounding a corner there ahead, framed by the walls of a narrow passage, is the front of the Treasury, the surviving showpiece from the Nabatean kingdom that ruled this desert trade route from the 4th century BC to the 2nd AD.

The first impression was that it was much bigger than I expected. A full 30 metres high, the façade is intricately carved out of the solid red rock face. Four lofty classical pillars support the entrance. The chisel marks made by those who hacked it out by hand were clearly visible. I felt humbled by the thought of the incredible effort required to build the necessary scaffolding and the skills that had fashioned thousands of tons of rock in such an accurate and awe-inspiring manner.

The tourist trail now opened out and wandered down the wider gorge past more stunningly carved buildings and ended where it narrowed again and our trek began. Ahead lay the challenge, which had been the main reason we had come to Petra – the long and difficult gorge leading down for about ten miles to the rock and sand desert of the Wadi Araba. To the best of our knowledge, a party led by Tony Howard had climbed up this gorge but no westerners had ever descended it.

Up till this point I had been rather self-conscious about the bulging rucksacks we were carrying but now they felt more suited to the terrain. There was a small stream and initially the narrow flood plain was cultivated by the Bedouin. Huge well featured red sandstone walls towered overhead and I couldn't help but admire some very fine crack lines that just called out to be climbed, but we didn't have the equipment and Nicki was getting into full expedition 'we must move on' mode.

Soon we were fighting our way through dense vegetation to the top of the first step in the gorge. Here the stream tumbled down a 70-degree rock face for around 100 metres. There was no obvious way to continue.

'Any suggestions?'

Nicki clearly expected me – the experienced mountaineer – to have the solution to this problem. I peered hopefully over the edge, noting that our single thirty-metre rope was inadequate for abseiling hundred-metre drops. We could break the abseil but that would mean using intermediate anchor points and we had very few pieces of equipment with us.

'Perhaps we could climb down that way?' Nicki was pointing at a water-worn log protruding from a hole to one side of the watercourse. We scrambled carefully down. It wasn't too difficult but with a big drop down below, we moved cautiously. The holds led to the piece of wood which, on closer inspection, had clearly been placed there to aid progress over a difficult section. It seemed as if this upper section, at least, was well frequented by the Bedouin locals.

A short length of outrageously tatty rope hung from the wood. It was sufficient to pass a difficult section and allow us to scramble on down to the foot of the waterfall. Now we were in the depths of the gorge. Steep slopes interspersed with vertical walls towered 100m above us on both sides. The way on was obvious and we picked our way on down the stream bed, squeezing between huge jammed boulders and wading in waist-deep water. The wading wouldn't have been so bad except for the fact that it was cold. Low temperatures were not exactly what we had expected in Jordan but the normally cloudless sky was becoming increasingly obscured by a layer of high cloud and there was no doubt about it … it was cold. We sat shivering on a large boulder looking hesitantly at an obviously deep section of wading ahead.

'Do you think it might rain?'

Nicki's question focused the mind on the most serious aspect of this venture. It doesn't rain very much in this part of the world but when it does the run off is such that tiny streams such as ours can rapidly be transformed into raging torrents.

We peered warily upwards. No doubt about it – the weather was looking increasingly threatening. In fact, as we sat there the first drops of rain pattered down. Nicki was studying the vertical walls on either side of the narrow deep section ahead.

'Better get through this quickly.'

I couldn't help but agree. The water here was so deep that the only way to keep our rucksacks dry was to hold them on our heads. At one point a huge boulder wedged across the canyon forced us to duck down until we were up to our necks with the rucksacks at nose level. When the floor opened out somewhat we were able to escape the water and gain a scree slope. With uncharacteristic foresight we had brought woolly jumpers and waterproofs which we now struggled into. It felt very strange to be pulling on this kind of equipment in such a usually hot and arid part of the world. This said, it was raining harder now but our little stream, probably the only one for miles, was not yet looking in any way threatening. All the same, the next section looked particularly committing; the gorge narrowed and a long section of deep murky water could be seen to cover the bottom. Swimming would be necessary. This in itself was OK but the gorge curled out of sight and there was no way of knowing how long this section might go on for, but to fail to complete it would result in a challenging swim back against the flow.

The skies gave us a clear signal. We sat there miserably considering our predicament. Nicki spoke first.

'I hope you've got a decent Christmas present for me.'

I had completely forgotten it was Christmas day. Also, a more distressing thought from someone keen to pursue the relationship, I didn't have a present of any kind laid on, let alone a decent one. The thought also struck me that my chosen evening meal of noodles and mashed potato might not go down well as a romantic Christmas dinner.

On one side of the gorge a scree slope appeared to give access to a shelf above the vertical walls that dropped sheer to the bottom. We were still in with a chance of descending the entire gorge if not in the perfect floor-hugging style that we would have preferred.

The boulders of the scree slope were dripping wet but free from moss or vegetation of any kind. This kind of weather was clearly a marked departure from the norm and it felt somewhat incongruous to be struggling up a middle eastern scree slope in now pouring rain and full waterproofs. Our nice, sunbaked Christmas trip to the ever-warm middle east was not turning out quite as planned.

But at least progress was being made. The shelf allowed easy movement for a few hundred yards and then it was possible to drop back down to the bottom of the gorge. Looking up the way we would have come down I could see vertical walls dropping into more stretches of deep water. At one point a huge smooth green boulder was wedged right the way across. I was glad we hadn't come that way.

As dusk approached, the watercourse widened and a small over-hung flat area was visible on the far side. It looked to provide a sound camping site for Christmas type activity and I waded across the six-inch-deep stream to take a closer look. Whilst doing so I was aware of a low, rumbling sound. As I reached the far side though I could see that half a mile upstream a spectacular waterfall was plunging down the vertical side-wall. Either we had somehow missed it as we descended the gorge or it had appeared in a remarkably short time.

A shout from behind changed the focus of my attention. Nicki was about halfway across the thirty-foot watercourse in ankle-deep water. The stunted bushes growing from the upstream sandbanks were shaking under the strain of a foot high wall of water that was advancing at a running pace. Nicki also accelerated; it was touch and go for a few moments until she reached my side just ahead of the water. We were both aware of the dangers of flash floods but the sheer volume of water from one very localised source had caught us seriously by surprise. What would have happened if the flash flood had struck earlier, whilst we were wading narrow chest deep sections and ducking under wedged boulders. It didn't take much to calculate that the water levels in the narrow sections of gorge must have been at least two metres high.

It was two rather chastened gorge descenders that turned to address the task of tent pitching and Christmas dinner preparing.

'I'm getting wet.'

'Shit.' Packing for Jordan I hadn't bothered to dig out a fully waterproof tent. The last straw was when the gas cylinder ran out and I had to admit that the spares were back in Petra where we had left our surplus gear. Lukewarm tea, together with digestive biscuits, mashed potato and noodles, all consumed in a damp tent did not bode well for romantic action. Nicki seemed to take all this in her stride – a tremendous boost to the chances of our relationship being a success I mused as I downed another mug of cold tea.

Breakfast of water and Weetabix with cold water, was another hurdle, but that too was successfully negotiated when she was actually heard to say that she 'enjoyed this sort of thing'.

Outside it was cold, and misty. The cloud level had risen slightly and there was definitely snow on the upper slopes. Our plan was to return to Petra over the mountains and while the snow itself was a surprise it was not a huge problem. The poor visibility though could make things much more difficult. The whole Petra upland area is a deserted sandstone plateau cut by a series of vertical sided narrow gullies or *siqs*. We had experienced one of these on our approach to Petra and could easily imagine the problems they might cause if we tried to force a route through the clouds. Getting lost in a misty, snowy landscape, criss-crossed with narrow gorges could be pushing Nicki's tolerance a little too far. I wasn't keen either. An alternative plan was required.

There was only one obvious possibility. The Petra gorge disgorges into the Wadi Araba, a huge open dry valley straddling the border between Jordan and Israel. We knew that a road ran down the Wadi Araba on the Jordanian side of the border. This went to Aqaba on the Red Sea from where we would be able to get transport back to our gear in Petra. A description in Tony Howard's guide to Jordan gave us a rough idea of where to go. With uncharacteristic foresight we also had a compass. From where we were the ground ahead looked sufficiently inhospitable to make the plan fall into the 'very challenging' category. Below us the gorge opened out and the stream flowed sluggishly between rock outcrops. Away from the water there was virtually no vegetation, little more than a rubble-strewn desert. With the dank mist the visibility was poor. The first priority was to follow the stream and get out into the open Wadi from where we might be able to locate the small village that the guidebook referred to. If that failed, the road, running north-south, should be easy to find if we took a westerly compass bearing. The village, Bir Madhkur, seemed more attractive ... it might even provide us with a second breakfast.

At first the going was pleasant, sandy strips alongside the watercourse allowed fast progress and rocky outcrops on either side made for interesting and varied scenery. Some of them looked to provide idyllic climbing. Soon though the ground opened out and the stream soaked away into the desert landscape.

Soon two large Bedouin tents loomed out of the mist. I found this amazing. The landscape was so harsh and unaccommodating that it was difficult to see why any local might want to come here.

But this was no time to pontificate on the whys and wherefores of the situation. The Bedouin dogs had seen us and were approaching menacingly. Nicki had spent a year living with tribal Ladhakis in the Himalayas and had experience of vicious dogs.

'Stones ... pick up some stones.'

In fact it had been an instinctive reaction. We both stood there with handfuls of stones. The dogs were perhaps fifty yards away and approaching slowly but noisily. The tents were fifty yards or so behind the dogs. I couldn't help but think that the Bedouin might not be too pleased to see us stoning their dogs. Also I wasn't convinced that it would work very well and feared that the end result could be ferocious animals running towards us with bared fangs as we ineffectually scrabbled to pick up more stones. Nicki threw her first stone.

'You wouldn't do that to Nanda.' I was thinking of her recently acquired Labrador puppy.

'This is different.'

She had a point. They were still heading our way and looked unlikely to greet us with a friendly Labrador-type nuzzle.

The stone missed its target but had a positive effect. They stopped moving forward. I threw one of mine just to make sure. It appeared that the dogs were used to having rocks thrown at them and presumably feared that we were much more accurate throwers than we actually were.

We sneaked past, giving dogs and tents a wide berth. Interestingly despite the ferocious barking and obvious occupancy of the tents we never saw anyone taking the slightest interest in what might be going on. I wondered if anyone would have paid any attention if the dogs had torn us limb from limb.

Ploughing on through the mist, we were surprised to find occasional signs of habitation; the usual sort of rubbish – a discarded rubber shoe, the odd plastic bag, a cigarette end here and there. And there was what we called 'the clothes tree'. It was just about the only tree that we had seen since exiting from the gorge. A proper tree, perhaps five metres high and with a good selection of gnarled but solid looking branches. How it had come to be adorned with scraps of clothing remained a mystery. High up in one branch there appeared to be the remains of a dead animal. We scurried past, wondering vaguely if it might be the focus of some sort of religious ritual.

Our elation at first spotting the settlement of Bir Madhkur was short-lived. Nicki declared it to be the 'biggest shit-hole' she had ever set eyes upon. It certainly did seem to lack a certain something. In fact I'm not sure to this day that this was actually Bir Madhkur or whether it was a settlement at all. It was more a row of perhaps ten grey concrete shelters, some occupied by domestic animals and one appearing to have a family living in it. Most of the cells had no roof and the whole construction appeared to be largely abandoned. Why anyone should want to build a row of single-storey, single-cell concrete structures in such an arid and inhospitable place was quite beyond me. There didn't seem to be a water supply of any kind. There was no vegetation at all and, judging by the sand swept against the walls, the position on a rounded rib made the place particularly exposed to sandstorms. The one resident family was not very friendly and hopes of a pleasant coffee and breakfast were out of the question. We didn't even bother to stop.

But our rudimentary map was correct. Not only had it enabled us to follow a compass bearing to find Bir Madhkur but there was, as it promised, a motorable track leading straight for the Amman/Aqaba road. Our route-finding problems seemed to be over.

Half a mile away was a hill adorned with what appeared to be a military building of some kind. As we walked down the road a figure appeared from the building and started shouting in Arabic. We hesitated:

'What do you reckon?'

The empty expanse of the Wadi Araba opened around us.

'Not much point in running.'

The figure was waving a gun and there really was no doubt that he urgently wanted to speak to us. We waited for him to catch us up.

He was young, perhaps thirteen years old, and appeared mentally sub-normal. I watched warily as he fingered the gun, balancing up the pros and cons of trying to stop him pointing it at us. He kept pointing to the hill station and beckoning. I was scared. This loud-mouthed youth looked dangerously out of control. We were wary of accompanying him except as an absolute last resort. Smiles, diplomacy and a firm approach seemed the best tactic. The handshakes were tense but we sensed a slight softening. He stopped pointing towards the hill fort and instead fixed us with a piercing stare.

'We have come from Petra and are going to Aqaba,' Nicki announced authoritatively.

Trying hard to smile broadly, we bade him farewell and headed decisively along the track leading across the Wadi Araba. As we set off our unwanted escort persisted in accompanying us along the track. We walked together in this manner for perhaps thirty minutes. The skies were clearing and an isolated building, more like a concrete shed, fifty yards from the track, had been visible for the last five minutes.

Our unwanted companion was gesturing with his gun again and clearly wanting us to accompany him to this unappealing structure.

There were no doors or windows in the sides we could see – just drab sandblasted, sun-baked cement. Round the corner a dark green door was wide open and there, kneeling on what looked like a pile of camel skins, was a man. He stared at us intently as our hanger-on spoke. His initial expression – not exactly friendly – darkened considerably as we stood there. He was perhaps fifty-five years old, of a slim build with thin features and aggressive frown. I felt increasingly uncomfortable. It was pretty obvious that there was nothing but trouble for us here.

'Best to be moving on,' I announced in a routine sort of a way.

I must admit that I feel a lot more comfortable coping with difficult natural challenges than erratic humans with firearms. We both made movements away from the hut. My fingers were so firmly crossed ... we really had no way at all of predicting how they might react. It was a tense time. Five yards ... no reaction. Ten yards ... no reaction.

We arrived back at the track and turned right towards the Amman/ Aqaba road. We could see the hut out of the corners of our eyes. They were standing facing us talking between themselves. As we walked on they separated, the younger one staying at the hut, the older one moving in the same direction as us but parallel to the track. It was frightening to see that he was still showing an interest but encouraging that, for whatever reason, he had clearly decided not to confront us head on. And so we continued, perhaps a hundred yards apart.

The terrain was now a flat, desolate, boulder-strewn desert. Visibility had improved and we could see for miles. Why then was there no sign of the road? The map showed it running north to south. We were walking exactly due west. Even with our dubious talents with the compass surely we couldn't have missed it. Perhaps five miles ahead was a line of low hills which I took to be in Israel. About two miles ahead and half a mile to the south was a cluster of substantial white buildings. Presumably they were on a road, if not *the* road ... but where were the cars? Surely we should be approaching the main Amman/Aqaba highway. From the map this was one of Jordan's main highways; it seemed reasonable to expect it to be teeming with cars and lorries.

We were about a few hundred yards away when we spotted the first vehicle. It looked like something out of Star Wars ... a huge articulated lorry with a box girder-like trailer was heading steadily southwards.

It was all beginning to add up to a potentially awkward situation. The close proximity to the Israeli border, the extreme sensitivity of the boy and man, and now increasing signs that the road we had been heading for was not a normal public highway. I regretted more and more the decision to leave our passports in Petra.

It was a road and a fine tarmac one at that. But by the time we reached it we had not seen any other vehicles. It felt somehow ludicrous leaving the track, turning sharp left and continuing in the direction of Aqaba, fifty miles to the south.

'Should make it in two or three days,' I quipped.

Black clouds still hung over the mountains but the skies had cleared over the Wadi Araba and the tarmac strip snaked across the flat expanse into a shimmering heat haze. We plodded tediously along the side of the road, heading for the white buildings that we had spotted earlier. Our shadow took up position fifty yards out into the desert on the other side. I noticed that he was now carrying his gun in his hand.

We carried on plodding along the road. It is amazing how familiarity can breed disinterest. I couldn't help but recall my horror when I realised that the young lad we had met first was fingering a firearm.

'He's running forward now,' observed Nicki in a slightly more concerned voice.

I looked over. The man was keeping parallel to us but was clearly intent on getting to the white buildings before us.

As we arrived there were perhaps ten men standing outside with our 'friend' proudly at their head. It seemed to be a military ambulance station and, perhaps unsurprisingly in view of the lack of traffic and lack of people, there was absolutely nothing going on. This of course meant they had unlimited time for us. The man who appeared to be in charge sported a heavy beard and had a smattering of English. He greeted us with a smile. 'We are your friends. You must eat with us.'

The room we were led into had smooth grey concrete walls and floors, a simple table and six chairs. With just one small window the interior was distinctly dark and had a rather oppressive, intimidating feel. Nicki and I were given a chair each whilst the men scrabbled between themselves for the remaining four. It was immediately apparent that there was a strict hierarchy here. Soon all was relatively calm. All the chairs were occupied and those who couldn't get their bums on seats perched with one buttock on the edge of the table. Everyone leaned forward and looked expectantly towards the man with the beard.

'You have come from Petra,' he announced gravely. He stared intimidatingly, his eyes exploring us, taking in our matted hair and dirty rumpled clothes. Suddenly he burst out into raucous laughter and the others, as if on cue, joined in. It was difficult to gauge his feelings; the mood seemed to swing from one extreme to the other within seconds.

'You are tourists?' he declared, banging the rickety steel table and invoking further roars of laughter. Nicki stepped in with a description of how we had descended the gorge from Petra and had intended to return to Petra over the mountains.

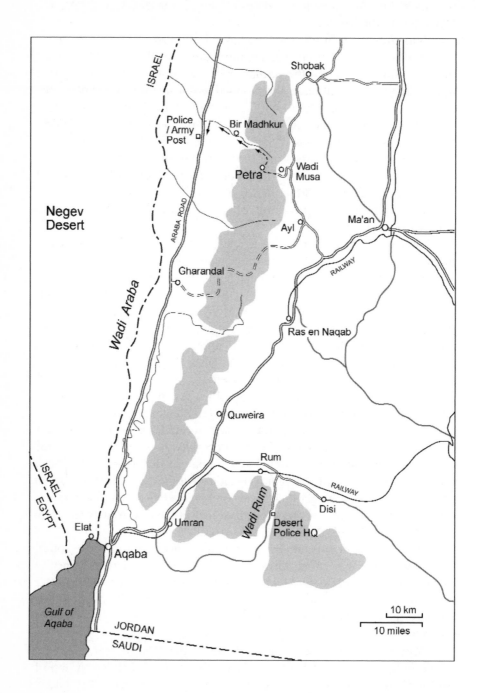

'But now,' she concluded, 'the weather is bad in the mountains and so we want to return to Petra via Aqaba.'

Nicki's words appeared to transfix them. Perhaps it was that these men were not used to women speaking out or perhaps they were simply frustrated by a posting which appeared to be totally boring and 100 per cent female-free. Either way they appeared not to know how to react. Robust exchanges in Arabic followed, punctuated by occasional shouts in the direction of the kitchen. We were not addressed again until scrambled egg on toast and black coffee were in front of us. The gap in conversation must have been at least five minutes and felt longer. I was beginning to feel slightly happier. This was certainly more relaxing than trying to placate gun-toting nomads of questionable mental state.

The bearded man addressed us again.

'Open your bags ... please.'

The use of the word 'please' after a few seconds hesitation seemed to prompt a further wave of inexplicable hilarity. This was not the easiest atmosphere to judge with any degree of certainty.

Our sodden rope was examined, squeezed and prodded with interest.

'Your passports?'

Our host listened intently to our convoluted explanation. His response was unexpected.

'You must go to Aqaba,' he announced.

'Finish your food. I will arrange a car.'

The driver of the car that he flagged down did not seem over-enamoured with the position he found himself in. Presumably he was a fairly senior businessman who had special authority to use the road. His initial attitude made it pretty clear that he had been driving contentedly south on his own but now he had suddenly acquired two unwanted dirty passengers who were in danger of staining his cloth upholstery. Unfortunately for him the road was clearly controlled by the military and any attempt to drop us off prematurely would doubtless have got him into all sorts of trouble. He was stuck with taking us to Aqaba and after a bit he clearly decided that he should make the best of a bad job.

And so the two hours to Aqaba passed in halting conversation about his refrigeration business and our lives as taxman and watercolour restorer. It is possible that neither of us really understood the other but the time passed quickly as we sped along the single strip of black tarmac cutting through the arid flats of the Wadi Araba. We saw no real settlements of any kind until the outskirts of Aqaba when one of the first roadside buildings was a police check post. Our driver stopped and a uniformed man poked his head in through the window.

'Passports?'

Our account of their existence in the lids of our rucksacks at a hotel we were not staying at in Petra was sounding less convincing with repetition. Phone calls were made. Return calls were waited for. It was several hours later, when we were climbing into a taxi that I spotted the white Mercedes we had arrived in. It was still parked by the side of the building.

The staff in the hotel that we were dropped at in Aqaba required identification. A signed statement from the checkpoint police was deemed acceptable and so, an hour later I was back at the police post.

The Mercedes driver was just leaving as I arrived. I forgave his black look in response to my wave as I headed back to the building.

I steeled myself for a further ordeal of questioning but the officials were clearly tired of me and I was soon heading back to downtown Aqaba clutching an Arabic clearance note.

'Bus to Petra, please.'

This didn't seem too unreasonable a thing to say at the bus station. After all Aqaba is a pretty major town and Petra a pretty well known and not too distant, tourist attraction.

'No ... no buses today. Snow on the road.'

'Snow? In Jordan? On the road?'

It was surprising enough to see a dusting of snow on the tops but this really was something else. It was also a pain in the neck to put it mildly, and it was why we ended up in a taxi with a local Aqaba driver who had promised to take us to Petra and then back to Wadi Rum – a distance of a couple of hundred miles including his return to Aqaba.

He drove too fast, he chain-smoked, the heater didn't work, and Nicki and I huddled nervously in the back seat as we hurtled across the darkened desert. Whenever he felt the car starting to slide in the snow, our driver's attempt to save the situation consisted of raising both hands from the steering wheel and summoning the assistance of Allah. Twice we had to get out to help him to push the vehicle back onto the road. He blamed the conditions, saying there had been no snow like this in Jordan for forty years. We were not going to contradict him.

After retrieving our baggage, passports, etc from the hotel at Petra we headed back south. When at last we arrived at the village of Wadi Rum our driver cheerfully accepted payment of a sum we worked out might just cover the cost of petrol. The fuel gauge was reading empty as he dropped us off and his tail lights receded into the distance on a desert track with no petrol station for miles.

Wadi Rum was warm and dry, in fact very dry. As the sun rose on the small climbers' campsite the stark arid beauty of the place was immediately apparent. The village was situated on a strip of flat sandy desert between huge walls rising sheer for 600 metres. At one point a spring at the foot of the rock encouraged a green dash of vegetation but the overwhelming feel of the place was one of arid desert punctuated by steep-sided mountains with rounded tops. Perched incongruously in all this was a rough campsite with large plastic shields for sandstorm protection but a newly built bunkhouse with cooking facilities and rest room gave a hint that there was something special about this place which attracted people from afar. Ten or so climbers from France and Italy completed the scene. The array of western styles and brightly coloured clothing heightened the sharp contrast between the small tourist community and the much larger Bedouin settlement.

Towering above the campsite was the huge red sandstone wall of Jebel Rum. Various modern climbs tackle this wall but our aims were more modest. The Bedouin are renowned for their climbing abilities and Bedouin youths had somehow reached the top of Jebel Rum via a line near the left end of the face. Yet the mountain appeared steep and impregnable to all but serious rock climbers. The idea of an unroped Bedouin ascent and, perhaps even more remarkable, safe descent seemed inconceivable. But the guidebook was insistent. Somewhere up there was an AD grade route called Steps of Assaf. These 'traditional' climbs by the Bedouin were originally an offshoot from hunting expeditions but they evidenced a natural and recognised climbing talent.[1]

As we walked towards the foot of Steps of Assaf we could imagine the excitement felt by Tony Howard's team. The topography was difficult to anticipate. What we had thought was a deep wide chimney was in fact a narrow passage with 500-metre vertical walls which led deep into the mountain. It was another *siq*. The mountains that look so rounded from a distance are in fact frequently cleaved by these *siqs*, which complicate summit navigation and, as we now knew, can become lethal watercourses after heavy rain.

We sneaked round under the huge red walls overlooking the village. It was intimidating but at the point where the walls turned into the *siq* there was a blunt rib that appeared to provide at least a possibility. We scrambled hopefully upwards over fragile sandstone edges until a short

---

[1] In 1952 Sheikh Hamdan guided the first recorded European ascent by Charmian Longstaff and Sylvia Branford. In the 1970s and 1980s Hammad Hamdan (son of Sheikh Hamdan) made quite a local reputation by climbing numerous difficult lines for his own pleasure, without using any modern equipment. Foreign interest in climbing in Jordan did not really take off until 1984 when a British team led by Tony Howard was invited by the Jordanian Ministry of Tourism and with the help of local Bedouin climbers/hunters thoroughly explored the potential of the Wadi Rum area. Their subsequent articles and photographs in the mountaineering press inspired other climbers and undoubtedly led directly to the current popularity of this remarkable desert outpost. The subsequent guide-book reinforced the interest.

overhanging section barred the way. At one point a metre high pile of stones looked to give enough height to reach above the overhang.

'Looks unethical" I pointed out as Nicki wobbled disconcertingly.

I couldn't help but notice that a cairn collapse could have most unwelcome consequences. These Bedouin boys are certainly not averse to a bit of adrenalin flow in their climbing ventures.

The cairn held firm. On we went, bobbing and weaving up steep and intimidating terrain – but always with cairns or cut holds to assist on difficult steps. The Bedouin route-finding never ceased to amaze. Time and time again impossible-looking steps were outflanked by cunning manoeuvres and higher and higher we rose above the surrounding desert. The final step was thirty-metres high and involved some slightly more technical climbing. Finally we stood on the summit plateau of Jebel Rum. I say plateau in the broadest sense. The terrain was one of smoothly rounded humps separated by slots of varying depth. I could not resist drawing comparisons to a sea of rounded sun-bronzed buttocks on a Mediterranean beach and gleefully clambered over them in search of the highest one. This was easier said than done. Steep-sided slots, some apparently bottomless, necessitated long detours and soon I began to fear that I might not be able to find my way back to the point where we had gained access to this weird and wonderful landscape. The day was threatening to draw to a close and a night on the tops without sleeping bags would be a chilly experience. I suggested that a descent might be in order and stood firm in the face of expressions of disappointment in being so near yet so far.

The day ended with a series of abseils and awkward down-climbing by headtorch. There was no moon and it was pitch black by the time we regained the campsite and rest room. We collapsed exhausted whilst an Italian climbing team enthusiastically plied us with wine.

Back in Aqaba I was to be introduced to an aspect of my wife-to-be's personality that has caused considerable grief and many excess baggage arguments on mountaineering trips over the years. Her philosophy is to ensure that items of ethnic interest are brought home from every place that she deems of sufficient interest. Over the years I have returned from climbing trips with items varying from two Indian brass buckets to an aluminium kettle to thirty metres of best Pakistani Kardi from Dehli.

I hate shopping. I stare morosely at everything on offer, fret that I am paying too much and am rarely satisfied with my purchase. So it was with a sense of shock and amazement that I witnessed the rapid accumulation of Arabic coffee pots, huge rugs, a Bedouin drum and various other bits and pieces. Nicki was positively in her element.

'These will look lovely at home' she enthused.

'You live in a small flat' I pointed out. 'And excess baggage is about £10 a kilo.'

But such enthusiasm was not to be quashed by negative comments.

We had arranged our flights as part of a package group and I had to admire the skill with which our luggage mountain was blended with the more modest bags of the other passengers. Potential excess baggage problems were thus solved. Import duty fears at Heathrow fell by the wayside with a suitably smiling flirty approach.

Back in London we collapsed in around a huge pile of 'shopping' in the middle of the floor. Nowadays it is spread attractively around our house but such a vision was difficult to imagine then. I just wondered where we would put it all.

A satisfied feeling came over me as I contemplated the criteria necessary for maximum holiday pleasure: new places, adventure, challenges, uncertainty, interest, ethnic action and wild, preferably mountainous, terrain. That Nicki clearly shared such pleasures, left me with a positive feeling about our relationship too.

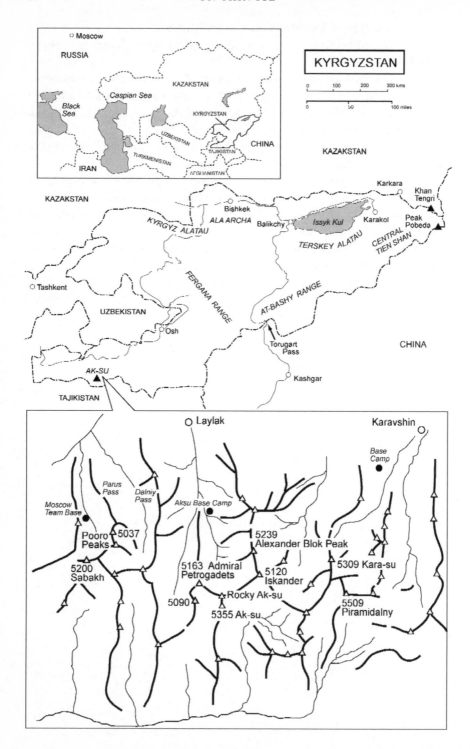

3

Abseil Training on Ak-su

*The Pamir Alai range – Bishkek airport's facilities – viewing the Ala Archa range –
Laylak Base Camp – saunas and acclimatisation – Ak-su traversed –
attempt on Pooro East – bus ride to Osh – Pic Lenin earthquake press report*

'Watch out!'

I had lost control. There was no doubt about it.

I had balanced my huge rucksack on the handrail of the London Underground escalator, confident that I would easily be able to hold it. But I was wrong. The escalator was packed and as my bag slipped swiftly down towards the lady in front of me I could do nothing at all to stop it. Her large and instantly aggressive partner proved adept at fielding her but the rucksack careered onwards before fortuitously wedging itself against the emergency stop button. My frantic efforts to retrieve it and avoid physical violence resulted in me ripping the nail of my index finger clean off. It was an inauspicious start and was to be the most serious injury suffered by the rather wordy British Mountaineering and Mountain Biking expedition to AK Cy[1] (Ak-su) in the Laylak Valley of Kyrgyzstan (aka Khirgistan).

Ak-su is a spectacular rock peak in the Pamir Alai, a range of spires in southern Kyrgyzstan that extends to the west into Tajikistan where the peaks assume a more alpine character. These two small countries were then frontier states of the USSR on its border with the Sinkiang region of China. The Pamir Alai forms an inner group of 4000-5000-metre peaks – a sort of Yosemite Valley and Alps combined. The USSR/China border to the east is defined by the higher Pamir and Tien Shan, ranges that boast several major peaks around 7500 metres in height.

We were the early beneficiaries of Mr Gorbachev's *glasnost* policies which had prompted a relaxation in the previous restrictions to this strategic frontier area. One year after our visit it became an independent republic. Kyrgyzstan is about the size of England and Wales with a

---

[1] At the time of our trip AK Cy seemed the correct name for the mountain but Ak-su has become the accepted international form, as used here. This will not match earlier journal and magazine articles.

population of nearly 5 million and the capital city is Bishkek (previously known as Frunze). The highest peak in the Pamir Alai is Pirimidalny or Pyramide (5500m), at that time thought unclimbed until Vitali Abalakov's ascent in 1947 became more widely known. Notwithstanding renamings, broken history and general uncertainties, there appeared to be many possibilities for exploratory mountaineering.

The plan was that four climbers – Jerry Gore, Crag Jones, Chris Watts and I – would try to make the first ascent of the North Face of Ak-su (5300m), whilst Nicki and Siobhan Sheridan would explore the area by mountain bike.

I had known Chris for ten years and had spent many happy weekends driving from London with him to climb in obscure parts of Britain. The image of him coiling his considerable length behind the wheel of his Austin minivan is still painfully vivid. We had also climbed together in the greater ranges, enjoying success on Taulliraju (Peru) in 1982 and failure on Bojohagur Duanasir (Pakistan) in 1984. Originally a biking road-racer from the flatlands of Norfolk, he developed an interest in rock climbing and mountaineering when he started to work for the outdoor gear shop in London where he met his partner Siobhan Sheridan and they had later gone into the gear distribution business. His ice and mixed climbing abilities are formidable and can be combined with immense determination which only emerges from an otherwise laid back manner when the going gets tough. He also has the valuable ability to keep calm in difficult situations. Once while bivouacking under the Chandelle of the Frêney Pillar, I stirred, thought I was home with my girlfriend and leant over and kissed him. I was mortified at the feeling of whiskers and awoke frantically. Chris seemed to take it all completely in his stride. It was pitch black but I could imagine him peering quizzically in my direction with one of his very wide range of middle-of-the-road expressions. It was only many years later that I admitted the incident only to learn that he had slept on blissfully unaware of my advances. When Chris is happy he looks very happy and when sad he looks very sad. But between there is a poker player's impassiveness that is difficult to read. He could be terrified and you wouldn't know. But the photographs of the unclimbed North Face of Ak-su made him look very happy. It was a rather special-looking mountain.

Crag Jones was another I had shared trips with in Britain, the Alps and the Himalaya. He had now brought along his climbing partner Jerry Gore, who I only knew by reputation as a muscular ex-army rock climber and mountaineer with a formidable list of routes to his credit.

The Russians had only just begun to allow foreign teams into the Pamir Alai and its proximity to the Chinese border had meant that even Russian climbers had been kept out until 1982. With its pioneering potential and relatively easy access it sounded to be an ideal area for a three to four-week trip. We felt rather pleased with ourselves for having secured the necessary permits to become the first British climbers ever to visit the region.

But there was a problem. Internal strife was still a notable feature of the political climate and by the time the six of us were on the huge expanse of concrete runway at Bishkek's airport our hosts were looking distinctly uncomfortable. We had managed to obtain permission to visit the area via the Sports Committee in Moscow but it was clear that they had sub-contracted the local work to one of the numerous fledgling adventure companies of the post-glasnost USSR who were not happy about the idea.

Valery, the man responsible for us, had planned to fly us in from the much closer town of Osh, around which, only a few days before our arrival, an estimated 500 people had been killed, so movement in that area was out of the question. We would have to fly direct from Bishkek. Our hosts made it clear that they would prefer us to visit the Ala Archa range close to Bishkek.

Having set our hearts on Ak-su we were reluctant to change plans.

'We show you Ala Archa range.'

Visions of spending half the trip bumping around in a truck crossed my mind. I objected, stressing our limited time.

'It will take one hour.'

Blank looks all round.

'By helicopter.'

The thought of the cost of hiring even a small helicopter was distressing. Here though the 'free market' clearly wasn't operating commercially. There would be no extra charge we were told. There seemed no need to make any more excuses and in we clambered. The helicopter was enormous, perhaps twenty metres long and eight metres wide with bright yellow supplementary fuel tanks lining both sides and taking up much of the internal space. The fuel tanks served as seats which made it feel as if we were sitting in a huge flying petrol bomb. To cope with its weight the machine was equipped with enormous engines, which drowned conversation but soon got our flying tank airborne over the 4500-metre mountains of the Ala Archa range.

This was an unprecedented experience for all of us. In the Western Alps such a flight would have cost more than we hoped to spend on the whole trip here. And this was, in effect, just a bonus. I peered intently out through the porthole windows. The scenery was magnificent with the huge rolling plains of southern Russia rising sharply into the spectacular snow and ice-covered peaks of the Ala Archa range. Though 700 metres lower than the main peaks of the Ak-su area it couldn't be denied that they did appear to offer steep and appealing mixed routes of the highest calibre. We registered it in our minds for the future but all of us were still mentally geared up for the Ak-su area.

Back at Bishkek airport the Russians were keen to emphasise the delights of the local mountains.

'They don't look much good for biking,' commented Nicki.

'This is a mountaineering trip. Biking is secondary,' announced Jerry.

I could sense hackles rising.

Further internal exchanges followed, before a unified front could be mustered and then, with remarkably little objection, our hosts abandoned their Ala Archa hard sell and agreed that the helicopter would take us all the way from Bishkek to our base. We didn't really have a clue how far that might be but from the Russians comments we judged that it was about 200 miles and certainly a lot further than the Ala Archa range. The helicopter running costs appeared of minimal significance.

I had assumed that as soon as the decision had been made we would all get into the helicopter and take off. But no, it seemed that more 'equipment' was needed, so much so that a small truck was necessary to bring it over to the helicopter! Mostly it was the usual sort of stuff, tents, food and vodka, but there were a few extra items. The full-size domestic stove with three big gas cylinders even caused the pilot to raise his eyebrows. These Russians really do like a bit of luxury at Base Camp.

Whilst all this was going on Jerry had gone off to find the toilet. He came back relieved but insistent that we too should check out the facilities. Feeling in need myself I wandered over to the hole in the concrete that he had pointed out. It was close to the edge of the runway and on closer inspection was not a proper toilet at all. It appeared to be a disused storage tank of some kind. Whatever it was, the whole five-metre square floor area was completely covered in decomposing turds, with more recent additions adorning the steps leading down to the quagmire. The buzzing bluebottle noises reverberated at a disconcertingly loud volume. Doing my business as quickly as possible I retreated to the helicopter.

'Nice, was it?' enquired Jerry mischievously.

In all my travels I had never come across such a repulsive 'facility'.

Jerry and I exchanged details whilst the others decided to hang on with crossed legs, squeezed buttocks and whatever else was necessary.

I lost track of the length of the flight. Suffice to say it was long enough for the combination of noise, fumes and vibration to give me a memorable headache. However it was impossible to ignore the panorama of spectacular peaks that dominated the horizon. We had seen very few photographs before the trip but we recognised Pyramide and, closer to hand now, the sweeping North Face of Ak-su that we had come to try.

The helicopter pilot was clearly moved by something other than the view. He and the co-pilot were engaged in an animated conversation, which involved more arm waving than I felt advisable in their line of employment. The problem, it seemed, was the weight. So much stuff had been piled on board that the poor helicopter was straining badly in its efforts to get up to Base Camp. I began to have visions of a multi-day carry or worse. The end result was the six of us, along with Valery and our three assistants, jumping out from a low hover position, suffering bombardment with our own rucksacks and then having to walk uphill for thirty minutes to arrive at the official Laylak Base Camp at around 4000 metres. It could have been worse. At least we didn't have to carry the stove!

Base Camp was lush and idyllic. Unfortunately, and much to our surprise, it was also extremely popular. We might well be the first European team to visit this area, but since it had been opened to the Russians in 1982, word had obviously got around and we were welcomed with interest by a large group. In true Russian style they were immediately friendly, plied us with copious quantities of vodka and then tried to sell us titanium ice screws. These are desirable items. On a previous trip to the Caucasus Victor Saunders had caused complete confusion when the check-in staff at Moscow airport discovered that his bulky hand luggage consisted of nothing whatsoever except Russian titanium ice screws – all made with best quality titanium from the Soyuz space programme.

Meanwhile our Russian hosts concentrated on erecting tents whilst we supposedly super-fit westerners sat quietly contemplating our altitude headaches which now enhanced the original fume and vibration-induced ones. Our feelings were not exactly elated by one of the Russians showing us a topo indicating that the supposedly 'unclimbed' North Face of Ak-su already had several routes on it.

Crag absorbed himself in his usual pastime of packing and repacking his sack for no obvious reason. I knew Crag well and over the past decade I had witnessed his unprompted repacking sessions at the most unexpected and inconvenient occasions. Crag, short for Caradoc, is an ever jovial character with strong Welsh roots and his own unique way of tackling life's challenges. In one memorable incident, he swam, totally naked, some forty metres out to North Gaulton sea stack off Orkney, whilst at the same time trying (unsuccessfully but to the great amusement of the rest of the party) to attach inflated black bin liners to the rope to stop it from sinking. Some years later he became the first Welshman to climb Everest.

While Crag unpacked and re-packed, Jerry embarked on a military-looking training session of muscle-flexing. Bemused by this energetic floorshow, the rest of us nursed our headaches and sipped tea from ornate china bowls that had somehow survived the helicopter drop.

'We need to build a sauna,' announced Valery, noticing that some of us needed pepping up in some way.

I knew that saunas were very important to Russians but the construction of a tent sauna was something new to me. Soon a substantial pile of granite boulders had accumulated and a tent frame was put over the top. I watched intrigued as huge quantities of fire lighters and wood were stuffed in between the rocks and lit. As soon as the smoke had died down, and a good set of glowing embers had formed, a huge sheet of plastic was thrown over the frame, followed by a tent flysheet. Camp chairs were arranged and a large container was filled full of water and placed next to the pile of stones. It appeared to be an outrageously Heath-Robinson affair but then these people were undoubted experts in the field and keen to show us the therapeutic qualities of their fine construction.

'Better go for it.' Nicki was presumably feeling rather better than most of us.

Somehow it felt rather odd, sitting there starkers around a big pile of boiling hot stones. The effect of pouring cold water on the stones was very impressive. Soon all of us were sweating profusely in what felt to be 100 per cent humidity. 'Don't touch the sides,' shouted Valery, as Chris swayed dangerously towards the plastic liner. I poked an experimental finger towards the plastic – it was indeed outrageously hot.

'OK ... the river!' Valery was enthusiastically pointing out of the door to the glacial stream. In Britain the sight of a large number of naked bodies sprinting from a steam-spewing tent towards a freezing stream would be greeted with interest. Here it was clearly the norm and little attention was paid. The river though sorted out the men from the boys. It wasn't just the willy-shrinking, nipple-hardening cold, the rocks it was bowling along in its fast flowing current offered, if anything, an even greater challenge. Getting body bits caught between them was excruciatingly painful. After this bracing regime our headaches capitulated and we were soon ready for new and more pleasurable challenges – a huge evening meal and copious quantities of vodka.

We had organised this trip through the Soviet Sports Committee in Moscow and had applied to join the first ever 'Laylak International Camp' in the Ak-su region. As 1990 was the first time western mountaineers had been allowed into the area we had expected a full camp, but it was becoming increasingly clear that we were the sole international participants, with Valery in charge and three helpers, plus a 'mountain guide', to ensure that we were adequately catered for.

Sitting in what was to us unaccustomed camping luxury, the Russians were keen to talk and, despite the language difficulties, we gained some interesting insights into the ethics, methods and styles of climbing that had developed in the Soviet Union.

Most climbing was, it seemed, organised on a club level, with the state prepared to lend financial support, which was the only realistic way that most active Soviet climbers could guarantee access to equipment and be sure of getting permission to visit the mountains. Regulations and financial constraints severely limited the alternatives. Everything, it seemed, was regulated, even for 'amateur' climbers who did not partake in the institutionalised competition systems. Mountaineers had to do two routes of a certain grade and then wait until the following season before being permitted to attempt anything at the next level of difficulty.

Competition climbing was an important feature of the Soviet scene and was organised by the Central Sports Committee and also by the Trade Unions. I had come across Soviet rock climbing competitions before but Valery's description made it clear that the mountaineering competitions were altogether more lavish and structured events. Teams had to choose a suitably spectacular (preferably unclimbed) line and then study the route for several days, to observe possible objective dangers, before submitting a written plan of action. Assuming the plan was approved the team was then let loose onto the objective. Points would be lost for bad practice such as deviating from the plan, using too much aid or not rotating the lead climbers. The whole affair was scored by a series of judges who followed proceedings with powerful binoculars and medals were then awarded to the victors amidst much ceremonial activity. As far as we could work out many Russians seemed to frown upon such competitions and regard them as not being in the true spirit of mountaineering. However they undoubtedly conferred a respected status on the winning climbers and opened the door to further funds which could ultimately include state-sponsored trips to the Himalaya. Perhaps because of the advent of *perestroika* and the swingeing cut-backs on state sponsorship the Russians present felt that the days of competition climbing were numbered.

Whether the days of competition climbing were drawing to a close or not, they had already left their mark on the mountains of Kyrgyzstan. Competitions were inevitably focused on the most attractive and challenging faces and in the Turkestan range this meant that hard and serious challenges such as the North Faces of Sabac (5300m) and Ak-su (5355m) had several routes on them, whereas easier, equally attractive but less difficult objectives remained untouched.

Whether or not it was a competition target the whole approach to a difficult new climb was alien to us. Constant use was made of radios and, once completed, the route would be comprehensively documented in booklet form with every imaginable manner of information included. This method of pioneering has certainly established numerous impressive achievements – all the more remarkable when it is borne in mind that equipment is generally of dubious quality, so improvisation, innovation and toughness are required to a far greater level than in western mountaineering.

Times were changing however. In the past the Soviets did not take kindly to solo ascents or even alpine-style efforts, but now all Valery asked was that we didn't kill ourselves.

'It would cause so much paperwork,' he grinned.

This said, our dismissing their offers of radios, bolts and support team was met with total bewilderment. They clearly regarded such things as absolutely essential if risks were to be kept to an acceptable level.

The evening was long and enjoyable with much food and vodka consumed by all and we were treated by our hosts to enthusiastic renditions of an apparently endless stream of songs. In comparison, our tuneless efforts seemed pathetic. The Russians just couldn't believe that we didn't have a more extensive repertoire and plied us liberally with vodka in a presumed effort to help us overcome inhibitions. We woke in a bemused and hungover state, marvelling at the damage we had done to our bodies after just one evening at Base Camp.

To my amazement there was another British person at breakfast. To this day I know not how he had managed to secure permission to visit this area but his name was David and it transpired that he was on some kind of trekking holiday with a private Russian guide. In true Russian fashion they had dropped in on us for a sociable breakfast. David was tucking into the local delicacies as I approached and fell into conversation with him.

'I am told this will fill me with boundless energy,' he announced, pointing at a small pile of sticky brown stuff on his plate. Feeling nauseous anyway, I peered unenthusiastically as Valery launched forth with a spirited support of this dubious substance.

'I think you call it "Masschit". We mix it with tree sap and think highly of its medicinal properties.'

David looked worried.

'Mouse shit?' I suggested.

'Yes, yes. Sorry for my English,' continued Valery.

David looked ill. He began frantically to spit out lumps of mouse shit mixed with tree sap as Valery watched aghast. Seldom, I suspected, had such a highly regarded substance been treated with such disdain. David and his guide headed off a few minutes later, making for a challenging-looking pass into the next valley. I could only conclude that his taste in exploratory cuisine was less adventurous than his urge for exciting treks. I tried a quick nibble. It wasn't too bad really. In fact I brought some (in liquid form) home and am still able to treat visitors with it to this day.

We were keen to get to know our surroundings as soon as possible so, after a leisurely stomach-stretching breakfast, all six of us joined a Russian climber, Sergei, in walking up to the foot of the North Face of Ak-su. This was about a four-hour walk through lush alpine vegetation and along an easy-angled glacier to the foot of the 1500-metre wall. Although the temperature dropped considerably as we gained height, Sergei continued to sport only a pair of underpants which, judging by the attire of others, appeared to be standard Soviet wear until it became colder than 0°C.

From directly below Ak-su we could see that the face was less icy than in the photographs and consisted largely of vertical rock walls of compact granite. Also, it seemed that our 'unclimbed' face had at least three lines on it. Further enquiries revealed that there were two reasons for this. Firstly the Ak-su Valley provides the easiest access to the range and secondly a high standard mountaineering competition was held here in 1986.

Sergei did not have anything like a written guidebook but he did seem very knowledgeable about the area and pointed out a fine-looking buttress towards the right-hand side of the face which he thought was unclimbed. Chris and I decided to give it a go, whilst Jerry and Crag opted to try an existing direct route up the middle of the face which ranked as the only 6c climb in the area. Meanwhile Nicki and Siobhan decided that the mountain tracks were unsuited for biking and instead began to draw up plans to cycle to a large lake about sixty miles away.

Valery now taxed himself as to whether he might be classed as 'reckless' if he allowed the only foreigners on the international camp to either die on the hardest climb in the area or be lost forever cycling through remote, terrorist-infested areas. He clearly felt deeply disturbed at the prospect but his brief was (within reason) to allow us to play as we wished. Poor Valery. He spent much time fretting with his head in his hands as Nicki and Jerry did their best to convince him that there was really nothing to worry about. Meanwhile Chris and I kept a low profile, surfacing only to refuse the repeated offer of a one-kilo radio. Eventually amicable conclusions were reached all round. Jerry and Crag would sign a statement noting that Valery had emphasised the 'extreme' danger of their proposed line, whilst Nicki and Siobhan decided that the combination of lurking terrorists and no map was not a good one. Instead they would explore closer parts of the range which were more Valery-approved.

Chris and I pitched our little tent at the foot of the face and settled down to watch the setting sun picking out the lines. A monstrous tower dominated the lower section of 'our' spur and it looked best to gain the col behind this via a clearly dangerous couloir on the right. An early start would, we hoped, find everything frozen and still. Looking across to Jerry and Crag's line, we could see them on the glacier and hear intermittent rockfall down their proposed route. Doubtless they would be out early in the morning as well.

The alarm was greeted with resounding lethargy. I fumbled around with the stove whilst Chris stuck his head out of the door, complained of a splitting headache and was promptly sick. His normally placid demeanour had changed to one of real misery. Pain-killers were consumed and the alarm was reset for 5.30. The second attempt was also not entirely successful. Chris built on his bad start to the day by losing his belay plate beneath an immovable boulder and it was not until 7am that we were off across the glacier. So much for an early start.

Moving as fast as our energy reserves would allow, we traversed beneath a huge tottering ice cliff and by midday we were at the foot of a 150-metre rock wall below the col between the gendarme and the main face.

It had been an unpleasant and dangerous start to the climb and now our sacks felt monstrously heavy as we struggled in the full heat of the afternoon sun. Progress slowed to a near halt. We had brought rock boots along for difficult pitches, but this ground seemed to consist of over-hanging chimneys smattered with ice and numerous downward-pointing flakes, perfectly designed to complicate any sack-hauling. The rock boots stayed firmly hidden as we sweated with big boots, sacks and dripping overhangs.

'Slack' I cried for what seemed like the hundredth time.

The absence of Chris's belay plate meant that proceedings were often delayed as he fought to feed the ropes through an obscure knot which he assured me would operate in the same way as a belay plate. It certainly jammed when the ropes were being fed through it in belay mode. I just hoped that it would never be tested in the opposite direction. A full afternoon of swearing saw us emerge suddenly onto the col where Chris's optimism was rewarded as we could pitch the tent on a luxurious platform.

Above the col the rock became smoother and a great sheet of granite soared up for over 100 metres. There were a couple of thin finger cracks visible and, with the sun now warming the rock, it seemed sensible to get the rock boots out and climb a pitch or two before dark.

Although I have religiously taken rock boots to alpine ranges for years, this was the first time that I had actually carried them on a route. It felt very strange to be up there on a big mountain teetering about in flimsy footwear that I had always associated with pleasant outcrops. For some reason I felt clumsy and frightened. I climbed poorly and, with feet flailing, trying to free climb on damp rock, progress was painfully slow. After an hour I had climbed about thirty metres and was contemplating aiding a nasty leaning crack when I spotted something rather unnatural above me ... a bolt! Sergei it seemed had been wrong. There was only one single bolt in this vast sea of granite but, try as we might we couldn't convince ourselves that this had appeared without a human body having been there to place it. Back on the ledge we took stock of our position. It was disappointing to realise that somebody had been here before but, looking on the bright side, we were not carrying bolts ourselves and this find meant that if there were any really blank sections above there might at least be some bolt holes there to give us a chance.[2]

We were awoken at 7am by the sound of an impressive avalanche thundering down our approach couloir. With the benefit of hindsight it now seemed a particularly silly way to have started the route. Above us the rope snaked up to the Soviet bolt. It was at this point that the inconvenience of not bringing a pair of jumars to climb up ropes caught up with us. I dislike rope climbing intensely and Chris seemed equally unhappy at the prospect. Nevertheless he contrived to regain our high point and press on, using some aid to gain a suitable stance. It was almost midday by the time we had half-climbed, half-prusiked and sack-hauled up two smooth vertical pitches to a welcome ice band. Both of us were suffering sprained hands but were now able to look down on the huge gendarme that dominated the lower section of the route.

Progress continued in a tortuous and erratic manner. The hauling was the worst. Leading difficult rock with a sack proved impracticable and, as the angle eased slightly, the hauled sacks became increasingly jammed and we gathered impressive blisters as we tugged and pulled to free them.

I was just sorting myself out midway up a particularly nasty-looking pitch when I inexcusably dropped my belay plate. Long shall I remember my distress as I witnessed the old hawser-laid piece of rope attached to it spiralling down the face. Now we had both lost our belay plates and we had been planning to use them to abseil.

---

[2] Later we were to discover that a Soviet competition team had, in fact, reached this point by climbing a line to the left of the gendarme and then continued up much the same line that we were to follow. Their start, it has to be said, is far preferable to ours. [See article in *Alpinist* 4, 2003. *Editor*]

A couple of tricky mixed pitches ended in an uncomfortably sloping sitting bivouac and a night punctuated with intense discussions on how one might abseil using karabiners clipped together to make a brake.

Chris is deeply into mountaineering equipment, techniques, clothing and things, so I had rather hoped that his ignorance in the field of karabiner brakes had been feigned. It was thus distressing when I had to conclude that he was in fact as ignorant as I was on the subject. I at least had the benefit of Steve Sustad using the system in front of me only six weeks or so before. I remembered him saying how lethal the technique could be and how easy it was to drop the karabiners. Chris was surprisingly ungrateful when I imparted this useful information. Other possibilities were limited. Both of us were well aware of traditional abseiling techniques but wrapping the rope around the body to produce enough friction to control the slide didn't seem very appealing on the long steep abseils that we would undoubtedly face. Personally I could never work out how traditional abseilers managed to cope with long steep sections. I had been taught the technique on the ten-metre sandstone outcrops of South-East England and my chief recollections are of extreme pain and great relief on arriving at the bottom, by when I had usually given up abseiling and resorted to descending hand over hand. The prospect of revisiting traditional abseil techniques on the open walls of Ak-su was unthinkable.

The night was long and uncomfortable, with plenty of time to clip karabiners into different combinations, but by morning we were pretty sure that we had sorted out a workable system for when the need arose.

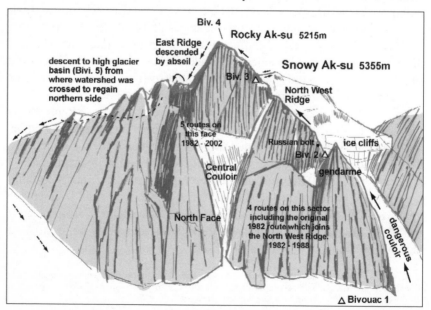

We were to put our theories into practice sooner than expected as the next day started with superb granite climbing which suddenly ended atop a spectacular gendarme. An abseil down the far side seemed the only practical solution. Chris, in the lead, wimped out and lowered, whilst I bravely tested our preferred combination with the protection of both a prusik knot and a safety rope. It seemed a ridiculous place to be practising but all appeared well and another gendarme gave us a second chance to rehearse before reaching the 5215-metre summit of rocky Ak-su.

The views were now spectacular. To the east lay Pirimidalny (5500m), the highest peak in the range, whilst to the west the Sabac area (5300m), looked particularly exciting. To the south an endless panorama of barely touched mountains stretched away into the distance, whilst to the north the Central Asian Steppes rolled interminably away into the distance.

Ak-su has two distinctly separate summits with the southernmost – Snowy Ak-su (5355m) – being the highest. Sergei had told us that we should allow four hours to traverse between the summits. If we allowed four each way that would see us back at 8pm – an hour before dark. After four perfect days the weather was at last showing signs of deteriorating. I was keen, Chris wasn't so sure. After a dither it was 1pm by the time we had sorted out the gear and made the decision to go for it.

Only twenty metres from the summit a short abseil proved to be necessary. The ridge continued down in an awkward but never desperate manner to a snowy col beyond which a long snowy ridge led to the realistically named snowy Ak-su. Altitude was now taking its toll and stamina was becoming notable by its absence. The ridge was icy and the wind strengthening by 5.30pm when we collapsed onto the shaly summit and our dream of the past year turned into reality.

As we returned along the ridge a deep throbbing sound reverberated around us. Louder and louder it got until a huge ex-Aeroflot helicopter was visible heading straight for us. As it drew level Nicki and Siobhan could be seen waving enthusiastically from an open door. In such situations I always falter. My natural tendency is to wave back but I have too much experience of the unwanted attention of helicopters and know it is all too easy for signals to be interpreted in the wrong way. Instead, much to Chris's amusement, I did my best to convey a 'hello' and 'no problem' greeting all in one movement. The whole experience felt surreal. After five days climbing one tends to feel out on a limb, or at least in a suitably remote and difficult-to-reach spot. To have a thirty second glimpse of friends wearing casual clothing just 100 metres away was disconcerting. Feeling thereby disorientated, we retraced our steps to rocky Ak-su and spent an uncomfortable night squeezed under rocky blocks forming the summit, very aware that our fleeting visitors were doubtless gorging themselves on Base Camp hospitality.

Our descent route, the East Ridge, was not really a ridge at all but a steep buttress peppered with overhangs and sporting a Russian 5b rating.

A few exciting prusik-protected initial abseils built confidence in our karabiner brakes which was good preparation for what was to come. Somehow we lost the easiest line and I found myself committed to a long free abseil with an energetic swing to regain rock at the end ... a manoeuvre that will always remain deeply ingrained in my memory. The relief when Chris joined me and we were able to regain the ropes was palpable. With normal abseiling resumed we descended steadily down a long and tortuous narrow ridge as it grew dark, intent on reaching the safety of the flat glacier. Eventually after further hair-raising manoeuvres on the final abseils, we reached the flat glacier and by midnight had the tent pitched and were tucked into our sleeping bags discussing the route.

It had been a wearing six days on both mind and body. We had not climbed a really eye-catching line, the start had been stupidly dangerous and the climb itself had offered only periodic difficulties. But we had reached the summit, traversed the mountain and got down safely despite all the abseiling worries. All in all it had been an intense experience that we had greatly enjoyed.

Back in Base Camp Valery, pleased to have us back safe and sound, felt it his duty to concern himself with our slimmed physiques. Vast quantities of food miraculously appeared and much concern was apparent as we proved ourselves incapable of making any recognisable impression on it.

Vodka and champagne helped wash things down but Russian hospitality knows no bounds. A tent sauna was prepared, gifts ranging from caviar to ice fifis were distributed and, in line with local customs, even the ubiquitous mouse excreta was produced to 'restore our vitality'.

Life felt pretty good really.

Crag and Jerry had less luck. Their intended line on the North Face looked superb but the lower section was badly exposed to ice and rockfall once the sun had hit the upper reaches of the face. Their plan, like ours, was to start early and get clear of the danger area in good time. Unfortunately the difficulties were extreme right from the start and a desperate aid pitch took four hours to lead. This would have been bad enough normally but fresh snow on the upper reaches of the face began to melt as Jerry was climbing. Soon he was engulfed in a full-scale waterfall and both climbers rapidly became soaked through to their underclothes. A rock piercing Jerry's helmet (remarkably he escaped with no physical injury) was the last straw and they retreated safely to Base Camp, much to Valery's relief. By the time Chris and I returned Crag and Jerry were off again, this time to attempt the memorably named Alexander Blok Peak.

Nicki and Siobhan had found that the local mountain tracks tended to be too rough and precipitous for biking but the (barely) motorable tracks in the valleys had enabled them to cover plenty of miles and get a good look at some other parts of the range. Their enthusiasm levels suggested that the Ak-su area was not the only part worth a visit and I was keen to do some exploring in the week that remained.

When we first got down from Ak-su I had noticed how much more acclimatised I was and how much easier it was to walk up the short slope to the toilet. In that short, euphoric phase I had agreed to walk for two days over intervening ridges to gain the Achat Valley beneath the spectacular peak of Sabac and the unclimbed Pooro peaks. As soon as the four of us set out though, all my energy seemed to have drained away. At the end of day Nicki and I opted for a circuitous route via the valley systems, whilst Chris and Siobhan decided to try a more direct approach.

Our arrival at the Moscow Mountaineering Club's summer camp at Achat came as something of a shock to our systems. The club had hired a helicopter to ferry in all equipment and nothing had been left to chance. Of the twenty or so tents the cook tent was the obvious focal point and we quickly found ourselves shepherded in its direction and encouraged to partake of a wide variety of unpronounceable but very tasty delicacies.

'The sauna is ready for you.'

The call should have been more expected than it was. After all it was already very clear to us that saunas are an important part of Soviet life and after experiences at Ak-su and in the Altai we already knew that remoteness is not an obstacle. Here though, for some reason we failed to understand, the sauna system was operated on a single sex basis with ladies second. Nicki had to wait until it was almost dark – which made the 'cool-off in the glacial torrent' sessions particularly challenging for her.

By dusk the following day there was still no sign of Chris and Siobhan and our hosts were taking it upon themselves to ensure that we were in no way hindered by the absence of the equipment the others were carrying. Their hospitality appeared to have no bounds. Not only did they clear a store tent for our sleeping quarters but a hawser-laid rope was put at our disposal, along with an impressive array of home-made equipment. It seemed that they were keen to give us every encouragement to attempt the unclimbed peaks that were the focal point of their camp and even went as far as to suggest that we try Pooro East which they thought might be a suitable objective for us.

Morning dawned drearily and heralded the unsuccessful return of a team from the camp who had been trying the first ascent of Pooro West. They looked soggy and dishevelled in their absorbent cotton anoraks and we were uncomfortably aware that we attracted envious glances in our embarrassingly brightly coloured Gore-Tex clothing.

A long, tedious 40-50-degree snow slope led to a col at the start of the difficulties on Pooro East. The drop down the far side was unexpected and breathtaking. It must have been overhanging for at least 200 metres and the crest of the ridge itself was a severely undercut rock flake which we had unknowingly climbed up the easy side of. We lay down and clung to the edge, peering down like two small children.

Above us the ridge was narrow and crenellated and generally looked far more intimidating than I had expected. The first step was a twenty-metre vertical to overhanging rock section which looked most feasible by traversing out over the abyss on the Uriem side.

'What if I come off?' enquired Nicki staring questioningly down the huge overhanging wall.

'Well ... er, then you prusik up the rope.'

I could sense that my response was unconvincing. The thought of dangling over a huge drop on an apparently ancient Russian rope of dubious origin was not one which filled me with confidence. Against this background the onset of snow proved to be the excuse we were looking for. I can't say that I felt too much disappointment as we glissaded down steep snow slopes to be welcomed by yet another sauna session.

Two days later we were back at Base Camp. The other four were already there and welcomed my arrival with great glee – I had hitched a ride on an outrageously flatulent horse. My embarrassment was all the greater as Nicki – who had stuck to walking, had arrived a good hour earlier.

Chris and Siobhan were in relaxed mode, having given up on their high-level route and enjoyed some scenic exploring. Crag and the normally hyper-enthusiastic Jerry were looking slightly chastened, having ferried all their gear up to Ak-su's South Ridge and Alexander Blok Peak's West Wall only to be beaten back by the weather on both occasions.

It was nearly time for us to leave but our Russian hosts were clearly having difficulty organising something. Jerry was quick to move into decisive military mode.

'Helicopter tomorrow, please.'

Awkward looks from the Russians. I wondered for a moment whether Jerry's 'shout it loudly, keep it simple style' was not getting through. But no ... It seemed that there was indeed a problem.

'It is a problem. No helicopter' mumbled Valery.

It transpired that there had been some sort of mountaineering emergency on Pic Lenin in the Pamirs and 'our' helicopter was indisposed. Worried looks all round on the Russian side.

'We need a military vehicle,' announced Jerry, pointing excitedly at the six-wheel-drive monster that had appeared at Base Camp.

But Valery was not listening. His head was in his hands now.

'Osh … there are problems in Osh. Your plane to Moscow; it is supposed to fly from Osh.'

By the following morning Jerry's wish had come true and another ex-army vehicle had arrived to ferry our equipment down to the road-head where a ramshackle bus was waiting with 'Osh' helpfully written on a piece of paper sellotaped to the windscreen.

The road quickly left the mountains and we found ourselves on a dead straight dusty track crossing a flat, arid plain. To our south the Ak-su mountains rose in a jagged, snow-capped backdrop, whilst to the north the plains faded into the hazy horizon. Through the shimmering heat haze a huge statue gradually became visible. Lenin … Standing twenty metres high in all his concrete glory, and behind him a concrete skyscraper town looking for all the world as if it had been lifted, lock, stock and barrel from European Russia and transported here. Our bus stopped so that we could admire the statue close up. Presumably the idea was that we should pay homage to the great man but the close proximity of the obvious *raison d'être* of the town proved a far more interesting distraction. Never before had I seen an open cast mine of such proportions. The scale was simply enormous. Inside the huge scar on the landscape, giant-sized dumper trucks crawled back and forth and meccano-like conveyor belts loaded with ore snaked their way across the landscape. The atmosphere of the whole complex was ramshackle; the buildings were lop-sided, the conveyor belts clanked and groaned, the lorries spluttered and belched fumes … but somehow, in the best possible Heath-Robinson tradition, it all seemed to function smoothly.

Prior to this we had only seen sporadic settlements. Now, as we headed deeper into Kyrgyzstan, more and more indigenous towns and villages were apparent. The contast between their typical third world central Asian characteristics and those of the concrete Russian town that we had passed could hardly have been more marked. Nothing could have brought home more directly the vivid reality of Stalin's policy of spreading european Russians throughout the Soviet Union. We pondered the situation over a sweet tea and rice and dahl stop at a Kyrgyz roadside café. By 1990 Gorbachov's *glasnost* and *perestroika* policies were already bringing down the central control that had existed under the old regime and ethnic clashes were becoming a feature of the area. We didn't envy the isolated pockets of European Russians standing out so obviously amongst the overwhelming Kyrgyz majority.

As the miles rolled by the road to Osh showed increasing signs of conflict. Soldiers became a more frequent sight and by the time our bus entered the town tanks on street corners were a regular feature. Ethnic unrest had come to Osh. Valery was worried. He took his responsibilities towards us very seriously. 'We will get you to the Rescue Command Building,' he announced, doubtless assuming that this bold statement would reassure us in some way. In fact, it simply conjured up images of the nerve centre of a panic situation until it transpired that we were actually arriving at the Russian equivalent of the local mountain rescue post, a rather pleasant and comfortable wooden building in a secluded position on the outskirts of the town. It was here that we first heard details about a serious avalanche on Pic Lenin and understood why our helicopter had abandoned us for more important duties. Initial reports suggested that a fairly major earthquake had occurred which had triggered a huge sérac fall. It appeared that at least a hundred people were involved (the final death toll was forty) and all available rescue services had been directed to Pic Lenin. The control centre, apparently usually a hive of activity, appeared deserted apart from a couple of harassed co-ordinators. But in comparison to the tank-ridden streets it was a haven of calm and tranquillity where we could recover whilst Valery somehow arranged for a coach, complete with armed guards, to take us to the airport where he could finally class his job as done. We were seen on the plane to Moscow and there had been no mishaps. The relief was plainly visible in his smile.

The airport didn't look very familiar, but we simply assumed that it must be Moscow's domestic airport, with which we were less familiar, than the international one. Our luggage had been stacked into the main seating area of the plane and we dutifully lugged it out across the runway and through the terminal building. It all seemed a bit low key. No officials seemed to be very interested in us and we soon found ourselves outside the airport at a taxi rank. The delectable Olga from the Sports Committee was supposed to be meeting us here and her absence did, it must be admitted, prompt suspicion that all was not well. Our efforts to get a taxi to the Hotel Sport confirmed our fears.

'Hotel Sport, pashalsta' I tried in my best Russian.

'Nyet.' The answer was unequivocal.

There was something wrong. Why should all these taxi drivers refuse a lucrative fare?

An English-speaking lady came to our rescue. It transpired that we had got off somewhere in the Urals. Moscow was still a couple of hours' flight away. It was perhaps fortunate that true capitalism appeared not to have filtered through to this part of Russia. If it had we could well have found ourselves 'enjoying' a very long and expensive taxi-ride. Fortunately the plane was still on the ground and the air hostesses watched with ill-concealed hilarity as we sheepishly lugged all our gear back on for the last leg to Moscow.

Back in London I contemplated the trip. Russia was increasingly opening her mountain areas, the potential was enormous and the people fantastically welcoming. I sensed I would have to return.

There was a memorable postscript to the Pic Lenin affair. Back in Britain I received a telephone call from a daily national newspaper. It was a roving reporter out for an action-packed story.

'You have just come back from Pic Lenin,' he informed me.

'No, I haven't,' I protested.

Having clarified that Ak-su was somewhere near Pic Lenin, he blasted forth with his prepared questions.

'Did you feel the earthquake?'

'No, I didn't.'

'How about the severe aftershocks?'

'No. Can't help you there. But I was probably bouncing along in a bus on an unmetalled road when they occurred.'

'Oh … What about the rescue efforts. Did you see any evidence of these? Helicopters and things?'

'Not directly. As far as I know all available helicopters were sent to Pic Lenin but I didn't actually see them.'

My answers were not conducive to a good story. Nevertheless the next day *The Daily Telegraph* carried a report on the incident:

Mr Mick Fowler, a British mountaineer on an expedition on a neighbouring peak when the disaster struck said: 'It must have been a very small earthquake, because no-one felt it where we were … Our bunkhouse was the centre for rescue operations, with helicopters coming and going all night.'

My faith in the accuracy of newspaper reports dropped to a new low.

4

Taweche: North-East Buttress

Early Taweche history – bonding with Littlejohn – liaison officer and sirdar concerns –
fixing the initial pitch – hacking a bivouac ledge – the Torture Tube – steep ice pitches –
contemplating wet feet and 8000m challenges – the summit – clever descent techniques

Sustad was not sounding happy. 'It's a real bummer. I just can't make it
– it's the trip I was most looking forward to this year and now the bloody
doctor tells me I can't go.'

He was in an uncharacteristically abusive mood. The problem was his
toe. It had gone an unhealthy black colour and begun to smell badly after
a frostbite injury incurred during a South American epic. He didn't seem
too worried about the imminent loss of a useful digit and was far more
concerned that he was going to miss out on a crack at Taweche's North-
East Buttress. This distressed him.

Steve was one of my regular climbing partners who had been with
me on Cerro Kishtwar two years earlier. This was just the sort of trip he
would have liked – a multi-pitched route of great challenge on a peak of
manageable height in a marvellous situation.

Taweche (6542m) is ten miles south-west of Everest. It was first
climbed in 1974[1] and by 1995 had had about ten ascents – almost all by
the first ascent line. Our attention was drawn to a magnificent mixed-
buttress line forming the north-east corner of the mountain. I first became
aware of this feature from a photograph in the 1991 North Face catalogue.

'East Faces are pretty inspiring too ...' said the caption. I couldn't
help but agree. The American climbers Jeff Lowe and John Roskelley had
climbed the stunning couloir line up the centre of the East Face in the
winter of 1988 but the objectively safer North-East Buttress remained
unclimbed. A couple of teams had sniffed around it but only the French
in 1990 had made any real impression. They reached a shoulder at around
5700 metres that marked the start of the continuously steep main section

[1] The first ascent was made in the pre-monsoon season of 1974 by Louis Debost and Paul Gendre, members
of a French expedition led by Yannick Seigneur. Three other members of the party climbed it during the
following days. This was a party of Chamonix guides who were in the region (ostensibly) to investigate high-
altitude ski potential. They climbed the peak without official permission, taking the route up the South-East
Face used in 1963 by a US/NZ expedition (led by Sir Edmund Hillary) that had gained a point just seventy
metres below the summit.

of the spur. The *American Alpine Journal* reported that they were stopped by a combination of technical difficulty and powder snow. They went post-monsoon, when it is colder and more prone to powdery conditions. We chose pre-monsoon, when we reasoned we could expect less settled weather but, hopefully, less powder snow.

As usual we had arranged to climb strictly as two teams of two.

Mike Morrison and Chris Watts made up one team, Steve Sustad and I the other. Steve's toe problem meant that we were a person short. But who could replace him? Finding someone willing to spend six weeks in Nepal with only three weeks' notice is difficult enough. To find someone who I would also feel comfortable climbing with seemed a virtual impossibility.

I phoned around hopefully. I couldn't cancel the trip now but whoever would be able to make it? The answer came quite quickly – Pat Littlejohn.

Pat is one of those legendary figures who was high on my list of rock climbing heroes during my formative years. I particularly remember feeling terribly humbled when he was quoted in a climbing magazine criticising those who cluttered Savage God, his climb in Devon, with hammered nuts because they couldn't do it properly. He didn't know who the culprit was but the gist of his comments was completely justified; a young Fowler had got terribly into extremis and had to ashamedly abandon his gear. A man of modest character and immense achievement, Pat is perhaps best known as the first ascensionist of a vast number of top quality, high standard rock climbs throughout the UK, particularly on the more remote and intimidating sea cliffs. Perhaps because of our mutual enthusiasm for rarely visited spots we had hardly ever bumped into each other. However I was very aware that we shared a passion for adventurous and committing climbs tackled with a strictly ground up ethic. By 1995 he was Director of the International School of Mountaineering in Leysin, Switzerland, although he spent most of the year living in North Wales with his partner Eira and their two children. His activities seemed to mainly emanate from the International School and, increasingly, involved guiding expeditions to various exciting-looking areas close to the Russia/ China border area. He was a busy man with heavy family and work schedules – but an inspiring photograph can work wonders on a full diary.

It was strange and out of character for me to arrange to climb in the Himalaya with someone whom I had never climbed with before. Not only that but Pat was, in my eyes, more a rock climber than a Himalayan climber. But sometimes the chemistry of confidence, judgement and respect seems just right. Nicki agreed. She takes an interest in my big mountain climbing partners and was more than comfortable with our decision to take our first climbing steps together on Taweche's North-East Buttress.

And so three weeks later four of us were squeezed into a heavily loaded ex-Aeroflot helicopter experiencing Everest Air's inflight catering services en-route to Lukla from Kathmandu. About twenty of us sat crunched together with our knees hard against a huge central mound of cargo. The air hostess first passed round cotton wool ear bungs and then a plate of boiled sweets. Luxury travel indeed – and a lot quicker than the nine or so days' walk from the road-head. Modern Nepal is well within reach of us restricted holiday boys.

Only Chris Watts had been to Nepal before. The rest of us marvelled at the intricate terrace-work below and stared gob-smacked at the huge mountains ahead. I had heard all about the airstrip at Lukla but, though I knew it to be memorably spectacular, I had at least expected brick-sized rocks to be swept to one side. Sturdy specimens, these small planes. I was glad to be in a nice helicopter which simply plonked itself down in a clearing at the top of the runway, covering the village in yet another film of dust.

Unfortunately, it had not been possible to get all of our gear on the same helicopter as ourselves. Such are the joys of popular areas. In fact most of the next week was spent worrying about when a flight might have space for our pile of essentials, last seen at Kathmandu. Theoretically our liaison officer should have been able to offer assistance in sorting out these problems. In fact he was 'busy' in Kathmandu for the entire time that it took us to get to Base Camp. The number of superfluous employees that we were forced to have was to become something of a sore point. Not only did we have an absent liaison officer, there was also a cook to look after him, a kitchen boy to help the cook and a sirdar to manage the employees, particularly the porters – of which there were none. All this was disturbingly expensive and increasingly irritating.

When the liaison officer did eventually arrive he spent one night at Base Camp (where we had provided him with tent, sleeping bag, cook, kitchen boy, etc.) before deciding that it was too cold and lonely there so he would spend the duration relaxing with a fellow liaison officer in the wondrously named Peace Zone Rest House in Pheriche, the small settlement directly below Taweche. It was no great loss not to have him at Base Camp but it was galling to have to pay his food and accommodation costs when we had provided everything for him at Base Camp. This feeling of being ripped off deepened when it became clear that he expected us to pay him his daily rate for the period when he wasn't even there. Also it transpired that he was a government employee and not only did he receive his salary whilst he was with us but he also received overtime payments for the weekends and evenings that he was away from home.

'Not like the British civil service,' ribbed Mike.

I did some wistful calculations. On the same basis, if a Nepalese climbing expedition came to Britain to climb, say, Beachy Head, as their liaison officer I could expect to receive something like £100,000 over and above my normal salary for sitting in a local pub chatting to mates for three weeks. No surprise then that the Nepalese Tourist Ministry like to keep their jobs in house!

As it happened our main concern was our sirdar. The liaison officer was always recognised as a bureaucratic necessity and the cook and kitchen boy were hard-working, great company, of benefit to us and relatively cheap. The role of the sirdar was far less obvious. The idea seemed to be that he should look after porters and the like but as we had only four yaks and one Yak-driver there wasn't exactly a lot for him to do, particularly after we had arrived at Base Camp. So we paid him off.

Ang Phurba was a nice enough chap but was clearly used to lucrative work with much larger Everest expeditions. The fact that he wasn't really needed was emphasised by his propensity to disappear for long periods, surfacing occasionally to ask for money for one reason or another.

And so our financially disgruntled but otherwise high spirited team made its way along the Everest trail for five days, eventually to establish a Base Camp (with, miraculously, all our gear) under the north-eastern side of Taweche which looked challenging.

Taweche (not to be confused with the lower Taboche just to its north) rises prominently on the western side of the wide valley south-west of the Everest massif where the highest Sherpa settlements, Pheriche and Dingboche, are situated. At the end of this valley the previously amiable Everest trail continues north heading steeply uphill to the huts at Lobuche and the snout of the Khumbu Glacier. The Taweche route heads in the opposite direction up long grassy slopes and moraine to the Tshola Glacier where flat areas of moraine provide obvious campsites.

The North-East Buttress looked pretty fearsome from close up but my inability to acclimatise quickly had left me so under the weather that I barely noticed.

My head hurt. Base Camp just was over 5000m but it did seem unfair that everyone else appeared fine, when all I could do was lie comatose in the tent uttering the occasional groan. Every now and then Pat would peer anxiously through the door and urge me to try his latest boulder problem.

'Are you sure you're OK?' Clearly he was used to fitter, more lively partners.

'Perfectly normal,' I would groan in response to his regular looks of concern. The others, who knew me better, confirmed the truth of my answer. After several similar trials on high mountains I concluded that fast acclimatisation was not really my forte.

After a couple of days, though, it was time to sniff around the buttress and check out both the route and my body's ability to cope with the higher altitude. We staggered listlessly around on the lower part of the buttress. On the north side the snow consistency was the much-feared bottomless powder, whilst to the south it was just horribly steep and difficult, with plenty of loose rock. After a couple of days of acclimatising we retreated to Base Camp to consider. Both ropes had been cut and my knee was painfully twisted. Not a good start. On the bright side, my head didn't hurt quite so much now.

A decision was made to follow the line of the French attempt up an obvious diagonal ramp, reaching the crest of the buttress at the point where it steepened and looked horribly difficult. I delayed action for two days, using the hurt knee excuse, whilst Pat oozed energy and even bounded up to the foot of the face to check things out. I was beginning to understand how he has kept up a prolific output of hard new rock climbs for near on thirty years. The man's energy reserves and enthusiasm level seemed unfathomably deep.

Pat reported that the first seventy metres were nastily steep, technical and clearly time-consuming. This obstacle unfortunately led to an easing of the angle which the morning sun would render exposed to falling rocks. Putting ethical qualms to one side, we decided to fix our ropes up this section so that we could jumar up and pass the exposed ground early in the morning when it was still frozen.

And so at 8am on 18 April 1995 I tied on to the rope beneath Taweche and prepared to climb my first ever pitch with Pat Littlejohn. It looked very steep and challenging. But Pat is the sort of person who inspires great confidence. Despite not having undertaken anything quite like this before, he seemed totally unfazed by the large overhangs and lack of any immediately obvious line. His enthusiasm for getting started was palpable and infectious.

'Your lead, Patrick.' It seemed the obvious thing to say.

Pat, though, was staring at me curiously,

'Where are your rock boots?' he enquired.

There was indeed a notable contrast in our footwear. The Fowler feet were cosily encased in plastic double boots, complete with all enveloping super gaiters whereas Littlejohn's were rammed into some rather dainty-looking rock slippers.

'I'll do fine in these,' I assured my clearly sceptical partner.

At least it seemed to convince him that the first pitch was, as I suggested, his lead. I settled down to watch the master in action. There was clearly a very hard section at five metres. Pat wiggled a good wire into a flaky crack and set about sorting out the difficult sequence ahead. I watched mesmerised as he made repeated efforts, utilise tiny crumbling layaways on an overhanging wall. There was none of the grunting or urgent shouts of 'Watch me' that I tend to emit on such occasions.

'Isn't, it good enough to pull on?' I enquired, pointing at the wire, whilst marvelling at the strictly puritanical Littlejohn ethics.

A curious look came my way before he made an outrageous series of moves and established himself in a wide bridge amidst more overhangs.

My efforts to second the pitch somehow lacked the Littlejohn finesse. I could blame it on the heavy sack, the big boots or even the altitude. In fact I excused my performance by referring to myself as a 'mountaineer'.

'Mountaineers wear big boots, carry sacks and pull on gear,' I explained to the bemused Littlejohn.

Notwithstanding these nuances in style, the day was successful and by nightfall we were back in Base Camp with our expedient if unethical rope fixed on the first seventy metres and nearly all of our gear at the top end. Another rest day and then, ten days after arriving at Base Camp, it was time to go for it.

Meanwhile Morrison and Watts had also been nosing around the base of the buttress but Mike's acclimatisation process seemed even slower than mine and as we set off they put off any decision about what they might attempt until Mike was feeling better.

Rising at 2am or so is never my idea of fun but for us it was judged necessary to get out of the rockfall danger zone before the sun came up. We were though rather surprised to see Ang Phurba suddenly make an appearance. We hadn't seen him since arriving at Base Camp and I had assumed that, as there was nothing for him to do, he had descended to the tea house he ran lower down the valley. But no, here he was, in person, fully dressed, complete with big boots, in the middle of the night, asking that we pay him a salary advance! Our response is unprintable. Apart from anything else we were dressed to leave for the mountain, had hidden our money and passports and had no wish whatsoever to advertise where they were. Somewhat to my surprise, on being told that we would pay when we got down, he left and went back to bed. All very odd. From this point on we found it most amusing to ask each other for money at the least convenient moment possible.

But at last we were off. No more bureaucracy and financial nego-tiations for now, just the North-East Buttress of Taweche to climb.

Staggering up the snow slopes beneath the face, I was surprised to hear a shout from above and, through the gloom, see a dark cylindrical shape heading erratically towards a large crevasse about twenty metres ahead of me. I recognised it immediately, our bivouac tent, without which we stood no chance of success. Pat was waving the broken carrying strap and gesticulating wildly. Running at altitude is not something that I am very good at, particularly whilst waving axes and wearing crampons. Fortunately, the tent veered in my direction and a combination of wavering sprint, followed by a faultless dive (although I say it myself), saw the tent back in our hands.

After this thrilling little interlude, our attention was turned to the joys of jumaring up to our gear. Pat seemed to be good at this. He flowed gracefully up over overhangs and disappeared, moving strongly upwards. My turn merely provided me with an opportunity to demonstrate my comparative incompetence. The rucksack pulled me backwards to the point of inversion and somehow, whatever I did, the sling lengths seemed to be wrong. Progress looked to be impossible. I contemplated leaving my rucksack behind and pulling it up afterwards but numerous downward pointing spikes led me to decide against this. Eventually, having rigged up a complex arrangement of slings to (inadequately) support my sack, I succeeded in gasping my way up towards an incredulous Pat who could not understand how someone who has been climbing for so long could be so poor at jumaring.

As a result of my slow jumaring we were much later than we had planned and the first rocks were already bouncing down the face as we stepped onto the exposed foot of the prominent ramp line leading up right to the shoulder. Shortly after the rocks came the heat. Himalayan sun never ceases to amaze me. Most people know about the frostbite risks and assume the weather on mountains is continually cold; few seem aware of the energy-sapping sun and the risks of Himalayan sun-stroke.

Apart from slow acclimatisation I boast the additional failing of being not too good in the heat. Pitch after pitch, we alternated our way up the ramp, keeping well out to the right edge where we were less exposed to rockfall. The difficulties were mainly moderate but the sun was taking its toll. Not only were our bodies suffering but the icy trickle in the corner of the ramp was rapidly growing into a torrent full of bouncing boulders and shattering ice blocks.

Luckily the right edge of the ramp was reasonably hospitable. Only the really freak bouncers could reach us here. I began to feel a bit happier. Pat was good company and amazingly proficient. The rock quality left plenty of room for improvement however, with steep slabby grooves lined with precariously poised veneers of crud. We picked our way cautiously upwards heading for the French high point. With luck there would be a good bivouac spot there.

Needless to say, we arrived as the last rays of daylight faded, to find nothing but a razor-sharp arête of solid ice. It looked as if we were in for a bum-ledge bivi. Pat, though, was keen for some creature comforts and feeling more energetic than I was.

'We'll just chop the top off and pitch the tent.'

I looked at him uncertainly. The energy involved in this exercise would be immense. Also, I couldn't help but remember the problems caused when Sustad and I broke three axes out of four whilst attempting something similar on Cerro Kishtwar. But Littlejohn was not to be denied. Ice chips flew as pickaxe blows rained down hard. Every now and then I contributed a token swing with my axe, but it was, I have to admit, pretty feeble compared with Pat's resilient pounding. Thus mesmerised, I was privileged to witness the single-handed transformation of a solid ice ridge into a very acceptable tent platform. It certainly seemed that these super-fit guide types had their uses.

Next morning I peered hopefully upwards, expecting that a night's rest would have moderated the previous evening's impression of fearful problems to come. But the difficulty was still readily apparent and beyond the shoulder the angle increased to over 70 degrees. After a few pots of tea and a Muesli bar we packed the tent and set to work. It had been an unusually comfortable night and I felt refreshed and ready to go. I reflected that hacking out good bivouac ledges might indeed be worth the effort – particularly if the effort was made by one's partner.

The way lay up a series of ice-streaked corners connected by challenging rock traverses. At the end of the knife-edge crest forming the shoulder there was a bolt, the last sign of the French effort in 1990, and then the first rock traverse fell to me.

'Looks about Grade III,' came wafting up from below, as I rubbed my nose against the verticality and contemplated placing a peg behind a selection of dubious flakes. Either Pat's judgement on this difficulty business was a bit awry or there was a heavy hint of sarcasm in his voice that I had missed. Either way, extremis soon followed. Wild pulls on flaky pinch-grips and strenuously spectacular layaways seemed mildly out of place on the Himalayan severity menu. There must have been something slightly difficult about it as even Pat took back the Grade III rating and complained of a pulled shoulder afterwards. But he did make it look horribly easy.

The difficulties continued. I suppose we knew they would, but one must, of course, remain optimistic that a break might allow some height to be gained quickly. Here, though, it didn't.

The buttress has two distinct steep sections or steps, one above the lower ramp and the other forming a daunting headwall above the upper right-leaning ramp lines we had seen through binoculars. We were now on the lower step,where the main feature is a prominent, friable pinnacle. The aim was to turn this on the left and gain height to reach those upper ramp lines. In the colder winter conditions Roskelley and Lowe had made their height using an icy depression in the centre of the great face to our left, but in the morning sun of the early summer their line was a veritable skittle alley of falling rocks and ice, whereas ours (apart from the initial pitches) was comparatively safe.

Icy grooves and difficult rock cracks slowed progress to the extent that we only managed five pitches before the usual afternoon storms (which had miraculously held off the day before) moved in and Pat was once again called upon to exercise his excavation skills and magic up a ledge for the night. Perhaps he was tiring slightly for, when I squeezed into the tent first, I was uncomfortably aware that one-third of the floor space was hanging in mid-air. Looking back towards the entrance, I was treated to the sight of waves of spindrift pouring in, whilst Pat stood there fighting to sort out the gear before zipping us in. We sat huddled together listening to the wind and snow. There was no doubt about it – these afternoon storms were becoming distinctly tiresome. The mornings, though, were invariably bright and sunny and had to be taken full advantage of. On we went. Steep icy grooves with delightful white ice, which occasionally took placements good enough to allow clipped-in rests – a novelty for the super-ethical Littlejohn. On one pitch I was forced to remove my sack and climb a difficult leaning crack on wedged ice picks with a couple of insecure aid points. In the interests of speed Pat jumared, something that neither of us liked doing. It was though a relief for me to see that our ethics were converging as we became more stretched. We were moving slowly but steadily upwards, onto a prominent ramp.

After an uneventful third bivouac the ramp line led, as expected, round to the right-hand side of the buttress and a whole new panorama. Here, below and to our right, the unclimbed North Face fell sharply away, Droites-like, looking very cold and challenging. Up above, we had seen what we hoped would be snow/ice streaks from Base Camp but from this angle they were hidden above vertical rock walls.

The afternoon storms started whilst we were still in this rocky no-man's-land somewhere between the ramp and the white streaks leading towards the top. Spindrift roared down from up on high and progress soon became impossible. Forays to various prospective bivouac sites proved fruitless and we were beginning to get a little anxious before we spotted a small hole and possible snow patch up to the left. Getting there, though, looked to be extremely challenging.

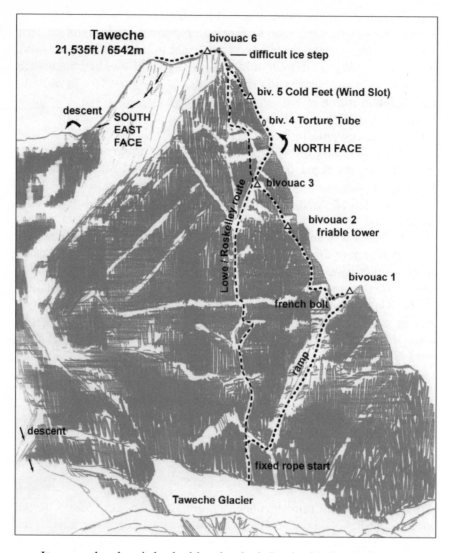

It was as hard as it looked but by dusk Pat had belayed, brought me
up and the two of us were peering into a 50cm wide ice tube which
funnelled down deep into our snow patch, which, of course, consisted of
iron-hard ice. An uncharacteristic look of concern was painted on Pat's
face.

'Looks very snug, Patrick,' I quipped, trying to be enthusiastic.

He still didn't seem too keen as I squirmed into my sleeping bag and
slid committingly into the slippery orifice. The angle eased after four
metres or so but it was particularly nasty and claustrophobic being stuck
at the bottom of a hole. I lay motionless, trying to quell a sense of rising

panic. I could lie quite comfortably on one side but my nose was hard against the ice and my hips were too broad to turn over. Could I last the night in this position? The chances felt no more than fifty-fifty.

After a few minutes the stove clanged down on top of me, as did Pat's boots which caught me painfully on the shoulder. Then, after a series of contortions of which any yoga expert would have been proud, I was just about to light the stove when a blast of spindrift posed a new problem. Up until this point I had at least been protected from the elements. Now the wind had obviously changed and it was as if a fireman had suddenly directed his hose down into my little bedroom. To begin with I abandoned my efforts to light the stove and fought to prevent the snow getting into my sleeping bag. But it was a losing battle. The snow just kept on coming. Soon it was beginning to block my only exit. Priorities changed fast as I abandoned the stove and boots and instead scrabbled to haul on Pat's legs and squirm back up the frictionless tube. Ultimately we settled down without our sleeping bags, wedged into the slightly under 45 degrees section of tube. It was an excruciatingly unpleasant night during which the endless hours passed with a rising tide of groans and moans about our respective problems. Particularly memorable were the two occasions on which I was called to semi-invert myself and make a brew with the stove hanging from the guy ropes of the tent which we had done our best to drape over our heads. For good reasons we christened this bivouac the Torture Tube.

Morning was impossible for me to appreciate. Firstly, Pat was above me and blocked out ninety per cent of the light; secondly, the entrance to our torture-tube faced north-west and thus was denied the warmth-giving

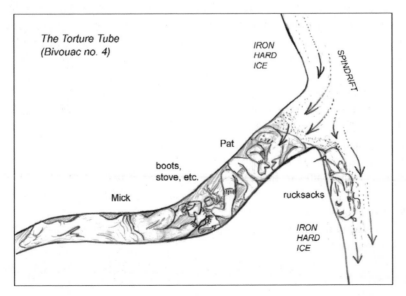

early morning sun. We crawled out, cold and stiff, but the view upwards was not over-encouraging. The sun was catching the face just above us, but there was no obvious line to follow and the angle was distressingly high. We moved up five metres, took a hanging belay in the sun and tried to remember what we had seen through binoculars from Base Camp. The time spent peering at the face was such that both of us had the most likely-looking line firmly imprinted on our minds. Somewhere up to our right were two snow/ice streaks, the right-hand one of which looked to give the most promising line to the top of the buttress. My main fear, when looking through the binoculars, had been that this streak might be bottomless powder snow on steep rock slabs. I had come across such ground in India a couple of years previously and knew how downright frightening it could be.

Tentatively we followed discontinuous streaks of snow, trending slightly rightwards. The first of the vertical streaks seen from Base Camp was obvious and appeared to end in a cul-de-sac of overhanging rock walls. It was, however, ice. Our hopes rose. The climbing conditions had, in fact, become excellent, even the very steepest snow bands being of fine hard névé. The second streak looked worrying, though. It was ice all right but it was steeper and thinner than expected. It clearly covered smooth rock slabs and these were visible enough for us to realise that the ice in general was very thin.

It was my pitch and it looked hard.

Unfortunately it was. Equally unfortunately we had only brought three ice screws. I clipped into my axe as soon as sensibly possible and contemplated our pure ice rack. Why ever had I insisted on cutting it down so much? Pat had pressed for more, but ever conscious of my inability to carry heavy loads, I had insisted that 'one on each belay and one for a runner' would be OK. That had assumed that all three would be bomb-proof. My first effort bottomed against the rock after only five centimetres. Five metres higher I managed to get one in halfway, and felt slightly better. Nevertheless it still felt a harrowing pitch: the whole of the North Face fell away beneath my feet and the last five metres was completely vertical and I had used all three screws before belaying at a rock.

The ground continued in a similarly precarious manner but with no obvious rock cracks to head for. I was glad that it was now Pat's lead. But I was in for a shock. A short groove, which had offered an escape from the icy openness, stopped the master in his tracks.

'Coming down,' came from up to my right, as he fought his way back to the stance.

This was worrying. The Littlejohn climbing machine was not easily repulsed! Failure was not something that I had considered. His next

JORDAN 1988

1 Approaching the ancient ruins of Petra.

2 *(below)* A flooded section of the gorge west of Petra.

3 *(inset)* A storm in the mountains soon made the higher reaches of the gorge a scene of raging waterfalls that quickly reached the lower gorge which we had passed just in time.

4 *(left)* We camped where gorge ended and next day trekked west over arid hills towards Wadi Araba. Nicki carries her wet clothes from the previous day's adventures.

5 *(overleaf)* The spectacular scene on the classic Steps of Assaf at Wadi Rum. First climbed in 1952 it gave a fine climb to the top of the plateau.

5 On the Steps of Assaf above Wadi Rum.

KYRGYZSTAN 6 - 7 In 1990 we visited one of the best mountain areas of the old Soviet Union. At Bishkek, Valery *(inset)*, our 'minder', had organised a helicopter to take us to the official camp near Osh. *(above)* Nicki, Crag Jones (packing his sack) and Jerry Gore (in red) by our pile of gear.

8 *(below)* Rocky Ak-su's fine northern rock face fronts the higher Snowy Ak-su's summit on the right. We climbed Rocky Ak-su's North Ridge on the right, traversed to and from the snow summit and descended the steep East Ridge on the left.

9 *(top left)* On Ak-su we rapidly gained height by following a dangerous couloir on the right to the face – moving left at the top to a bivouac site behind a gendarme.

10 *(above left)* On the hard pitch above the gendarme I was mortified to find a bolt just above this point suggesting that the route had been climbed before.

11 - 12 *(far right)* Chris Watts climbed this steep pitch close to the summit of Rocky Ak-su near the end of a fine rock climb up the ridge. We dumped most of our gear and climbed the connecting ridge to Snowy Ak-su *(above centre)* with fine views north-east to Alexander Blok Peak.

13 - 14 *(right)* After returning to bivouac on the summit of Rocky Ak-su we made a long abseil descent down the steep East Ridge to where the angle eased *(far right)* and we could gain a high snowfield below the face.

NEPAL 1995

15 Taweche's North-East Buttress *(left)* throws down a fine challenge. After careful study we opted for a line up the ramp and the crest of the buttress (avoiding the tower) to gain the two high ice ledges that led round to the icy North Face where we hoped to find suitable finishing pitches.

16 - 17 With the sun loosening ice and rocks on the face above, Pat Littlejohn hastens up the ramp *(top right)* towards the safety of the skyline notch where a bivouac ledge was hacked out of the crest of an ice ridge *(right centre)*.

18 - 19 I follow a steep pitch on the second day *(below)* as bad weather brings climbing to an early halt. The third pitch next day *(far right)* gave difficult mixed climbing using torqued ice axes.

TAWECHE (continued) 20 - 21 In the afternoon bad weather, finding a bivi site became unlikely as I moved round onto the steep North Face *(left)*. Eventually Pat found an ice hole. In this 'Torture Tube' *(above)* I displayed distress and Pat added to the misery by squeezing down above me as the spindrift began.

22 - 23 Next day we were soon in action on the North Face *(upper photo)* enjoying several fine ice pitches *(right)* made more exciting by our frugality in taking just three ice screws – one for each belay and one for a runner.

INDIA 1997 Changabang's North Face was the target for several ambitious climbers after an abortive attempt in 1996. 24 The two driving figures in both years were Roger Payne and Julie-Ann Clyma (seen here below Kalanka and Changabang while acclimatising). The route was based on the obvious snow shoulder (Second Icefield) seen on the face above Julie-Ann. The following photo sequence shows Steve Sustad and me on various pitches on the route.

25 Day 1 / Pitch 1 The route moves left from this point to the obvious groove line.

26 Day 2 / Pitch 2 A thin ice veneer allowed progress up the groove line.

27 Day 2 / Pitch 3 The afternoon spindrift begins.

28 Day 4 / Pitch 1 Glassy icefields became both taxing and boring after a time.

29 - 32 *(left)* Day 4 / Pitch 5 The steep rocks above the Second Icefield. *(above left)* Day 6 On the Third Icefield. Andy Cave climbs to join Brendan Murphy at the top of the ice tongue. We camped for two nights at this point awaiting progress. *(above right)* Steve Sustad leads a mixed pitch above Bivouac 5 (Day 7) – note the steel plated anti-balling crampons that later failed in their function with serious consequences. *(below)* Day 8 / Pitch 2 One of the fine mixed pitches high on the face.

CHANGABANG 1997

33 - 36 *(top left)* In poor weather we were forced to bivouac during the descent of Kalanka's South Face. *(centre)* Abseiling down the ice cliff after the avalanche. *(above)* Our view of the accident scene next day. *(left)* At Shipton's Col.

37 *(right)* Brendan Murphy in Dehli. His fine Changabang success ended in tragedy.

38 - 40 *(below)* Andy Cave, myself and Steve Sustad after our safe but sad return from a multi-day epic.

PERU 1998

Siula Chico looked the ideal challenge for a new Andean trip made more interesting as I teamed up with Simon Yates returning to the scene of his Siula Grande epic with Joe Simpson. In the event we found that in the warm year of El Niño Siula Chico's ice encrustations were dangerously unstable and the lower slopes were bare of snow. It was just too risky.

41 *(right)* Loading mules in the main street of Cajatambo.

42 *(below)* Simon Yates below Siula Chico's steeper walls

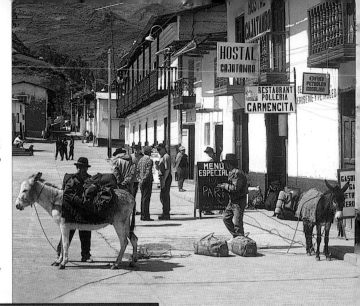

43 Siula Chico

44 Simon Yates and Mike Morrison in the Huayllapa 'hotel'

45 *(photomontage)* Siula Grande and Siula Chico seen from a viewpoint above Base Camp. The Simpson/Yates epic took place on the lower left snow slopes of the Grande and afterwards Joe Simpson crawled and stumbled down the glacier and lower moraine slopes to regain Base Camp.

46 *(above)* On the Chico, even with early starts, huge ice chandeliers, were soon crashing down the face.

moves, however, were even more worrying. Amidst comments about the ice looking thicker over to our left, he lowered down the vertical section of the previous pitch and traversed ten metres to gain his preferred position. The absence of screws meant that, from the second's point of view, the adrenalin flow was building up rapidly. I did not relish the prospect of seconding.

Pat continued impressively upwards, always trending slightly left, and thereby increasing the already frightening pendulum potential. Eventually he was able to slip in one of our big steel screws right up to the hilt and belay. I followed gibbering and, much against the grain, leaving a sling and karabiner for a back rope. Even so, the ropes hung clear from the face which at this point was thrillingly exposed with matchless vistas in all directions. I confess that I was unable to give my full attention to this splendid prospect, being preoccupied with climbing difficulties at this point.

By the time I had joined him, the views had disappeared and the afternoon dose of bad weather was imminent and bivouac sites were looking, if anything, even more non-existent than the night before. We fumbled on for a couple more exciting pitches before spotting a hole piercing the icy crest of the buttress just to our left. Holes were not popular after the previous night's antics. But this one looked slightly more friendly. It was clearly wind-formed but at least had a vaguely flat floor and was not so claustrophobic as the Torture Tube. Somewhere, not far above us, we sensed the top of the buttress. But mist swirled around, denying essential visibility. It could be one pitch, it could be five. Fearful of a night hanging in slings on the exposed open face, the decision was made. We would make the best of it.

It was impossible to pitch the tent properly in the cramped 'Wind Slot' but the poles were half in and we did, at least, manage to get inside our sleeping bags. I lay there warm and cosy, thankful that I had suffered the night before in order to make sure that my sleeping bag stayed dry. Outside the clouds were dropping down into the valley and the majestic mountains of the Everest group were revealed in all their splendour. Farther east the huge bulk of Makalu was instantly recognisable. The faces of Lhotse and Makalu in particular sport Taweche-like problems but at altitudes in excess of 8000 metres. Would I ever try such routes? I lay there in my scenic bedroom contemplating. The time commitment would be substantially greater, perhaps ten weeks away, compared with the three to four weeks required for peaks around 6500 metres. But even if I did have the time, would I be drawn to try? I thought about the greater extremes. Bivouacs like the Torture Tube but even colder. Exhaustion like at 6500 metres but far worse. Impaired judgement from lack of oxygen. Visually it all looked very appealing but in all mountaineering there is an element of balancing risk against reward. Maybe the risks of such climbing are just too high? For the moment at least I am happy to leave them for others.

'I need some help with my feet. They're really cold.'

Pat's sleeping bag was on the thin side and this was obviously now causing a problem. While I am scrupulous about cutting down on weight in general I do like a warm sleeping bag and work on the basis that the less energy used in keeping warm the more one has available for the climb itself. Pat had a lighter bag, and with the temperature dropping to –25°C he was probably feeling the cold.

In our constricted environment some intricate contortions had taken place to manipulate ourselves into positions to be able to get damp, cold Littlejohn feet pressed against my nice, warm Fowler body. Inevitably all the exertions resulted in the poles collapsing even more. I lay there contemplating these weighty problems amidst a degree of claustrophobia brought on by my head being at the bottom end of an ice-encrusted, collapsed tent and the curious intimacy involved in cuddling a pair of cold male feet. Usually only Nicki, by now my wife of four years, was allowed to get cold feet anywhere near me. I think we both felt slightly awkward. Even though these were very famous feet this was taking admiration a little far – we didn't know each other *that* well.

Mountaineering certainly prompts ready acceptance of a degree of intimacy that would normally be taboo. Earlier on we had both had to crap in front of each other on a tiny stance and now we lay in our curiously intimate sleeping position. With heads at opposite ends of the fabric, conversation was difficult and we dozed with our own thoughts. With luck we would get to the top of the buttress tomorrow. If we didn't we would probably have failed and be faced with a horrendous descent. That was an uncomfortable thought that I preferred not to dwell on.

The morning dawned crystal clear but, even so, it was still difficult to judge how far we had to go. The first Littlejohn lead of the day looked worryingly difficult but beyond that it was impossible to be specific. Steep ice just stretched up into the distance, eventually merging with the dark blue sky.

Rather to our surprise it was only two pitches later that a very cautious team, maximising the protection potential with three ice screws, pulled over the sharp crest of the ridge to complete the first ascent of Taweche's North-East Buttress.

A sudden clearing revealed the summit to be some way off.

Apart from slow acclimatisation and being unable to climb well in heat I am a self-confessed, incompetent snow-plodder. My regular climbing partners know this and it must have become increasingly apparent to Pat over the next few hours. He, though, ploughed on bravely whilst I floundered behind. At one point a short, difficult snow step impeded progress and gave Pat such concern that he borrowed my axe, with its large homemade adze, in order to overcome it. A complete whiteout all afternoon resulted in the wonderful sensation of bivouacking in a totally unknown location and waking up in a fabulously scenic position surprisingly close to the summit.

By 7.30am we were 'so far forgetting ourselves' to be found shaking hands on the highest point – a wonderfully reserved British gesture that somehow failed to sum up the feelings of the moment. I recall we even added a small hug too. Tilman would have been ashamed of that bit. There had been forty-three pitches of climbing, lots of uncertainty and a night that I have no hesitation in describing as the most uncomfortable of my life. But we had done it! All we had to do now was descend safely. I sat down in the deep powdery snow, full of relief, happiness and exhaustion. Pat enthused at the view and snapped away frantically. The panorama was indeed amazing. Near at hand we were now higher than Cholatse which was no longer obscuring the view. Menlungtse, Cho Oyu and Shisha Pangma and a whole host of unclimbed peaks reared their heads in that direction. Elsewhere the view down towards Lukla and the foothills beyond was open whilst to the north and east the spectacular peak of Ama Dablam drew my attention in front of the awe-inspiring bulk of Makalu and Everest. It was all very elevating just swivelling round on my bum and photographing it all. Taweche was certainly a very fine vantage point.

'Lots for the future,' enthused Pat.

It did indeed seem that objectives in this part of the world were unlikely to run out in our lifetimes. But it was cold on top. And getting down was recognised as rather important. We trudged back in our deep powdery steps to where we had left the tent and our sacks.

The obvious way down was to the south. We knew that previous ascensionists had gone down this way but the first part was an open ice face with no sign whatsoever of previous climbers.

'Retrievable ice screw abseils,' prescribed Pat enthusiastically.

Doubtless these guide chaps demonstrate such things all the time. To me though this was a technique I had only ever read about in 'how to do it' books. I wasn't sure this was a good place to learn. And the image of having to climb back up ropes attached to a half-out ice screw immediately sprang to mind. But Littlejohn confidence swept all aside, clearly unconcerned about such negative thoughts. A length of cord was produced and rapidly transformed into a prusik knot connecting the ropes to the first ice screw. Meanwhile I opted for the 'leave it to the expert' approach and sat back marvelling at the intensity of Himalayan sun on south faces. Give me a nice cold north face any day.

Pat knew his stuff. Time after time I found myself jumping into action to avoid the gnashing teeth of a descending ice screw. Magic! And we were descending fast too. Down onto a small glacier, a comfortable bivouac, and then a final fifteen or so abseils before we could see Mike Morrison and Chris Watts at the foot of the face. Inevitably, at this point, the rope became inextricably stuck thereby enabling them to have much entertainment at our expense. But the end result was as planned. A final abseil down a steep rock wall saw us reunited with our friends after eight days. It was a strange, and, for me, unique feeling to finish a Himalayan abseil descent, and suddenly be relaxing with friends on completely safe ground just thirty minutes or so from Base Camp. The others had not had such a successful time. Mike had been suffering recurring illness problems which prevented any serious climbing and both he and Chris were looking rather dejected. I have to admit that Pat and I were probably a little wearing as we prattled on non-stop about our climb until the others insisted on carrying our rucksacks, at which point we bounded ahead, wallowing in the incomparable elation of Himalayan success.

Down in Base Camp our cook and kitchen boy greeted us with cups of tea. Ang Phurba was there too.

'Congratulations,' he said 'I have recalculated how much you owe me.'

Welcome back to twentieth-century Nepal! A new Switzerland struggling confidently towards bright sunny uplands of tourist affluence?

5

Scottish Winter Climbing

A series of minivans – memorising the Tremadoc guide – Raven's Direct –
in and out of the CIC Hut – racing Moran – Deep Gash Gully –
racing Nisbet – the Fly Direct – Elliott's Downfall – filming in Applecross

My grandmother always used to say that reminiscing is a sign of old age. It is something I have done for many years. I suppose I could be ageing prematurely but I take the view that if you can derive pleasure from past experiences long after the event that can't all be bad.

It was whilst I was squeezed into the Torture Tube on Taweche, with my nose hard against hero Littlejohn's boots, that I contemplated what good training Scottish winter climbing had been for this sort of thing, not the bivouacs but just the general undercurrent of masochism, and, most importantly, the willpower to push through something occasionally unpleasant at the time in the knowledge that things will get better and the retrospective pleasure of the experience as a whole will make it all more than worthwhile.

The attractions of multi-day, alpine-style climbing on steep Himalayan terrain and the pleasures that lead Londoners to rave about Scottish winter climbing are not readily understood by the average person. I have to admit that I too have struggled to come to terms with both. Perhaps though, that is one of the attractions. Successes that are won too easily are inevitably those that are the least rewarding.

Let me turn the clock back. My first attempts to savour the joys of Scottish winter climbing were back in the mid-1970s. At that time I was based in London, pennies were tight and I depended on the cheapest possible reliable form of transport – in those days an Austin minivan. I got through thirteen in all before moving on to other vehicles. By buying them second-hand from small businesses, running up perhaps 25,000 miles on weekend climbing trips and then selling them six months later as a private owner, I usually broke even or made a small profit. There were two engine sizes, 850cc and 1000cc. The 1000cc engines were much better but somehow I tended to end up with 850cc ones. Either way, the drive to Scotland seemed to be a long way, although we were spurred on by stories we had been told about glorious, crisp, clear days and fantastic climbing.

The usual form was to keep the driver awake through the night by quizzes based on climbing guidebooks. This has left me with an encyclopaedic knowledge of the Crew/Harris 1970 guidebook to Tremadoc. Why this should be so, when so many more hours were spent testing each other on the Scottish guides, I do not know – but if anyone is interested I can still, to this day, reel off the graded list of Tremadoc extremes in the 1970 guide. (Best steer clear of me at parties, when too much alcohol tends to prompt recitals whether asked for or not!)

My regular climbing partners in those early days were Mike Morrison and John Stevenson, both south Londoners who, like me, had an urge to escape the 'smoke'[1] whenever possible. Mike remains one of my regular climbing partners to this day and was, of course, part of the Taweche team. One of my earliest Scottish memories is of our trio arriving in Glen Coe intent on spending a week front-pointing up crisply frozen classics. The rain poured incessantly and the water by the Clachaig Inn was ankle deep. In the then harshly cold confines of the public bar (up to then the only place I had ever worn my down jacket), we were just in time to hear the well known guide Terry Taylor say how good Zero Gully on Ben Nevis had been the day before. We were gutted. Were we too late? Had we missed the 'conditions'?

'What do you think about tomorrow?' we enquired naively.

'Only one way to find out,' came the calm and practical reply.

But we hadn't learnt the game by then. We equated wind and rain in Glen Coe to wind and rain on the Ben (bad mistake!), and spent a whole week drinking in the Clachaig and splashing our way up wet snow slopes. I remember John Stevenson being particularly excited when he was able to find a section of ice substantial enough to get four or five consecutive placements in. Looking back, Ben Nevis was probably in excellent condition or, as Gordon Smith – a keen activist of the time – once entered into the CIC Hut log book: 'Ground conditions excellent, air conditions disgusting.'

I liked that comment; to me it summed up the unique flavour of Scottish winter climbing. I have also been known to use it in the Himalaya.

One week in particular sticks in my mind as the turning point in my attitude to the Scottish winter.

1978 had seen magnificent conditions in North Wales, and Mike Morrison and I had spent a superb week ticking off unclimbed, or rarely repeated, ice streaks throughout Snowdonia. It wasn't that we were particularly talented. It was simply that, after a series of lean years, winter

---

[1] London was at that time still nicknamed 'The Big Smoke' dating from the days of coal fires, smog and foul air. These days it might be more accurately described as 'The Great Fume' because of its transport pollution.

climbing was nowhere near as popular as it is today. We couldn't help but conclude that, if Snowdonia plums like the 100-metre Craig Rhaeadr water-falls in the Llanberis Pass were unclimbed, then the scope for adventurous action in Scotland must be unlimited. So in 1979, Victor Saunders, a friend from the North London Mountaineering Club, and I got together to take advantage of two unfilled places, booked by the Croydon Mountaineering Club, in the Charles Inglis Clark Hut on Ben Nevis.

It was the first time that I remember climbing with Victor. True to form, he had introduced some uncertainty into the proceedings by arranging that we would give a lift to a friend of his. I never did work out quite who this chap was, but on the drive up it became clear that, whilst we had decided to climb in Glen Coe on the Saturday, he wanted to be dropped off in Fort William, twenty miles further. For some reason I refused to let anyone else drive, with the result that, by the time the trusty minivan had rumbled its way from London up to Fort William and back to Glen Coe, I was falling asleep badly and not feeling at my perkiest. I can still vividly recall hallucinating and swerving sharply to avoid imaginary (well I think they were!) animals on the road. In contrast, Saunders who had snoozed gently all the way up, was nauseatingly enthusiastic. Somehow we struggled up Raven's Direct before returning to Fort William and taking up our places at the hut late that night.

Times had moved on since our early week splashing about in Glen Coe and, in the intervening years, I had made a couple more attempts to get into winter climbing on the Ben. Success had been very limited. Once, Mike Morrison and I camped about half an hour short of the hut. We managed to climb Zero Gully, but my main memory is of our much prized tent freezing to the ground and the bottom parting company with the rest when we tried to prise it away.

On another occasion, Phill Thomas and I tried to camp outside the hut itself. Arriving in the dark and discovering that we had left the poles in the van, we tried to use the fabric to construct a bivouac of sorts against the wall of the hut. It was a foul night, and at about 9pm a very refined-sounding gentleman ventured out to complain firstly that we were breaking rules by using the hut wall as a shelter, and secondly we were irresponsible in not treating the Highland weather with the respect it deserved. The tone of his voice was such that we felt inclined to take up semi-permanent residence. But as the night progressed, the cold seeped in and discomfort grew, to the extent that a foray down to Fort William to pick up the poles was deemed in order. Come the morning, there was much unhappiness when our plans to be the first away were thwarted by he who had upset us the previous night stepping briskly from the cosy interior and striding purposefully up ahead of us.

But this time I was inside the hut for the first time. It all seemed so unethically easy. The Ben was there on our doorstep, and Victor was his usual irrepressible self with a long tick list of routes to do. Success on new winter routes in Wales had led me to view the Ben differently from previous visits and I couldn't help but notice a thin ice streak dribbling down the right-hand side of Carn Dearg Buttress. The classic routes attracted us more to begin with, but by late in the week we decided to give it a go and managed Shield Direct, our first new winter line in Scotland. I clearly remember feeling that, if obvious ice streaks were unclimbed on popular crags like the Ben, then the possibilities elsewhere in the Highlands must be immense. I also remember the route being heralded as the first Scottish Grade VI. Victor and I had graded it V, and never did quite understand how it came to be rated VI before anyone had repeated it. Not to worry; it was good for the ego!

By the end of the week I was knackered. It was tough going to climb big routes every day, even from the luxury of the CIC hut. The hut was only convenient for the Ben, and looked like being a one-off experience anyway. A different approach would be necessary if we were to make any impact on the more remote crags up in the North-West.

For some years, a group of us from London spent a week or so roaming Scotland between Christmas and the New Year. The weather was invariably poor, and most of the time was spent checking out various drinking spots in the North-West. But, in between the sheets of rain we did manage to explore some of the areas that we were interested in. Applecross, Torridon, Achnashellach – all names that I had heard of, read about and longed to visit. And all of them appeared to have unclimbed ice streaks adorning rarely visited corries. We managed a few routes, things like Sheet Whitening in Applecross, on these early ventures, but they tended to be one-offs from the road or outings from damp bivouacs under boulders. It wasn't until we had pinpointed venues and weekend trips started in earnest that we really got to grips with the almost unlimited severity on offer in the North-West.

Partly it was better roads that allowed the introduction of the weekly dash from London – but it was also a matter of learning from experience. I have never been the world's best walker (many would put it stronger than that), and experience was beginning to show that more than a couple of consecutive days on the Scottish hills led to increasing lethargy and unproductive use of time. Weekends were much better. I could keep going for two days, with the next five at the sedentary office desk to recover in. As for driving, the 650 miles each way became a bit more manageable when divided between four of us.

Fellow weekenders were not difficult to come across. I have always thought that one of the best things about London is that, whatever perverse urge one has for the weekend, like-minded characters always seem to materialise. This meant that there was always a full car, whether the venue was chalk cliffs on the south coast or ice streaks in the north of Scotland.

The North-West became a firm favourite, its relative remoteness and lack of people being particular attractions. It is interesting to note the increasing popularity of this area over the last twenty-five years. When I first started venturing this way in the late 1970s, a strong body of people wanted not to record climbs and keep the place a wilderness area. The guidebooks that did exist were hopelessly out of date, and it is fair to say that I cannot recall ever meeting another climber on the hills in winter. It was fantastic. By the mid to late 1980s we would meet the odd enthusiast, but these were virtually always people we knew. The 1990s saw a sea change. With glossy guidebooks sporting photos of instantly attractive climbs, the number of activists increased sharply and, shock horror, we began to come across other climbing parties that we didn't know!

But the North-West is a long way from the centres of population, and competition for the plethora of new lines was limited. Andy Nisbet, as ever, was in action on a broad front, as were people like Rab Anderson and Martin Moran. Martin in particular tended to have a similar eye for a line to me. On at least two occasions we ended up competing for the same route.

Deep Gash Gully, on Sgurr a'Mhadaidh was, for those in the know, an obvious Skye winter challenge. Frankly I was not completely 'in the know', but I was very aware of the guidebook description which referred to the summer climb as 'being deeply cut, normally damp, greasy and, at HVS, challenging'.

From previous jaunts in the area, particularly Waterpipe Gully, where Doug Scott and Colin Downer beat Victor Saunders and me to the first winter ascent by one day, I was vaguely aware that there was a gully of sorts up there, but I had no real idea about how good it might be. Jon Lincoln and I just about managed it in time to spend a relaxing evening at the Sligachan Inn by a roasting log fire with obligatory snoozing Labrador in situ. We didn't get round to recording our climb for a few weeks, in which time Martin had repeated it, thinking he was doing the first winter ascent. Sorry, Martin!

In line with the increasing popularity we had noticed elsewhere, other climbers were visible (in the distance admittedly) when we finished Deep Gash Gully in 1991. Even so the sight of an unattended car parked after dark on the Glenbrittle road was so unusual as to be brought to the attention of the police!

Other areas too produced their fair share of memorable action. Applecross became a favourite, and I well remember doing Gully-of-the-Gods on Bheinn Bhan with the classic East End character Simon Fenwick. This, we knew, had been attempted way back around 1960 by the intrepid duo of Chris Bonington and Tom Patey. We had sniffed around at the base during one of our Christmas/New Year forays, and so knew it to be an intimidating parallel-sided wet gully which might ice up well.

At my walking speed it took near on four hours to get to the foot of the crag, but it was worth it. We were rewarded with orgasmic conditions. Ice smeared the sides of the weeping fault line and it was one of those 'now or never' days.

Simon announced that he felt ill. He looked distinctly pale. Clearly he wasn't joking. But turning back now, when faced with such perfect conditions, was out of the question. We must have made an unusual first ascent team. At one point Simon stopped seconding and I spent some time pulling as hard as I've ever pulled, only to discover that he had clipped into a peg to be sick. But regular blasts of wind-whipped snow in the face were just what the doctor ordered – or perhaps good Scottish winter days are a tonic in themselves. Either way, the Fenwick body was evidently in better condition at the top than it had been at the bottom. Probably a first!

Andy Nisbet has long been one of the most prolific and respected activists on the Scottish winter scene. I first remember meeting him on the North Face of the Eiger way back in 1980, but it was some time later, at the roadside below Creag Meaghaidh, that I first recall coming across him in his native environment.

Victor Saunders and I had just completed a rather faltering drive from London. What with a miraculously disconnecting distributor cap and spells of challengingly slippery roads, we eventually arrived just in time to see a torch click on in a small roadside tent. A head poked out and the unmistakable outline of the Nisbet beard glistened in the moonlight. We regarded each other blearily, and spoke only enough to confirm that both teams were heading for the Pinnacle area. I didn't really need to know any more. I had already driven literally thousands of miles in an effort to nab the first full ascent of an obvious direct winter line based on the semi-sieged line of The Fly. The chances that Andy would be heading for the same line were distinctly high.

Nisbet was bound to be a speedy walker. Victor looked distressed, knowing that, with me present, we would inevitably lose any walking race. By the time we were ready to leave, the Nisbet team was already surging forth. I tried ineffectually to run after Victor – but it was clearly hopeless. The snow underfoot was crisp and frozen; there was one slim possibility that sprang to mind.

'The river bed!'

The end result was a first (and probably a last) in Fowler walking history. Victor and I crunched crisply along the smooth snow of the river bed whilst the Nisbet team followed the longer route along the path. We arrived perhaps five minutes before them, and stepped briskly on to the perfect ice streaks of Fly Direct.

All those miles of driving had been worthwhile; the conditions were the best I had ever seen on Creag Meaghaidh. White ice drooled down the lower slabs and choked the 200-metre corner line that formed the meat of the route. We twanged our way upwards, whilst Andy contented himself with yet another Nisbet first, the Midge, just to our right. It was one of those rare days when everything goes exactly according to plan. Lying in the sun on top of Creag Meaghaidh was a moment to be savoured. Victor was bouncing uncontrollably as he does when excited.

And so on the Sunday we found ourselves in Glen Coe, peering up at a hanging ice streak up and to the left of the well known column of Elliott's Downfall. Our approach had been interestingly unconventional, and at one point involved overcoming a particularly steep rock wall by clambering up a handy, if fragile, tree.

It wasn't until we were roping up beneath the line that Victor realised that he had left his axes behind.

'You lead and slide yours down the rope,' he suggested.

And so I set off on steep and brittle ice, clipping in just one of our two ropes.

The pitch was insecure and unnerving, to the extent that I felt increasingly uncomfortable with this arrangement. Eventually though, I pulled on to a ledge and belayed. Looking up, it was clear that we were above the main difficulties, and without a further thought I clipped both axes into the free rope and let them zoom off out of sight. The pitch was vertical for some distance, and the axes descended most efficiently. Regrettably I was unable to see Victor's strenuous efforts to run away from a couple of kilos of sharpened steel homing in on him – being tied onto the other end of the rope there was no escape and after fruitless exertions he bore the full force of two axes from fifty metres. A muffled cry reached me, and it was a not very pleased Victor Saunders who arrived at the stance some time later.

As he led off, I made very sure that the Fowler body was protected by an early runner in both ropes!

To me these recollections sum up a lot about Scottish winter climbing. Conditions are fickle, early starts wearing and success comes only to those that persevere. But the memories bite deeply, the friendships are warm and the pleasures long lasting. These are the important things. They apply to the Himalaya too; it's just the scale that's different.

I was collapsed at home in London one Monday evening, recovering pleasantly from the previous weekend on Ben Eighe's Triple Buttress, when the telephone awakened me from my doze. An urgent, crisp and enthusiastic voice spoke:

'Hello. Richard Else here from the film production company Triple Echo.'

It took me a minute or so to focus on what was being said. Clearly this man had not heard about the 'Mountaineers' Mountaineer' photographic fiasco as it transpired that he wanted me to star in a thirty-minute film about someone who had an overwhelming urge to drive from London to Scotland every weekend in order to clamber up steep bits of ice. It seemed that my years of devotion to the pleasures of Scottish ice had been brought to the attention of the outdoor filming industry.

'The exploratory aspect is important,' Richard was saying. 'We'll do some research and find something new for you to climb.'

I contemplated the prospect of getting paid for climbing an unclimbed ice line found by someone else in North-West Scotland. This sounded an offer that was too good to be true. I decided to keep quiet about my only previous attempt to perform for a professional photographer.

Steve Sustad and I rolled up outside the Loch Maree Hotel, near Glen Torridon, at about 4am on the Saturday morning. It had been a snowy drive but there was still time to settle down, in my slightly too short Citroën estate, for a couple of hours snooze before the action was likely to begin.

Steve and I had climbed together for many years, both on rock and ice in Britain and on big mountains abroad. A highly skilled carpenter, originally from Seattle, he had an English wife, Rose, and was now based just down the road from Nicki and me in North London. His approach to climbing and his character always appeared very un-American to me. As an extremely modest man he never spoke publicly about his climbs but his climbing achievements were such that he had acquired a tremendous reputation in mountaineering circles. On the drive up Steve had been telling me about the time his short pointed answers to searching questions once led an interviewer to describe him as the most difficult interviewee she had ever come across. It could be an interesting day or two ahead.

It wasn't until the dawn that I began to wonder about the timing. Usually we would be on the go well before now but it was 6.30am and there was no obvious action in the hotel. I was just contemplating stirring myself and making our presence known in some way when voices approached.

'Isn't that their car?'

'Do you think? Surely they would have come in?'

Steve pushed open the side door to meet Richard's relieved face. It was the first time we had met and I couldn't help but get the impression that he and his crew were used to rather more organised performers who arrived with many hours to spare. It appeared that they had woken up in the hotel, noted our apparent absence, and enjoyed a tense breakfast wondering where the hell the performers might be. It had been assumed that we would find our way into the hotel and so nobody had bothered to check the steamy windowed estate parked outside.

Richard though has built a reputation for straightforward honest filming and capturing situations as they are. So the discovery that the performers were dossing in their car whilst the crew enjoyed a luxury breakfast was greeted with both relief and enthusiasm. Steve and I were asked to hold our positions and eventually emerged to cameraman, soundman and producer all in full 'record the action' mode as we fought to get dressed and appear vaguely alert.

'Excellent. Great scene,' announced Richard with a beaming smile on his face. We were then introduced and allowed a bite to eat whilst the plans for the day were explained to us.

It was all a bit of a change from the one man band that had turned up to grab a few shots for *The Observer*. There were a few faces I recognised Brian Hall, a name well established in mountaineering folklore after a series of futuristic ascents with Al Rouse and Rab Carrington, was heading up a safety team, John Whittle, whom I first met in North Wales many years before, was here, as was Dave 'Cubby' Cuthbertson, one of Scotland's leading climbers. All to help the film crew capture some footage of Steve and me enjoying a typical winter weekend in Scotland. I began to understand why Richard's stress levels were rising before we were discovered.

'Cubby knows of a nice unclimbed ice streak at the head of the Applecross Pass,' announced Richard.

Cubby looked less then 100 per cent happy at this. I knew him fairly well having bumped into him quite a few times both on the crags and in various pubs. Like me, he devoted a substantial percentage of his time to seeking out and climbing new lines in Scotland. To find one and then hand the first ascent over to the Sassenach competition can't have come easily. Cubby though took it well, reminding me of the time back in 1977 when Phill Thomas and I arrived keen and raring to go at Creagh an Dubh Loch in the Cairngorms only to find Cubby and Murray

Hamilton just finishing the first free ascent of Giant, the exact objective that we had come to try.[1]

Soon a brand new Volvo estate was bouncing along the unmetalled track towards the radio mast overlooking the Bealach na Ba. It really is amazing where a hire car will go! The shortest walk in I have ever experienced in Scotland then led to a point overlooking the summit buttress of Sgurr a'Chaorachain. Steve and I had never been to this crag before. It was not huge, perhaps sixty metres high, but it did contain a couple of interesting looking icefalls, one of which sported a spectacular ice umbrella and looked exciting.

It was a very strange sensation to be climbing a new line with a cameraman and sound recording man dangling nearby. The climb itself went quite well: adrenalin flows were only moderate, nobody fell off, the cloud level stayed high and the film team seemed content with the end result. In fact it was an interview back down in the Torridon car park that produced the most unexpected results.

The scene in the car park was typical 'film team in action' – the sound man waved a huge fur-covered microphone around and the cameraman fiddled with his camera as cameramen do. Richard was in full interview mode and the safety crew stood nonchalantly around. After a couple of minutes a car drew into the car park, the driver got out, took one look at Richard's beard, strode right into the middle of the set and turned to face him:

'Hello. Are you Chris Bonington?'

Richard gave him a special withering look.

'No,' he said.

'Oh,' said the man, looking around the group of glaring faces. He then walked back to his car, got in and drove off.

Filming recommenced with hardly a word but the incident has left me with a curious urge to ask Richard if he is Chris Bonington every time I meet him.

---

[1] Paul Braithwaite and Nick Estcourt later claimed the first free ascent which they had made in 1974, but Cuthbertson and Hamilton believed they were making the first free ascent in 1977.

6

Changabang 1997: Bureaucratic Bliss

The 1996 attempt – two groups merge into one – organising efficiency –
beer money budgeted – baggage/customs problems in Britain and India overcome –
pre-hired transport to Rishikesh – we get healed in a temple

The average man tends to change his weekend activity with passing years. This thought rang loud and clear when one April weekend in 1997, I held an inverted position in a particularly smelly manhole whilst attempting to retrieve part of my wife's Sri Lankan shell collection.

I was off to attempt Changabang's unclimbed North Face the following weekend and, in years gone by, would have spent the last few weekends (and just about every other weekend throughout the year) getting in as much climbing as possible. Living now as a family man in Derbyshire should have made it all invitingly easy. Family life though is not conducive to such activities. It's not that I'm complaining; preferences change with circumstances. I'm just noting the difference.

The cause of the problem was Alec, our two-year-old, who had managed to successfully flush four or five potentially prize-winning shells down the toilet. Nicki had not been pleased. I had been in charge, hence my efforts which, I contemplated, were close to being beyond the call of duty. The really worrying factor was that the manhole was very deep and when my arm was in the best position to retrieve lost shells my ear was level with the discharge pipe from our neighbour's property. And I was uncomfortably aware that I had forgotten to ask them to hold fire. Hopefully the objective dangers would be less extreme on Changabang.

Sitting on the gravel at the side of the manhole I contemplated the results of my exertions. Three shells found and one surprisingly breathless body. Fortunately I seem to enjoy a fairly high level of inherent fitness but there was no doubt that a five-minute inverted struggle had induced some noticeably heavy breathing. Maintaining peak fitness is something I have real trouble with. Over the years I have concluded that only rock climbing and mountaineering have sufficient appeal to persuade me to exert my body. I admire those who can have pound the pavements at every opportunity. Such exertions are not for me.

And so I sat considering the demands the next few weeks would make on my system. Despite my best intentions I hadn't actually managed to do any training of any kind. In the past I'd at least gone as far as to condition my digestive system by spending plenty of time in some of Britain's worst curry houses. This time though, the Tandoori Nights takeaways from Castle Donington had appeared completely germ-free and of minimal use in preparing me for the joys of Indian roadside cuisine. I did note a bloody graze on my elbow where I had scraped it below the water line in the U bend. It was my only germ training and unlikely to have a positive effect on my resistance levels.

A voice over my shoulder interrupted this line of thought.

'Steve Sustad, for you ... not found my best white one yet then?'

I trooped into the house contemplating the challenge of the day.

'Steve, hello. How's the body?'

Steve Sustad was to be my partner on Changabang. We knew each other well. Not only had we climbed together lots in the UK but in 1993 we had enjoyed a successful trip to the Himalaya, making the first ascent of the spectacular Cerro Kishtwar. Steve is one of the world's toughest, most determined mountaineers. Losing a toe to frostbite on Aconcagua had prevented him joining me on the Taweche climb, but, true to form, his enthusiasm for Changabang was not dented in the slightest.

'Only a week to go. Have you got everything under control?'

This was a reasonable question but the honest answer was that I didn't really have a clue. All our personal climbing gear was ready but this expedition was to be a new experience for me in that all the bureaucracy and paperwork was out of our hands. Not that this was something to complain about, it was just different to what I was used to. Up to now I had always been closely involved with the frustration of doing battle with third world rules and regulations. In fact, my last expedition to India, with Steve in 1993, had involved a whole week of negotiations in Delhi before we were allowed to head off towards our peak; it had definitely been the bureaucratic crux of my climbing career. This time things were going to be different. Our leaders were the husband and wife team of Roger Payne and Julie-Ann Clyma.

Changabang stands in the Garhwal Himalaya on the northern rim of the Nanda Devi Sanctuary close to the India/China border. It is a strikingly spectacular mountain not visible from any road and the subject of much adulatory writing well before it was first climbed in 1974 by an Indo-British team led by Chris Bonington and Balwant Sandhu.

A flurry of activity thereafter saw several new lines established on the mountain's south and west sides until, in 1982, the Nanda Devi Sanctuary was closed by the Indian authorities for ecological reasons and the brief window of activity ended. Throughout this time the north side remained inaccessible behind the Inner Line, a restricted access area along the India/ China border, as it had done for many years. In fact, as far as I am aware, no western climbers had got close to the northern side of Changabang since Tom Longstaff's team crossed the Bagini Col in 1906 until 1996 when Roger Payne secured permission to attempt the North Face.[1]

The North Face itself, known about and admired since Longstaff's day, offered a superlative 800-metre mixed face. In the centre of the face, in the lower section, a slightly protruding buttress suggested several possibilities to half-height but thereafter a series of polished icefields separated by steep rock sections led up to a steep finger of ice giving a possible line through rock walls and up to the summit ridge icefields. This single possibility through the upper walls posed a lot of questions that could only be answered on closer acquaintance.

The 1996 Roger Payne, Julie-Ann Clyma, Brendan Murphy and Andy Perkins, climbing as a team of four, climbed to a point about halfway up the face, at which stage Andy Perkins' bowel problems caused much distress all round and made him so unwell that descent was their only option.

So in 1997 the North Face of Changabang was still unclimbed. The Indian system requires that peaks be booked and peak fees paid before climbers are allowed to attempt them. The system is basically a tax on climbing and is designed to put hard currency into the Indian coffers. On leaving India in 1996, Roger and Julie-Ann has been sufficiently impressed with Changabang to make a provisional reservation for 1997. Guiding tests meant that Andy Perkins couldn't make it in 1997 and so Brendan arranged to climb with Andy Cave.

Meanwhile Doug Scott, one of Britain's most experienced mountaineers, knowing that the North Face of Changabang was a fine objective, was also keen to take advantage of the relaxation of the access rules. As a member of Chris Bonington's team back in 1974 he had been in the successful first ascent party. Now he had gathered a team comprising Steve and me and the well-known American climbers, Greg Child and Alex Lowe. Doug had made a provisional pre-monsoon booking for 1997. A recipe for confusion and overcrowding was thus born which was only partially resolved when Doug, Greg and Alex decided to withdraw. The rest of us then joined forces under Roger and Julie-Ann's leadership. With the benefit of hindsight I now know that we all felt that six climbers was too many but at the time we were all drawn along in the optimistic hope that it would 'all be all right on the day'.

[1] Expeditions had been active in the Bagini Cirque in 1939, 1950 and 1978 – the latter when a Czech party made the first ascent of the North Face of Kalanka. The North Face of Changabang was a well known problem throughout this period.

Anyway the end result was that the Payne/Clyma pairing were very definitely our leaders, whilst the other ranks constituted Murphy, Cave, Sustad and Fowler as the foot soldiers. So when Steve Sustad interrupted my drain-searching to ask if everything was under control the honest answer was: 'I haven't got a clue.'

In fact I did have some slight reason to be unsure. The previous week I had been one of the very few people to witness Roger Payne actually being a party to something that went organisationally wrong. The fact that I was equally to blame should not detract from the delightful air of incompetence that surrounded the one evening that I have tried to spend climbing with the then General Secretary of the British Mountaineering Council. Roger and I had both been collecting equipment for the Changabang climb and, not wishing to tempt car crime, we turned up at Staden Main Quarry in the Peak District sporting rucksacks overflowing with all manner of bulky Himalayan mountaineering equipment. But neither of us had brought any rock climbing equipment. A quick foray on the delightfully named Bicycle Repair Man ground to a halt when it became clear that neither of us was prepared to lead it with just hand-placed ice barbs (metal hooks) for protection. Other climbers stared at us in bewilderment, recognising Roger, and marvelling at the fact that a man with his reputation for efficiency could bring so much gear to the crag but still not have enough to climb with. Sheepishly we retreated to the pub to discuss the joys of Changabang where I was assured that, notwithstanding our Staden rebuff, everything was under control for the Changabang trip.

And so it proved. The last week before departure saw tickets arriving through the post, computer lists of food and other requirements being e-mailed around the country and faith in Payne/Clyma efficiency was back at one hundred per cent. A day or so before departure day I telephoned him with the usual sort of last minute questions:

'How much extra money are you taking?'

A silence compatible with complete incomprehension followed.

'Just money for gifts and the like; the rest's accounted for.'

I thought of all those computer lists. I had never seen anyone this organised before.

'Beer money?'

'No, shouldn't be any need. All budgeted for.'

I put the phone down reeling from organisational brain strain. I wondered what consumption per head he had accounted for. Steve drinks lots of beer ... had he accounted for that? My thoughts tailed off as I made a mental note to slip in a little cash.

The first time we were all together was at Heathrow. The others had flown down from Manchester and met us whilst Steve Sustad and I were frantically trying to convince the check-in staff that we – or rather our leader – had arranged thirty kilos of excess baggage per person. We were failing which, at about £10 per kilo, was not funny. Tempers were getting frayed and Steve was in the process of explaining what he was going to do if the assistant persisted when a cheery authoritative voice rent the air.

'Morning team. Good to see you looking harassed.'

The master bureaucrat team of Roger Payne and Julie-Ann Clyma appeared with Andy Cave and Brendan Murphy looking shell-shocked just behind. Roger's mother was also present. The check-in assistant was nonplussed by the arrival of reinforcements. Soon the supervisor was called. The queue behind us was growing and voices of discontent were clearly audible, whilst the Payne family machine moved into full persuasive mode. Bits of paper were waved, voices were raised and a photograph of Changabang was thrust to the fore.

'You must have a photograph of the mountain our expedition is to climb.'

The supervisor tried to refuse.

'It's very important,' stressed Roger. 'This is a government-sponsored expedition.'

Quite what was important was unclear to me but the Payne tactics did appear to be winning ground. Roger gave a detailed explanation of the line we intended to attempt and then moved on to explaining the government grant system for mountaineering expeditions and the embarrassment her lack of co-operation would cause the government.

By now the queue behind us was full of agitated passengers looking at their watches. Roger moved on to explaining that a possible solution was to unpack some heavy items like tinned food and leave them at the check-in desk. He stretched down to one of the bags, presumably willing to demonstrate what he meant. Anguished voices came from behind.

'No, no.' The supervisor was crumbling. 'On this occasion *only* you are allowed through.'

And so, nerves slightly frayed but all equipment intact, we boarded the plane. Steve and I had experienced our first sight of the ruthlessly efficient Payne/Clyma negotiating machine in action. I began to feel rather sorry for the host of minor Indian officials who we would shortly be encountering.

Delhi airport was hot, sweaty and action-packed and Steve and I duly started to haggle with taxi drivers over the fare into town. But we were called away. What was this? Roger was gesticulating towards a luxury minibus complete with curtains.

'Pre-booked,' he explained to an incredulous Steve. And so it continued, with pre-booked hotel and pre-booked transport to the road-head.

It was beginning to feel a bit like I'd imagine a package tour to be. Not that I was complaining. Soon questions of the 'Can I do something?' variety changed to 'What's happening next, leader?'

Roger delegated a Sustad/Fowler pairing to collect our freight from the much feared customs buildings at Delhi airport. We had previous experience of this and knew it to be a frustrating and miserable way to fritter away a full day. Our leader initially accompanied us but then had to rush off for a meeting, leaving us to handle matters with efficiency and despatch. Steve was less hopeful and had brought a book.

It didn't take long for things to go wrong. It seemed that we had somehow been left with 'visitor' passes and only Roger had an authorised 'action' pass. Why anyone should ever want to go to Delhi airport customs building as a 'visitor' was beyond me but it rapidly became clear that the officials were under orders not to deal with 'visitors'. There seemed no option but to return to the front gate and start the whole tedious process again. To make matters worse we were both fully aware that all the equipment had been freighted in under the Payne name and, at some point a passport entry was necessary which could bring the process to a grinding halt without the presence of our leader. He had promised to return as soon as his meeting finished but when would that be? We could do little but persevere and keep our fingers crossed.

It was whilst I was queuing for an action pass that I got the first inklings that my guts were not at their best. By the time we were back in the customs building proper, I could hold back no longer and rushed off in the direction of an appalling smell which I took to be the toilet, abandoning our hard fought place in the queue.

I squatted miserably over the turd-surrounded hole in the floor. The non-existent door lock made life difficult. Perhaps it was because I had just arrived straight from the genteel etiquette of rural England, but somehow I felt obliged to try and keep the door vaguely closed to others. The combination of squat, keep the door closed and not overbalance was a challenging one, the whole experience being enhanced by the small blue plastic cup full of water which substituted inadequately for the nice soft toilet tissue back home.

Steve was sweating profusely but looking relaxed when I returned. The queue had hardly moved but he had managed a few more pages of his book.

'All OK?'

'Double dripper,' I retorted.

We laughed together, noting how easily the tried and tested phrases slipped off the tongue after, for me, a couple of years' absence.

'Welcome to India,' we managed in unison.

The queues moved slowly but by mid-afternoon we had at least physically seen that the gear had arrived. I always regard this as a crucial uplifting moment, although past experience has shown that many challenges still remain, like this time showing my passport and then trying to impersonate the Mr Roger Payne who the paperwork said would be signing for the equipment. I fingered the wad of rupees that Roger had given me. This was a hurdle that could call for a nastily large bribe.

'Michael! Good to see you looking so well.'

Secretary Payne was back, wearing a spotless light yellow short-sleeved shirt and was smiling and apparently relaxed.

'Right, my man, these are our goods. Now come on, let me sign the forms ... here's a photo of the mountain we've come to climb ...'

There was no doubt about it; our leader was back. Bureaucratic insouciance smoothly replaced amateur bumbling and I slunk off thankfully to perfect my balancing act during another visit to the hole in the ground. Steve briefly looked up from his book and caught my eye.

'Enjoying your holiday, Michael?'

'Bastard,' I managed.

Life under Roger and Julie-Ann was super-organised; there was no doubt about that. UK-prepared typed shopping lists, complete with specified shopping venues, quickly led to a collection of stacked cardboard boxes, sealed and ready for transport all the way to Base Camp.

'Perhaps we should be doing more,' I ventured to Steve.

He looked at me with the quizzical look of a fully relaxed veteran of the expedition scene, capable of taking just about everything in his stride. When there is nothing to do Sustad is just brilliant at doing nothing.

'If they want to do it, let them do it.'

I took time to chew this over. Perhaps I was the only one who felt pangs of guilt over our unequal input? Whatever I felt, there was nothing to be done other than admire the Payne/Clyma team in their headlong drive to organise, socialise, network, build contacts and get us all to the mountain. They even found the time to give a lecture to the Indian Mountaineering Foundation and arranged for us all to enjoy the splendid hospitality of Manjit Singh Soin, head of one of India's leading adventure holiday companies.

In fact the aftermath of Manjit's hospitality left me with a nauseous hangover as we bounced through the suburbs of Delhi en route to the town of Rishikesh and the start of the Ganges gorge. Our transport was of course the curtained minibus that had collected us from the airport. I groaned unhealthily, noting that the others looked annoyingly perky. My alcohol tolerance levels have steadily dropped after peaking in my late teens. Now I sat there suffering from a throbbing head, a queasy stomach and a bowel still threatening to erupt at any moment.

'Good altitude training,' Steve assured me, noting my discomfort and doubtless thinking of the character-building experiences to come.

The road to Rishikesh bored its way through the muggy heat of the Indian plain. Monotonous motorway travel has yet to hit India. Instead our driver was faced with the non-stop hooting and excitement of Indian road travel. I never cease to be amazed at the number of different forms of transport in the sub-continent. We weaved and dodged our way round cycle-rickshaws, carts drawn by horses, buffalo and even a camel. Elephant transport was occasionally spotted and at one point we were held up for a good thirty minutes whilst an enormously long queue of water buffalo pulling sugar cane-laden carts ambled across the road.

It was interesting to watch the team's reactions to their surroundings. Steve, relaxed as ever, watched with a passing indifference. If something really spectacular occurred he would turn his head slightly but that was about as far as it went. Stretching for a camera at this stage of a trip was definitely not something that he would undertake lightly. At the other end of the scale was Andy Cave. He had borrowed a huge posh camera from Elaine Bull, his girlfriend, and had not yet fully mastered the innumerable buttons. But such problems did not prevent him snapping frantically at regular intervals. Meanwhile Brendan sat quietly reading, half-submerged under the collapsing piles of baggage, whilst Roger and Julie-Ann took selective shots that I had no doubt would turn out to be of excellent quality. And then there was me, leaning optimistically out of the window, ever hopeful of catching a really memorable shot, pressing the button a lot but never being quite sure of what I had photographed. You can learn a lot by just watching people.

Rishikesh has long been popular with the western hippy community. The town sits astride the Ganges at the point where it spews forth from the Himalayan foothills. We stopped here to stretch our legs and give our driver a rest before doing battle with endless hours of Himalayan hairpin bends. An aimless wander soon brought us to a sign pointing down an interesting narrow back alley. 'Temple' it said. But it didn't seem to lead anywhere. The alley opened out into a sort of private allotment/cannabis growing area. Brendan, suddenly caught short, was picking his way through the crops searching for a discreet spot round the corner of the next building when a perfect Queen's English voice made itself known.

'You are looking for the temple?'

The voice's owner looked anything but Queen's English material. A man of large stature, he had a huge grey beard and was dressed in a white shawl which brushed the ground.

'Er, Yes ... the temple,' replied Brendan awkwardly, picking his way back through the well tended vegetables. The man led us up some external stairs and into a large softly lit room. It appeared to be nothing more than an upstairs room in his house. The walls were adorned with religious artefacts, complete with numerous garland-laden photographs of him. We wandered around hesitantly in the five-metre-square room, feeling slightly uncomfortable under his close scrutiny. A flea-ridden disabled dog joined us – and proceeded to display great interest in Julie-Ann. The situation was beginning to have that special blend of uncertainty and farcical humour that tends to surface so often in India.

'You must sit down,' urged our religious leader.

At this Julie-Ann left the room and the dog transferred its attentions to Steve.

'Why are you here?'

Blank looks all around.

'Because we are nosy,' I whispered to Steve who was unsuccessfully fending off the dog's attentions.

'Are you in need of healing?'

Andy perked up. His shoulder had been causing him some grief for a few days now. The would-be healer noted the movement.

'You, sir. You have pain?'

Andy moved hesitantly forward. It was not at all clear what he was letting himself in for. The healer sat on a chair on one side of the room beneath photographs of himself. The five of us sat, backs to the wall, facing him. Every now and then more heads would appear at the door then disappear again.

'Sit down.' The healer motioned to the floor in front of him. 'And your pain, where is it?'

Andy motioned towards his shoulder.

'Shirt off.'

The rest of us waited expectantly. Andy sat down, looking vulnerable. A small blob of white cream was scooped up from a metal cup and transferred to his shoulder. A vigorous finger massage ensued, after which he was pronounced cured.

'How much do I owe you?'

'Nothing.'

Even Secretary Payne looked slightly taken aback. More takers were quick to move forward. It was interesting to note how many aches and pains were evident in an apparently fit and healthy mountaineering team. It is debatable quite why but after a couple of days no one mentioned their pains any more.

'You can always guarantee feeling good after a visit to these places,'
Sustad drawled sarcastically, scratching his dog flea bites.

Beyond Rishikesh the road contoured above the churning grey glacial
water of the River Ganges as we left the plains and entered the Himalayan
foothills. Little yellow warning signs began to appear:

                    PRESERVE LIFE   DROP SPEED
                    IGNORE MONKEY   ARRIVE SAFELY

Sure enough the occasional monkey could be seen, along with bare-
footed pilgrims plodding steadily towards the holy source of the Ganges.
The masochism level involved in being a pilgrim seemed disturbingly high.
The really dedicated wear nothing but an orange shawl. Bare feet plod on
sun-scorched tarmac and only begging provides any sustenance.

'Bit like Himalayan climbing in a different guise,' Steve observed.
'We just like it cold rather than hot and don't even have the chance of
scrounging any food.'

We arrived at Joshimath in the afternoon two days after leaving Delhi.

This is a fair sized town at an altitude of about 3000 metres. Strenuous
attempts are being made to turn it into a winter resort. A téléférique
adorns the hillside above the town but the place has a long way to go
before it becomes the Chamonix of the Himalaya. Maybe one day? For
us Joshimath was a place to buy our staple foods for Base Camp, along
with any other bits and pieces that we might need.

Out came another computer list from which Roger and Julie-Ann
delegated responsibilities.

'Mick, Steve, could you take on the potatoes, thirty pairs of porters
shoes and thirty pairs of socks?'

Steve and I wandered through the main street. Open sewers flowed
along each side of the road, their pungent smell mixing easily with the
noise and bustle of everyday Indian life. A man was having his armpits
shaved just outside a grain shop where the proprietors sat surrounded by
their wares. We kept an eye open for shoes, socks and potatoes.

Soon a tiny and very dark shoe shop was found. We stared glumly at
the limited range. A standard walking boot looked prohibitively expensive
and there was a definite absence of plastic sandals that, in our experience,
porters like best. Difficult business this choosing equipment for others. A
bit like buying Christmas presents for distant relations or fussy spouses. I
picked up a canvas boot that I had spotted lurking under a pair of very
out of place-looking ladies' sling-backs.

'They won't wear them,' said Steve dismissively. 'You wait.'

A bold decision was called for.

'Thirty pairs of your cheapest walking boots, please.'

A blank stare returned my request.

'We have only three pairs of these, sir.'

Three hours and innumerable shop visits behind us, we returned with thirty pairs of assorted footwear and about ten pairs of socks. That was about it for socks. They were in short supply in Joshimath. Perhaps the locals just weren't very keen on them. Either way Steve was still showing signs of concern over our varied porter purchases.

'Not worth it, you know. Endless scope for argument.'

I saw his point.

It was at about this time that I discovered Woody in the lining of my jacket. Woody, star character of the children's' video *Toy Story*, was a favourite of my two-year-old, Alec. Amidst difficult goodbyes at East Midlands airport he had hurled poor Woody out of Nicki's car window and somehow he had ended up in my pocket. I stood for a moment imagining the detailed house-searching and tearful wailing that would no doubt have ensued when Woody's disappearance was noted. A small package to England was definitely called for.

Andy Cave was at Joshimath post office when I arrived. He was not looking his usual calm and collected self.

'All I am trying to do is buy some bloody stamps!'

'Come to the wrong place then?' I enquired.

The sign 'Stamps' above one of the windows suggested that he had not. But getting hold of any stamps seemed easier said than done.

'I started over there,' said Andy, wearily pointing at a faded sign above an adjacent window. I glanced at the sign: 'Stamps 10am – 12 noon'.

'Now it's 1.45pm so I'm in this queue,' he explained.

I glanced at the sign above him: 'Stamps 12 noon – 2pm'. It looked right, if a little perplexing. Further windows on either side invited queues for stamps at different times of the day. Behind the windows was one open-plan office. It all seemed very strange.

Soon Andy came to the front of the queue and, much to our surprise, he secured an immediate result. It was my turn. Woody was now wrapped in a neatly addressed brown paper package. I pushed him through the window to the assistant behind.

'To England, please.'

A curious stare greeted my request.

'This is not a letter, sir.'

'I don't really care what it is but I do want to send it to England, please.'

'No. It is not a letter, sir.'

At that he stood up and headed off towards the back of the office. It began to look as if his shift had ended midway through dealing with poor Woody's postal problems. I glanced at my watch. Sure enough it had just gone 2pm. Angrily I tried to transfer my position to the front of the newly formed queue at the 2pm – 4pm window. But it was no good; a bustling throng elbowed me to the back. It is important to have a sense of humour and a long temper to get the most out of Indian bureaucracy.

Eventually the time came for me to try again.

'Can I post this to England, please?'

A new official peered at me quizzically.

'Sorry, sir. It is not a good size.'

'Don't worry, I'll pay the more expensive rate.'

'I'm sorry we can't take it. It is too big to be a letter and too small to be a parcel.'

Out came a post office table decreeing what sizes were classed as what. It seemed this was not a bribeable problem. Repackaging was a possibility but a glance at my watch showed that I was already well overdue at the hotel. Infuriating as it was, there was nothing I could do but hope that I could find the time to try again later.

I felt a little deflated by such a dismal failure. The whole incident had reminded me of my family and I experienced a pang of homesickness as I stepped carefully through the raw sewage flowing across the road. I reflected on my position. Tess was now five and Alec nearly three. Demands on my time were becoming more complicated as the years went by – the balancing act ever more difficult.

I was lost in such thoughts as I bumped into Roger who was returning from a porter-organising trip up the valley. He was still wearing his yellow short-sleeved shirt and looked incredibly clean and generally well turned out. I knew the porters had proved a real headache for him the previous year – something to do with porters being employed in Joshimath. This upset those at the road-head, where porters were in short supply, but those that were there felt that the work rightly belonged to them. It sounded the sort of sensitive and time-consuming balancing act that Roger loves battling with.

'All sorted then?' I enquired in a tongue-in-cheek sort of way. Even increasing familiarity with the Payne/Clyma expedition concept still left me unprepared for the crisp efficiency portrayed in his answer.

'Twenty porters from the local villages and sixteen from Joshimath. A bus will pick us up at 6am. Everything ready?'

I contemplated our efforts on the shoes and socks front and my inability to even send Woody back home. It struck me that between the rest of us we were also supposed to be buying sunglasses for the porters but somehow that seemed not to have happened either.

7

Changabang 1997: Acclimatisation

Josimath to Malari by bus – equipping the porters – Base Camp –
a trip towards Bagani Col – attempting Dunagiri Parvat –
concerns about too many climbers on the same route

At Joshimath the road divides, one branch leading to the Hindu temple at Badrinath and the other to summer pastures at Malari. Ours was the Malari road but it appeared that this was closed until the start of the summer pasture season, still a couple of weeks away. Secretary Payne had somehow managed to overcome this minor problem by hiring a bus into which we poured porters, our obligatory liaison officer, Narendra, ourselves, our equipment and provisions. Then we wound up the steep and spectacular valley beyond Joshimath. The scenery was truly idyllic. Snow-capped mountains were visible towering over the heavily forested lower slopes, at one point a steaming, yellow sulphurous spring oozed strikingly across the road.

Not far from the exit of the Rishi Ganga Gorge we stopped at a road-side tea shack.

The road being 'officially' closed seemed not to be adversely affect-ing the popularity of this small establishment and numerous people appeared from nowhere to marvel at the curious westerners. The Rishi Ganga Gorge had long captured my imagination as the only valley route into the fabled Nanda Devi Sanctuary, home of the Hindi snow gods. The section visible from the road was nothing out of the ordinary but I knew the epics of early adventurers and the story of Eric Shipton and Bill Tilman's first penetration right through into the Sanctuary back in 1934. The image of approaching idyllic meadows and the beautiful peak of Nanda Devi up an unknown and very difficult gorge strongly appealed to my imagination. But on this trip the gorge might just have a practical purpose as well.

Our plan, and it is easy to hatch such plans in the safety of rural England, was to climb Changabang's North Face and then descend to the upper reaches of the Changabang Glacier on the south side of the mountain. From there we would return to base by circumnavigating the mountain via the 5600-metre high Shipton's Col to the Rhamani Glacier on the Rishi side of the watershed. From there we hoped to cross the 5600-metre Bagini Col to gain the Upper Bagini Glacier and thence back to our Base Camp. Officially the Rishi Gorge that leads to Nanda Devi has been closed since 1982 but if something went horribly wrong on the south side of the mountain there was at least a possible, albeit inconvenient and politically sensitive, way out. We knew that after years of disuse the bridges would be down and the track possibly non-existent but at least it gave a last hope alternative.

The road continued up the valley towards Malari in the usual hair-raising Himalayan fashion. An unwelcome observation was the obvious nervousness of our driver. He appeared unable to drive in a smooth and unhurried manner. Everything from gear changes to steering movements was rushed and irregular. Beads of sweat stood out on his forehead. A minor landslide across the road looked likely to be a major challenge. I could see Steve shifting uncomfortably as we approached, something that doesn't normally happen. It shouldn't have been that intimidating an obstacle and tyre prints showed that other vehicles had managed to cross safely. Our man was cautious, edging his way slowly over the scree and slurry. As soon as the bus tilted he stopped. Not a good move. The porters looked nervous. Sustad is a good judge of such situations.

'Time to get off, Michael.'

Standing well back, it was readily apparent that the driver's 'let the clutch in sharply and accelerate hard' technique was not best suited to the problem. By now the rest of the team and even the porters had got off. The driver stopped his efforts, opened his door and peered thoughtfully at the position of the wheels. He got out and started to build up the scree slope on the outside edge of the back wheel. Another wheel-spinning effort was clearly on the cards.

'Abandon ship.' Roger's crisp instruction could not be ignored and his choice of metaphor indicated that he had his eye on the river below. 'Let's get the gear off.' Another crisp instruction, but not quite as relaxed as normal .

The driver stared incredulously, gesticulating that he was about to try again.

No one needed any encouragement. Gear bags rained down from the roof in a frantic effort to salvage all in the face of potential disaster. The driver was left with a completely empty bus and a rather crestfallen look appropriate for someone whose solitary optimism must have been rather dented by the resounding vote of thirty-five or so realists.

Soon the engine was revving hard again. Thirty-five hesitant helpers lifted and pushed at the same time, the wheels spun and the rocks flew. The porter next to me fell, hit hard in the leg, but no serious damage was done. At least the end result was that bus, occupants and luggage were over the danger area – albeit separately.

The end of the road was close by now. In fact, it was not really 'the end' but a lay-by a few kilometres short of the village of Jumma. The porters got off and we awaited the inevitable fights for the lightest or easiest loads. Soon though the Payne/Clyma collective authority was evident. Porters were neatly lined up and walking boots, socks and sunglasses were distributed. Even the huge variations and the fact that there weren't enough to go round seemed not to cause the expected rumpus. Many of the porters produced plastic bags and stuffed their pristine kit away for later. Their own plastic sandals without socks looked to be the preferred footwear.

'Told you so,' murmured Steve.

The track to the summer village of Dunagiri was extremely well maintained. Winding its way up through dense pine forests, it was not unlike the walks up to alpine meadows in the European Alps. But here we had the area almost to ourselves; the odd local passed us on the lower section but we had seen no westerners since leaving Joshimath and in fact saw none until we got back.

Moving up to the high pastures for the summer months has been a way of life for many Himalayan families for generations. The summer occupants of Dunagiri village had to walk for twelve to fourteen days from their valley homes to get here. Nevertheless, over the years, they have built up a formidably impressive track with dry-stone structures supporting a comfortably walkable path clinging tenuously to steep slopes. The last half a mile or so to Dunagiri was even paved with neatly arranged rocks dug from the surrounding fields. It resembled a highway leading to somewhere far more grand.

But Dunagiri itself was not at all the small collection of summer shacks that I had expected. Although completely deserted on our walk in, we called in on our return and learned that up to eighty families once stayed here from May through to October. Numbers have declined as new generations are increasingly drawn to the attractions of the lower valleys but even so there were thirty or so families in 1997 and the place enjoyed a bustling and healthy atmosphere.

We were told that the Indian authorities were keen to help preserve the traditional way of life and had helped to fund a reliable drinking water/irrigation system and a small school. The school building was left unlocked and provided excellent dry accommodation for us.

At a height of 3500 metres in Dunagiri village, my head was throbbing with the beginning of my usual altitude headache. Of greater concern was the surprisingly low temperature and the low snow level. Roger and

Julie-Ann had assured us that Base Camp would be in a delightful ablation valley full of lush grass and spring flowers. From Dunagiri village to Base Camp is a height gain of around 1000 metres. I began to suspect that it might be a snowfield this year.

Come the morning, the others rushed enthusiastically ahead whilst Steve opted to accompany me on my designated task of bringing up the rear. I think I was supposed to keep a general eye on the porters but if the truth be known this was only superficially possible as my walking pace left me so far behind that they were only visible as specks in the distance. Eventually even Steve could stand it no more and I was left to my own devices as I groaned through the sea of unstable boulders forming the terminal moraine of the Bagini Glacier.

At length, when I was still a good hour and a half from Base Camp, I spotted a group of porters who had already dropped their loads and were returning to the valley. I felt well satisfied to arrive only thirty minutes after the last porter. There was already lots of activity on the snowfield that was last year's grassy meadow. A clean-shaven Roger was directing building operations on the projecting stones which had been identified as the previous year's cook shelter. The others were busily heaving boulders about and generally creating an atmosphere of frantic activity. I sat down exhausted on my rucksack. My head throbbed acutely from the altitude and there was no way that I could match the effort that the others were putting in.

'A toilet hole needs to be dug over there.'

I was handed a trenching tool and dutifully wandered off in the direction Roger pointed to. A protruding rock at least allowed me to sit down whilst picking ineffectually at the frozen earth. I tried hard to convince myself that I was enjoying my holiday really. A voice in my ear interrupted my thoughts and focused my mind on the embarrassingly shallow hole that I had dug. It was Brendan Murphy.

'I know how you feel. Andy Perkins suffered so much that he nearly had to go down from here last year. Fancy a brew? It might help.'

They were words of sympathy that I found very touching. Brendan and I knew each other as climbing acquaintances before the trip but, our conversations had never really strayed much from climbing talk. I looked forward to getting to know him better.

Two days later I lay groaning in my tent. My head was still throbbing violently and I could hear Roger, Steve and Julie-Ann laughing and joking in the cook tent. Joining them was out of the question. It was all I could do to reach for more headache tablets. I lay and contemplated the fact that Andy and Brendan had left at 4am and were at that very moment heading towards the foot of the face. They seemed not to be affected by the altitude at all. Such active enthusiasm made me feel rather old and slow. I was glad to be climbing with Steve who had at least got up a difficult Himalayan peak with me and had experienced my slow acclimatisation and snail-like walking speed before. Despite my outwardly poor condition I think we both knew where we stood and remained inwardly confident that we would be ready to start up the face within the week. Such thoughts were all very positive but for the moment I could do nothing but lie horizontally in a nice warm sleeping bag and occasionally reach across for a pain-killer.

Four days after our arrival at Base Camp, the Cave/Murphy team returned from their initial exploration and I felt just about ready to tackle the challenging walk to a spot below the face that we rather grandly called Advanced Base Camp. The walk up to an altitude of about 5100 metres acted as a brutal reminder of the truly demoralising nature of unacclimatised activity. We were told to expect a six-hour walk – Steve and I arrived on the morning of our third day. The views were uplifting. Directly across the glacier from Advanced Base the virgin North Face of Changabang rose in an impressive steep wall peppered with a liberal amount of snow and ice.

Conditions were clearly quite different from the previous year. Brendan regularly commented on the lower temperatures and the amount of snow on the approach and yet the ice runnel by which the 1996 team had reached the icefields didn't seem to be there. It seemed inevitable that we would have to try a different, more direct line.

My first impression was that the face was huge and daunting but lacked an obvious eye-catching line of the sort that had attracted me on Spantik and Taweche. That said, the features that we had drooled over in Roger's photos were all too evident. The upper section in particular appeared challenging and I looked forward to getting to grips with it.

In places the ice was white, friendly and probably easy to climb. In other areas, a shiny green reflection revealed hard uncompromising shields which appeared to be stuck to near vertical ground. Try as we might, it was impossible to link up the white streaks; we were going to have to climb the white ice, green ice and mixed rock sections in between.

'Nice to have a bit of variety,' was the Sustad view. I peered at the green, featureless 55-degree ice slopes which formed a substantial part of the lower section. They looked technically boring and also physically knackering. I declined to comment.

Acclimatising is not much fun really. As I see it the main aim of the game is to spend as much time 'up high' as possible so as to get the body into a condition where it at least stands a chance of success on the main objective. Our plan was to maximise interest in this process by climbing up to the Bagini Col, over which we intended to return on our planned circuitous descent from the mountain. If we felt energetic we might even descend the far side to the Rhamani Glacier (from where Joe Tasker and Pete Boardman made their inspiring ascent of Changabang's West Face in 1976) and leave a food dump there.

Reality proved different. Day four from Base Camp saw Sustad and me wading through knee-deep snow on the upper Bagini Glacier. The temperature hovered around 4°C and the Bagini Col still 600m above us and nearly a mile at away; at least another two days to reach at our current rate.

Our position was now spectacular. Although farther away, we were now level with a point about 300 metres up the face and could get a better feel for the place. From here the line of weakness in the upper section of the face looked as if it could be lined with ice and now they were closer to hand Dunagiri Parvat and Bagini Peak had taken on a new grandeur. The unclimbed Dunagiri Parvat sported a fine granite buttress that looked particularly appealing.

As on the three previous days, we used heat exhaustion as an arguably valid excuse for bringing exertion to a close, pitched camp at 10am and settled down to a strenuous day of acclimatising by lying horizontally reading books and drinking endless cups of tea. We were just slipping into full relaxation mode when the sound of heavy breathing outside attracted our attention.

The Cave/Murphy team were powering their way up the glacier towards us, having left Base Camp that morning! My feeling of general exhaustion deepened. The potential for demoralisation is high when one is on a trip with such energetic youngsters (well, under thirty-five) and I made a mental note to try to be surrounded by slow and unhealthy types in the future.

At least, much to my relief, they decided not to carry on and we camped side by side that night. Perhaps our lethargy was catching but, come the morning, we managed to convince each other that the snow conditions were such that the Bagini Col would be avalanche-prone. The immense amount of energy that would have to be expended to get there also seemed to be a contributory factor. Sustad wisdom came to the rescue: 'It's important not to burn out too early on a trip.'

I heartily agreed and spent the rest of yet another day snoozing gently in my sleeping bag.

The acclimatisation process continued in a similar bland and unsatisfying manner. Steve and I climbed 300 metres up Dunagiri Parvat, whilst Andy and Brendan did likewise on a different spur of the same peak. The boredom potential was, however, increasing and, as we felt a little better, an urge to get under way on Changabang grew stronger. So Steve and I concluded that our acclimatisation programme was complete and headed back to Base Camp for some decent food and a proper rest before going for it.

It was a surprise for us to find Andy and Brendan already there. We had expected to be down first and ready to get on the face before them but they had coped with the boredom of acclimatisation even less well than we had and descended the day before. Roger and Julie-Ann had also been out acclimatising. Later that day they too arrived back at Base Camp feeling ready for Changabang. We always knew that there were a number of problems on this trip but the prospect of three teams in action on the face, one behind the other brought it into a sharp focus, only slightly relieved when it became clear that Roger and Julie-Ann intended to try a line well to the left of that preferred by the rest of us.

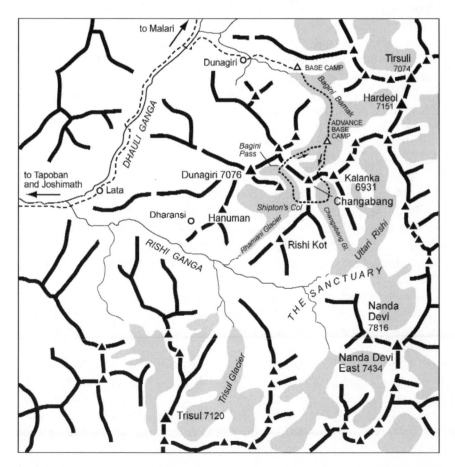

8

Changabang 1997: the North Face

*Remorseless ice slopes and afternoon spindrift – a potato feast –
disadvantages of two teams on the same route – enforced delay –
the fine upper section – top out – misadventure and a broken promise*

Steve and I sat at Advanced Base peering at the face through binoculars. Andy Cave and Brendan Murphy were picked out by the morning sun on the initial ice slopes and their progress had slowed to a crawl. We felt for them and noted that the midday sun over Changabang is so high in the sky that even the steep North Face gets it for most of the day. That is, of course, when it is not obscured by the incessant clouds that tend to boil up every afternoon. I felt better now. It was rather pleasant reclining in the tent eating excessively (stocking up for the route, we said), chatting away and occasionally stretching for the binoculars. It was a unanimous and easily reached decision that an extra day at Advanced Base would give the others a chance to get well under way.

'Best not to end up fighting over bivi ledges,' was the Sustad wise pronouncement of the day.

And so we set off two days behind them and Roger Payne and Julie-Ann Clyma, who were taking their different line, set off one day behind us. It was beginning to feel a bit crowded. We had not seen any westerners at all since leaving Joshimath and in all probability there were no climbers within a ten mile radius. And yet there were six of us on Changabang's North Face, four on the same route. As lovers of adventure and isolation, the irony of the situation did not escape us.

We had food for eight days and gas for ten. I had organised breakfast and Steve the evening meal. Breakfast had been easy; two small bags of Muesli-type stuff looked about right for sixteen servings. Steve's task was more challenging. Evening meals were to consist of mashed potato and noodles on alternate nights. Noodle quantities were pretty straight-forward, mashed potato not so. The problem was that the mashed potato packets claimed to do eighteen servings, whereas similar-sized, but different brand products that we had used thus far had only kept us going for six servings. Steve decided the eighteen servings must make up very small servings and stocked up accordingly.

We were at the foot of the face base at daybreak. Here a smooth steep wall barred access to the icy groove system 100 metres above us. After advanced inspection with binoculars and, less satisfactory, watching Andy and Brendan's progress two days earlier, we knew the best line to take. Nevertheless we were surprised by the angle. If conditions had been anything less than perfect we would have had real trouble but we were able to make good progress, gaining the groove system by a long passage of thin but solid ice sticking to the underlying rock. Thereafter progress was hindered by what was to become a usual pattern of heavy snowfall that quickly translated into a continuous stream of spindrift pouring down the groove.

Without spindrift the climbing would have been fun as it was a particularly nice groove line, very steep, but with only intermittent breaks in a covering of perfect white ice. It was disappointing to have to stop earlier than planned.

The evening found us perched on a foot-wide bum ledge, marvelling at the mashed potato liberally overflowing from the huge pan of our hanging stove. Steve decanted furiously into the lid and both our mugs. It was indeed impressive that such a small quantity of powder could be turned into such a vast quantity of potato. Perhaps we had found the ultimate hill food?

'Full of carbohydrate,' Steve assured me.

I dutifully struggled with the volume, keen not to commit the ultimate Himalayan sin of not eating my full allocation of food.

'Full of weight too?' I managed to comment between dry and powdery mouthfuls.

I was mindful of the unwieldy weight of our sacks which we had both been moaning about. But by the morning we had at least both recovered from the previous night's potato excess and were in position to take advantage of the standard morning fine weather. Unfortunately, the rigours of the night had been such that we somehow didn't get going until just gone 9am. Inexcusable really, when it was fully light by 5.30am.

In terms of climbing time, day two was not very impressive either. Our late start didn't help. The groove continued with superb Scottish Grade 5 climbing but by the time we had completed our fourth pitch the weather was such that a stop was inevitable. We sat huddled together, tucked into a snow spur beneath the first of a series of three greenish ice slopes, whilst a three-hour fabric-flapping storm buffeted our little tent. Unknown to us, up above, Andy and Brendan were caught out on difficult ground in this violent weather. Brendan fell twenty-metres and Andy suffered frostbite in his thumb. Meanwhile Roger and Julie-Ann were somewhere down to our left, where they spent a rough night standing up with their bivi bags over their heads. Relatively speaking Steve and I were pretty comfortable.

We were now at the foot of the first of the icefields. Photos taken the previous year showed these to have been largely snowy but this year they glistened hard and shiny, pure calf-wrenching stuff. In fact, it seemed that it was not just the ice slopes that were very different from the previous year. Brendan had recalled never wearing his duvet on the face in 1996. In 1997 all of us wore them leaving Base Camp and not a day went by without us wearing them on the route.

The ice was as hard as it looked and long precarious wobbles on front points were both tedious and wearing on mind and body. Steve eased the belay strain by tying his rucksack in to ice screws and sitting on it with his legs dangling free. It looked very strange but seemed to work well. A false line and a couple of more interesting pitches saw us bivouacking at the foot of the second icefield. Unfortunately, my adze, made for me by a blacksmith in Oswestry, had failed to stand up to the strain. I like a huge adze for tackling nasty overhanging Himalayan snow and had had one made for me back in 1995. The manufacturers had warned me then that it wasn't very strong but I suppose that after forty-three pitches of hard use on Taweche in Nepal I had become over-confident of its strength. My axe looked sort of naked without it. I kept my fingers crossed that we wouldn't come across too many overhanging powdery sections higher up.

Day four on the face consisted of another smooth icefield of hard ice and a hard mixed pitch leading out on to an icefield below the steep upper third of the face. From the icefield we could look out right to the snow rib which marked the high point of the 1996 attempt. It looked to be a long heavy-duty traverse away and I felt glad that a change in ice conditions since the previous year had tempted us to steer clear of the 1996 line and avoid the traverse.

On arriving at ice slope three (getting tedious by now these ice slopes) it was a pleasant but at the same time worrying discovery to find the Cave/Murphy team *in situ* on a tiny platform hacked out of the ice. They were about to spend their third night there.

'Thought we'd hang around a bit and enjoy the view,' explained Brendan mischievously.

The truth, of course, was slightly different. The vicious storm of two days ago had caught them on the hard pitch between the icefields. Climbing in such conditions must have been a real test of stamina. After Brendan's fall and a long cold lead by Andy, they managed to squeeze into their bivi at around midnight. Andy had some frostbite damage to his fingertips and, potentially more seriously, to his thumb. Understandably, they then felt that a recovery and recuperation day was in order. The following day they set out on the steep upper third of the face only to find that by the time the daily bad weather moved in, they were only about eighty metres up and without a hint of a bivi site in view. Tying their ropes together they returned to the icefield bivi and had the dubious pleasure of meeting Steve and me.

Too many people together increases the risk of rock and stonefall and makes uncomfortable bivouacs more likely. It is best to keep well clear of other climbers on a route like this. Having said that, it was an obvious pleasure to meet friends unexpectedly and enjoy the camaraderie. But what should we do now? Continue together or wait for Andy and Brendan to clear the way? The decision was far from clear-cut but Steve and I have a strong aversion to inactive days on the mountain. The others appeared indifferent and so the decision was made. We would team up as a four and proceed as best we could. As Andy and Brendan were just completing their sixth day on the face and had only eight days' food, there was another benefit in staying together and sharing round our mashed potato surplus.

And so the next morning saw Steve and me enjoying a lie-in whilst the others headed off up their ropes. The start was, in fact, delayed by some unhealthy-looking sunrise clouds and it was midday before Andy and Brendan reached the previous day's high point. Steve and I dithered as the hours ticked by. With the usual afternoon bad weather, it was unlikely that they would manage more than two or three pitches before being forced to stop. As far as we could see that meant that they wouldn't reach a bivi ledge good enough for two, let alone four. And to make matters worse, cloud was already swirling around them in line with the trend of the bad weather arriving earlier every day. We still had access to the ropes the others had climbed up and the gear was split fairly evenly between us. All in all there was no reason why we couldn't continue as independent teams of two if we wanted to.

Steve shouted up that we would stay put for the day and, in the absence of any violent objection, we prepared for an unwelcome day of relaxation. Being camped on a slight arête projecting from the third ice-field, we felt relatively safe from any falling debris. Little did we know how wrong we would be proved to be.

The ground that Brendan was leading on looked very hard and was sufficiently steep and icy for bits that he knocked down to fall more or less free to the ice slope, at which point they tended to cartwheel off in any direction that they fancied. At about 1pm a particularly loud noise signalled the approach of something notably unpleasant. I was struggling to put my boots on and clear the accumulating snow that was threatening to push us off our little ledge, whilst Steve was lying down waiting for me

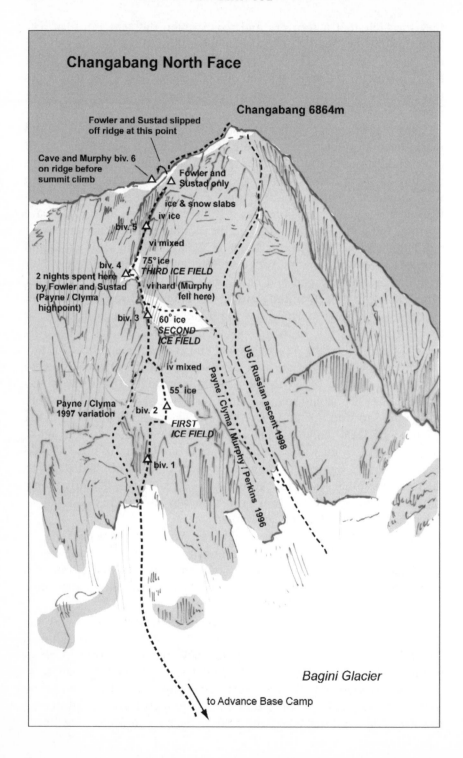

Changabang North Face

Changabang 6864m

Fowler and Sustad slipped
off ridge at this point

Cave and Murphy biv. 6
on ridge before
summit climb

Fowler and
Sustad only

ice & snow slabs

iv ice

biv. 5

vi mixed

75° ice
THIRD ICE FIELD

biv. 4

2 nights spent here
by Fowler and Sustad
(Payne / Clyma
highpoint)

vi hard (Murphy
fell here)

biv. 3   60° ice
*SECOND
ICE FIELD*

iv mixed

Payne / Clyma / Murphy / Perkins 1996

US / Russian ascent 1998

55° ice

Payne / Clyma
1997 variation   biv. 2

*FIRST
ICE FIELD*

biv. 1

Bagini Glacier

to Advance Base Camp

to get out of the way. We both pressed ourselves against the inner wall of the tent as a six-inch diameter flat piece of rock came straight through the back panel and ploughed into the groundsheet, missing Steve's head by perhaps 10cm. We were clearly not in as safe a position as we had hoped. I hurled some abuse up into the clouds and received an apologetic response but then they were hardly throwing things at us on purpose. Andy later described his horror at seeing the plate of rock home in on our tent. 'Like a heat-seeking missile,' he described it. But there was nowhere safer to move to and the remainder of the day was spent huddled against the side wall with our helmets on. It was much more frightening than the climbing. Steve did a wonderful job of sewing the tent up with a lurid pink bootlace that he happened to be carrying.

Our rest day had not been at all relaxing and the next morning it was not a refreshed team that climbed up the ropes that the others had left. The occasional piece of ice shot past, reminding us of their presence, but at least there was relief from the tedium of the knackering, featureless ice slopes. From the top of the ropes the ground was much more my cup of tea; mixed climbing up steep, thin ice runnels with lots of variety. I was really beginning to enjoy myself at the time, as opposed to the Himalayan norm of retrospective pleasure. Inevitably, it did not last.

By 11am the daily bad weather spell was already pouring waves of spindrift down on to us. Steve had headed off up a deepening groove system. His shouts of discomfort warned me in good time when particularly penetrating blasts of spindrift were approaching and our progress slowed to a crawl. Our bivouac justified our decision not to proceed as a team of four. The ledge wasn't even big enough for the two of us in a sitting position. We hung forlornly in the flapping tent fabric, dangling uncomfortably from tied-off ice screws. Midway through the night life seemed particularly miserable. The way we were hanging I couldn't avoid squeezing Steve hard into the fabric. Uncharacteristically, he was getting angry which I interpreted as him being so uncomfortable that I would have to adjust my position somehow. In retrospect I suspect that, like me, he was becoming tetchy about the situation in general. It felt ridiculous having two teams of two on the same line at the same time. Not only had we had to suffer a day of enforced inactivity and serious objective dangers but the sense of exploratory, adventurous climbing was seriously compromised by us following Andy and Brendan up the face. The crap-splattered ground leading to a couple of the bivi sites just about summed it up. Never again would we get ourselves into this situation.

But at the time I interpreted Steve's anger as a signal that I really had to sort out a different hanging position. There was a reasonable ice screw to one side but with a one-way zip entrance to the tent the only way to use it to take any of my weight off Steve was to puncture a hole in the fabric and clip in direct. I pondered this for a moment. Spindrift was continually rushing over the Gore-Tex tent fabric, whilst the nylon ground sheet was flat against the ice. Fearful of allowing spindrift to get inside, I chose to make a small hole in the nylon groundsheet. It was almost immediately obvious that I had made a serious error. Within ten minutes my tiny hole was a 30cm tear and spindrift was forcing its way inside. Keeping it out of my sleeping bag whilst suspended from a rope tied round my waist was a challenging way to spend a few hours. Meanwhile Steve groaned noisily next to me. He was in a bivi bag inside the tent and so was better off from the spindrift point of view, but had an even more uncomfortable section of bum-ledge than I did. I've had worse bivouacs, but an awful lot of better ones.

By the time we had sorted ourselves out the next day I was not feeling my best. It was also rather demoralising to realise that it was already snowing hard as Steve was leading the first pitch of the day at 8.15am. We managed a meagre two pitches that day before the first ledge in seven days of climbing provided all the temptation we needed to pitch the tent and assess our position.

'Still enjoying your holiday, Michael?'

'Most rewarding,' I responded. This was the end of day seven from Advanced Base so we should have had just one day's food left. Reality was much more encouraging. The mashed potato surplus was such that we had at least something to eat for a further five to six days. The gas, too, was lasting well. There was clearly no justifiable excuse to retreat and, after all, a bit of bad weather has to be expected when out on the mountain for so long.

As an added incentive, Roger and Julie-Ann's tent was now visible down on the ice field below and, of course, Andy and Brendan were somewhere up there above us.

The morning dawned perfect, with superb views right across the breadth of the Himalayan chain. We could see from Tibet in the north to the Indian plains in the south. Magnificent. I remember saying to Steve how lucky we were to be able to 'do this kind of thing'.

We were feeling confident now and guessed the top of the face to be only 150 metres or so above us. Route-finding looked to be a bit of a problem and, sure enough, we probably followed a more difficult line than we had to, but at least we enjoyed two wonderful mixed pitches through a steep rocky band which led to an ice slope and a final hard pitch with an exciting corniced exit on to the summit ridge.

And what a ridge, what a relief to be able to walk about after eight days on the face, and what a stunning view of Nanda Devi standing gloriously aloof in the middle of her forbidden sanctuary. The clouds were boiling, so we only caught a tantalising glimpse of the sun-struck summit, but that alone was enough to fire the imagination.

The climb had topped out well below the summit and we assessed that it would take the best part of a day to climb to the summit and back. This was, of course, the upper section of the ridge taken by the first ascent team in 1974. Andy and Brendan had been to the top that day and could be seen descending towards us but tracks going down the ridge suggested that their tent was a little lower down.

'Let's go and pitch the tent with the others,' suggested Steve.

To me the spot where we had joined the ridge looked okay for cutting out a good platform and would minimise the height gain necessary in the morning but Steve was already off. I wondered whether to call a halt but then the others probably had an even better site a bit lower down and it would be nice to have a good chat with them. Also they would probably appreciate some mashed potato, which I was getting pretty sick of. Despite my reservations, I said nothing, took up some coils and prepared to follow.

Steve had been having trouble with his crampons from the word go. They balled up with snow almost immediately and he slipped over stopping himself straight away. But I could see he was uncharacteristically uncomfortable. As he continued his heel sections balled up again after only one or two steps. I could see them slipping to one side. Suddenly one foot slipped away from beneath him on the balled up snow and he fell on to his side. Braking from that position was difficult as the still heavy rucksack tended to pull him back. I watched with horror as he started to slide down the south side of the ridge. I knew that it steepened markedly just below us and my quickly positioned ice-axe in the snow belay was not really up to any serious forces. I remember glancing up at the crest. Could I jump down the other side? No, it was too far above me, I braced myself. I had managed to get a waist belay and leant in to take the strain.

To begin with I felt I was in with a chance. I could feel my crampon points biting home and see Steve swinging round below me. But the further he swung the more the slope steepened and the strain grew.

Ultimately, I crumpled to one side and came on to the axe, I felt just a token resistance as I was dragged down. My feelings were of complete despair. All those promises to my wife and children.

'Be careful,' Nicki had said when I left.

'I will,' I'd cheerfully replied.

And yet here I was sliding fast down a snow slope, unable to stop and with a 1000-metre drop below.

I swear I saw their faces as I fell. More than fear was a tremendous feeling that I'd let them down. I was accelerating fast now and then free falling. A huge thump winded me and I was simultaneously aware of a sharp pain across my face. Then I stopped. I explored myself and my position cautiously. My nose was bleeding but my arms, legs and body seemed fine. The rope had wrapped itself around me in such a way that I couldn't easily move.

'Steve. You all right?'

I somehow knew then that Steve was only a couple of metres away but I couldn't squirm round to see him clearly. There was a terrible pregnant silence. He, too, was checking his body: 'My ribs hurt. Not feeling too good.' Steve is a tough man. I knew he would not be exaggerating. I also knew that he, like me, would be shocked and further injuries might come to light. Untangling myself from the rope was surprisingly difficult but it was encouraging that Steve too was able to free himself. We both stood there contemplating our position. I still had an incredibly strong vision of my family and the close call had had a deep emotional impact. I could feel the wetness of tears welling up in my eyes. The snow platform that we had come to a halt on was about seventy metres below the ridge and huge. It was already 5pm and the weather was far from settled. As we gathered our thoughts it was obvious that the only sensible thing to do was to stay put for the night and assess our position in the morning.

We later discovered that the other two had not seen us top out and did not know about our fall, being more concentrated on their own descent. Indeed when they saw our tent on the platform they were impressed that we had found such a good site.

9

Changabang 1997: Tragedy and Survival

Events on the descent across the South-East Face of Kalanka –
camp in the Inner Sanctuary – considering the Rishi Gorge escape –
crossing Shipton's Col – the Bagini Pass – return to Joshimath

Steve made nasty gurgling and groaning noises in his sleep. I could tell he was hurt but had he punctured a lung or got some other internal injury? There was no way of knowing and little I could do but keep my fingers crossed.

Morning dawned clear and bitterly cold. Steve found it difficult to move and was evidently in great pain.

'We'll have to go straight down the face from here,' he said.

My thoughts were unrepeatable.

I had no idea what was below us and viewed the suggestion as an absolute last resort. But his comment brought home to me how bad he must feel. There was no way he would normally suggest such an obviously dangerous way out. We packed up slowly, not speaking much, both lost in our own thoughts and certainly not touching any more on how we might get back to Base Camp from here.

Once upright, Steve was able to move around more easily than either of us had expected, although he was unable to carry much beyond his sleeping bag. Distressing as it was, we abandoned all of our non-essential equipment. Some of it was very expensive. We must have felt that the situation was serious!

Shouts from the Cave/Murphy team above naturally directed our thoughts towards getting back to the crest of the ridge which, fortunately, was approachable via a 55-degree snow and ice slope at one point. We managed to convey our predicament and headed diagonally up to them, gratefully taking up Andy's offer of a top rope which meant that Steve and I could climb together without having to waste time belaying.

And so we met up with Andy and Brendan for the second time on the route. This time we would stay together. Going up to the summit was out of the question for Steve and me and the decision to join together for the descent was easily made and unanimous. In fact, the others were having their fair share of problems too. Their food had now effectively run out and Andy appeared to have contracted secondary frostbite in his thumb. Steve, the acknowledged frostbite expert amongst us on the strength of having one toe less, confided in me that he thought that Andy could well have to have it amputated at the joint.

I recall sitting on the ridge thinking this was all getting rather out of hand. Never before had I experienced so much injury and danger on a route. In retrospect I think we all felt that having two pairs in action on the same route led to both making debatable decisions that might not have been made but for the presence of the other.

There were two possible ways of descending. Abseil directly down the face we had just climbed or make the far longer but hopefully less hazardous descent the south side of the mountain and then cross two largely unknown cols to return to our Advanced Base – all of this (with the exception of the final col) being effectively a descent of the first ascent route. Steve was keen to abseil or be lowered down the North Face, whereas the rest of us voted for the south side descent. This involved traversing along the knife-edge col between Changabang and Kalanka and then rising up a 100 metres or so to a system of glacial steps descending diagonally across the huge open South Face of Kalanka.

By that evening we were camped at the beginning of the glacial steps. The intervening day had involved a couple of slanting abseils on hard ice and some very steep bottomless powder slopes. All in all I was encouraged. Steve was able to walk strongly, and didn't seem to be as badly impaired as we had feared. Andy's thumb looked nasty but hardly seemed to affect him at all. Brendan was going strongly and, while I felt exhausted, it was no worse than I would normally expect on this sort of ground.

The next day looked to be the crucial descent day. If we could get down to the Changabang Glacier we would be in a more temperate climate, away from the objective dangers. We would then have two options, crossing the two cols as we had planned all along or, if things got really bad, trying to walk out via the politically closed Rishi Ganga Gorge. Either way we needed good visibility and fine weather to descend safely to the glacier.

Luck was not with us and the morning dawned grey with intermittent cloud. By the time we had been going for two hours it was snowing heavily and impossible to see the way ahead. I was uncomfortably aware of the avalanche risk inherent in the vast 40-degree snow slopes stretching up above us towards the summit of Kalanka.

A short section descending through a tricky series of ice cliffs brought us to a relatively sheltered spot beneath a solid-looking sérac where we stopped to consider our situation over a brew. By now heavy snow slides were intermittently pouring down runnels in the slope, a particularly nasty one having caught Brendan and me just before we reached the brew spot. It was difficult to decide what to do. It was still not midday and with so far still to go it was important to get a move on. But the objective danger was highest whilst it was still snowing and the lack of visibility made route-finding difficult too. Opinions were divided. I liked the idea of staying put but a slight clearing swung the majority view in favour of continuing and we ploughed on diagonally down, searching for an open couloir of mixed rock and snow which we knew led down about 700 metres to the Upper Changabang Glacier.

Visibility was intermittent and it soon became clear that we had descended too far. A huge line of ice cliffs stretched along below us and from what we knew of the face, we needed to be further up and further along the series of glacier steps. Brendan and Andy led the way as we strained 200 metres uphill through deep snow. Our lack of food and the time we had spent on the mountain were taking their toll but after what seemed a very long time we reached a level where we could continue traversing. It was only 100 metres to go to cross the open slope to where it seemed that the cliffs below us ended and, with luck, we would be able to gain the wide couloir that Andy and Brendan had seen on their summit day. The slope was 40 degrees, the snow knee-deep and the avalanche danger extreme.

Andy turned back to me: 'I'll just clip into a knot. Easier to unclip if the slope goes.'

I did the same. I think Brendan and Steve did too. There was nothing else that could be done to minimise the risk and we moved hesitantly onwards. I vowed to avoid routes with open slopes like this in the future.

The ice cliffs did seem to end at this point but visibility was such that it was impossible to see exactly where we were. It looked right but further descent was only possible by abseil. I went first but as I abseiled over the edge it became clear that the spot we had chosen was far from ideal. I was abseiling over the lip of a large sérac, hanging free and gently rotating. After thirty metres or so, I landed on 70-degree rock slabs which were exposed to anything falling out of the very unstable-looking sérac, I scrabbled ten metres or so to one side out of the fall line. Looking up, I could see that we were just a bit too far to the left and it would be much safer and easier all round if the others moved the rope about ten metres to the right where a relatively straightforward abseil would be possible. Cursing that I had left most of the equipment up above, I connected myself to a couple of tiny wire nuts (RPs), wedged the pick of my axes in a crack and shouted this news up to the others. I then disconnected myself from the abseil rope and settled down to wait. It was still snowing heavily and small snow slides intermittently swished past.

An ominous roaring sound gave warning of something more serious.

Looking up, I saw a dark cascade of a heavy snowslide take to the air almost directly above me. I was belayed in a shallow groove and stuck my nose as firmly into the back as it would go. Whatever happened I could not risk allowing the pressure of the snow to build up between my body and the mountain that would force me out onto my flimsy belay. The light darkened and heavy snow battered my helmet and shoulders. This was a nasty one, by far the heaviest so far; I prayed that there wouldn't be anything hard and painful mixed in with the snow. It probably lasted less than a minute but felt an awful lot longer. Eventually the pressure eased and I was able to shake off the loose snow. I was getting cold now. I wanted to put my duvet on, but was wary of doing so in case further avalanches came down. I decided to wait until after the next abseil – but what was going on up above? A long time had passed and nothing seemed to be happening. I shouted up, 'What's the problem? It's fine down here.'

After several increasingly insistent shouts, Andy's voice penetrated the mist.

'Is Brendan with you?'

This seemed a curious question. My alarm bells rang immediately. Of course he wasn't with me, the abseil rope hadn't even been moved.

'Oh … Fucking hell. He's gone!'

Andy had clearly clutched at a straw of hope in my 'It's fine' comment. The reality was that Brendan had been swept off by the snow slide whilst moving the abseil point. I looked down. Below me 150 metres of 70-degree mixed ground gave way to snow slopes broken by rock steps. There was no sign of Brendan and realistically no chance that he would have survived. Andy and Steve came down to me almost without a word.

Our abseiling proceeded carefully and quietly. There was little conversation. This was a new experience for Andy and me and we both sensed that its impact would grow rather than diminish as the days passed. Steve remained his usual stoical, reliable self. He hadn't really known Andy or Brendan before the trip but only thirty minutes or so before the accident he had commented to me what nice blokes they both were.

It was dark by the time we reached a decent bivouac spot on a protected spur. Andy shouted Brendan's name into the emptiness but, while we all dutifully strained our ears, the deafening silence was no surprise. We pitched the two little tents side by side and Steve suggested that he share with Andy. I half expected Andy to decline and the fact that he didn't somehow brought his personal distress into even sharper focus for me.

His frostbitten thumb was a worry but he also knew Brendan much better than Steve or I had done. He had just shared Brendan's first major Himalayan success and the elation of that had now turned so suddenly to despair. Brendan came from a large close-knit family and Andy knew that there would be a lot of distressing times ahead as the task of describing Brendan's last moments would inevitably fall mainly on his shoulders.

Also Andy and Steve had the image of Brendan's last moments on their minds. They had seen exactly what happened, seen Brendan venture out to place an ice screw, turn to them and shout 'it's a bomber' and then be swept away as he tried desperately to hang onto the head of the screw. He must have missed me by centimetres but I had seen nothing and had no such image in my mind. Yet I felt a cold and numbing loneliness as Andy and Steve shared one tent whilst I slept alone with my thoughts in the other.

47 The South Face of Kalanka with the ridge to Changabang on the left. The descent line took the obvious mid-height glacial shelf to its right end where the avalanche caught Brendan Murphy. We bivouacked on the rognon below the avalanche slope.

The weather the next day was glorious and by mid-morning we had returned to a spot where we could see the whole of the area where Brendan had presumably ended up. There was no sign of him at all. Andy shouted hopefully but there was no response. The sun was hitting the face by this time and the first snow slides of the day were already coming down. I was exhausted. I think we all were. It may well have been beyond us but, even if it hadn't been, it would certainly have been unjustifiably dangerous to search through avalanche debris beneath a huge hot Himalayan face. The most likely result would have been further fatalities. With a sense of reluctance and with huge sadness we turned our backs on the face and waded at a snail's pace through the soft snow and searing heat of the Upper Changabang Glacier to a safe spot where we could pitch the tents.

In the pre-1982 days expeditions visiting this spot would have been able to relax and walk easily down to a Base Camp the following day. Now the Nanda Devi Sanctuary below us offered little in the way of security. Not visited since the early 1980s and protected by the difficult Rishi Gorge, it was pretty clear to us that the old tracks would be extremely difficult to follow and the bridges long since swept away. Even with the track in good condition it used to be six porter days down to the road from the foot of the Changabang Glacier. In our condition and with the track disused for over ten years, it would doubtless take even longer and could prove impossible and we had enough mashed potato for only one day. The only alternative was traversing the mountain over Shipton's Col and the Bagini Pass[1] to regain the Upper Bagini Glacier but now, faced with the reality of two 500-metre climbs in our exhausted condition, it didn't seem quite so appealing. We spent the rest of the day lying flat out in the heat, talking about Brendan, staring back at his resting place and forward at the long slope leading up to the notch in the ridge that we hoped was Shipton's Col.

We started walking at midnight but, even so, the snow would frequently almost take our weight but then the crust would break at the last moment. The resultant jarring was totally enervating – excruciatingly painful for Steve. There was nothing but for him to keep going. Andy and I stopped occasionally to watch out for him. He was using our steps whenever he could but still frequently breaking through the crust. It is a measure of Steve's toughness that, once we had got going, I never seriously thought that he might not make it.

There was immense relief when Andy, who was in front, shouted down that the gap that we had been heading for sported an old fixed rope on the Rhamani side and was clearly Shipton's Col. But our hopes of an easy abseiling descent were dashed when we were faced with a smooth, vertical granite wall perhaps 100 metres high. At one point we all ended up hanging free, like a bunch of bananas, from a peg and a wire in the middle of a blank wall. I could feel my mind beginning to wander. This was too much. Lower down Steve admonished me for rigging the next abseil point from a single uncertain block when a crack nearby would take a bomb-proof peg. The incident brought home to me how tired I was. Double-checking each others' decisions became second nature.

---

[1] Shipton's Col was reached, but not crossed, by Shipton's Inner-Sanctuary Survey group in 1936. It was next reached by Martin Boysen and Doug Scott (members of the 1974 first ascent team) by an indirect climb from the Rhamani Glacier. The steep line directly to the col was then equipped with fixed ropes to allow access to the Inner Sanctuary below the South-East Faces of Changabang and Kalanka. The Bagini Pass was first crossed by Tom Longstaff's 1906 expedition *en route* to Trisul.

We camped on the flat Rhamani Glacier. The Bagini Pass was perhaps four miles away and 500 metres above us. On the far side was the Upper Bagini Glacier, leading down to our Advance Base Camp site where we had left some food. Conscious of the need to make progress whilst the snow was frozen, we set off at midnight again. Equally conscious of our state of exhaustion, we left everything that wasn't essential. Most of our pegs, nuts, one stove all but one gas cylinder, all got left. Steve expressed surprise when Andy didn't even make a move to pack up his tent.

'Why are you leaving it?' he asked.

Andy looked at him and said, 'It's shit or bust today.'

We just left it there pitched on the Rhamani Glacier.

We were lucky. The Rhamani Glacier, perfectly frozen, gave six or so kilometres of gradual height gain before the final 500-metre 45-50-degree slope to the Bagini Col provided a huge sting in the tail. Several times I caught myself falling asleep draped over my ice-axes. This was day thirteen for Steve and me and day fifteen for Andy. It struck me that this was how it could all end ... just falling asleep and not waking up again.

The sun caught us on the Pass. Previously we had been worried about our cold feet. Now the problem was the heat which had a debilitating effect on us and softened the slope horribly. We front-pointed, slipped, slithered and finally got down to the flat snow of the glacier.

Andy walked on ahead and I have an enduring image etched on my mind of him ploughing a lonely furrow in the enormous whiteness of the glacier with Changabang towering above. He looked so small and fragile. We should of course have been roped up but had abandoned the remaining ropes at the top of the Bagini Pass. We couldn't carry them any more.

Steve and I argued over the best way to descend the final 200 metres to Advanced Base. If I needed it, this was the final confirmation that things were getting a bit out of control as we never argue in the mountains. Even worse, we opted to take different lines. I scraped my hands nastily slipping down a steep icy section and Steve twisted his leg coming down a slope of soft snow covering hard ice. Ten hours after leaving the Rhamani Glacier and thirteen days after starting the face we finally crawled into the camp. We were nearly safe.

After a brew and some food Andy stood up.

'I'm worried about my thumb. I'll carry on to Base Camp.'

'Shouldn't we stay together? You might not make it tonight.'

But Andy was insistent. 'It's already smelling,' he said. 'I really must get down to that first aid kit.'

Steve and I couldn't face it. We just lay there and watched him head off.

'Strong bloke,' said Steve admiringly.

The walk down the next day was dire. An amazing amount of snow had melted and what had been easy snow slopes on the way up was now collapsing moraine which continually jarred Steve's ribs. Our pace was painfully slow. We just didn't seem to have any energy at all.

It was a relief to see Andy at Base Camp. He had ended up sleeping out and only arrived an hour or so before us. Roger and Julie-Ann were there, together with Narendra and our cook. They had only got back the day before us and had had their fair share of excitement, spending eleven days in all on the face. The weather had pinned them down on the third icefield and the spindrift had been such that they had to abort one attempt at an abseil descent and climb back up to their bivouac spot, where they then spent four days desperately trying to stop the accumulating snow pushing their tent off the mountain.

The porters arrived the next day. Roger said a few touching words about Brendan and we hobbled our separate ways, lost in our separate thoughts, down through the meadows to the now lively settlement of Dunagiri.

On the bus back to Joshimath, Steve, Narendra and I joined the throngs packed on the roof atop a high mound of bags. On the final approach to the town I caught sight of something out of the corner of my eye and shouted instinctively: 'Watch out!'

Narendra ducked frantically as a power cable gave him a resounding crack across the forehead. Others on the roof laughed but if he hadn't ducked we could easily have had a decapitation on our hands.

And what do I think of it all now? Andy's thumb has made a miraculous recovery and Steve's ribs (he'd broken four in several places) have healed well. But Brendan will never come back. I look back and remember the fantastic climbing high on the North Face, I remember the terrible sensation of falling down the south side, the endlessly falling snow and poor visibility on the descent, the shock of realising that Brendan was no longer with us, the enervating heat of the Changabang Glacier, the endless exhaustion of Shipton's Col and the Bagini Pass, the relief on getting down to Advanced Base Camp ... So many experiences.

Was it worth it? In bald terms the answer has to be of course not; nothing is worth the life of a friend. I have looked into the eyes of his loved ones and seen their grief. But Brendan died doing what he loved. He knew well the risks and balanced them against the rewards. Making the first ascent of Changabang's North Face was his first major success and if he was alive today I know we would still be toasting the good times and shared hardship in what was, for all of us, the adventure of a lifetime.

I move on to other climbs, remembering Brendan and hoping that I have learned from our experiences. The mountains? I love them still.

10

El Niño on Siula Chico:

A new family mandate – early ascents of Siula Chico and Siula Grande –
the El Niño effect – teaming up with Simon Yates – bus ride and Base Camp trek –
considering the Yates / Simpson epic – on Siula Chico's West Face

The Changabang tragedy inevitably caused questions to be raised at home over my mountaineering future.

The risk to reward ratio of climbing requires careful consideration and Nicki had always had unswerving faith in my judgement. Now though the loss of Brendan and the near miss experienced by Steve and me inevitably threw the whole subject into sharp focus. For a family man with two children I had to accept that the risks we ended up taking on Changabang were too high. But I like to think that we learn from our mistakes and whilst we can never eliminate risk in mountaineering, we can certainly reduce it to an acceptable level by choosing objectives carefully and exercising good judgement and caution on the mountains.

Nicki was fantastic. As one who has climbed herself she understands what drives me and knew my love of the mountains was such that giving up was never an option. But we both felt that the 'six weeks away on alternate years' regime that had been operating since we married in 1991 was now a problem. In climbing terms it had been productive, with routes on Cerro Kishtwar, Taweche and Changabang, but as the children grew six weeks was a long time to be away. The two years between each trip made it harder to get back to expedition fitness and growing work responsibilities also made a long absence difficult.

Shorter, more regular, mountaineering trips were the answer. This would leave me with sufficient leave to have family and climbing holidays each year. Also it would mean that taxpayers with intractable share valuation problems would not have to be told that Mr Fowler was away for six weeks. But where to go in three weeks? Most of the world's mountain ranges are increasingly easy to get to but three weeks is not long to get there, acclimatise, catch a weather window good enough to allow success and then get back. Careful planning would be essential.

Taulliraju's South Pillar in Peru, back in 1982, had been a three-week trip and such a good one that I longed to return to that part of the world.

And Siula Chico had been on my list of exciting objectives for years. At just over 6000 metres it forms one of the major summits of the Cordillera Huayhuash, a compact but spectacular range of mountains about 125 miles north east of Lima. I had first become aware of its existence back in 1985 when Joe Simpson and Simon Yates climbed the West Face of nearby Siula Grande and an article on their epic climb (and even more epic descent) appeared in the mountaineering press. A photograph published with that article showed, in the background, the West Buttress of Siula Chico. It offered a very steep mixed rock and ice challenge, seemingly free from objective dangers such as rockfalls and avalanches. I registered it in my mind as a worthy future objective.

It was to be sixteen years before it fitted into my plans and rose to the top of my list. Political problems were one reason for the long wait. The Cordillera Huayhuash was a centre of activity for the Sandero Luminoso (Shining Path) guerrilla movement. Between 1987 and 1995 this left-wing organisation was committed to overthrowing the government and mounted a campaign of extreme violence. Atrocities were initially directed against those suspected of supporting the government, but the perceived need to raise awareness of their cause resulted in Lima being subjected to a prolific bombing campaign in which tourists became ideal targets for raising the international profile.

One of my friends, Dave Wilkinson, endured a nasty experience at their hands. Camped in a hollow up in the mountains, his team was surprised by the appearance of several men on horseback. Initially they kept their distance but as darkness fell they closed in. Soon rocks started to fly towards the tent and the climbers were forced to don their helmets. Direct hits began to shred the tent and violent screams, which they took as dastardly threats, rent the air. In the darkness and confusion the climbers managed to escape but after a chilly night huddling under rocks they returned to their camp the next day to find it had been ransacked.

Such incidents kept almost all teams away from the Huayhuash for a few years but the capture of the Shining Path's leader, Abimael Guzman, in Lima in 1993 marked a turning point. By 1998 it was generally felt that danger levels had moderated enough to become acceptable, so, sixteen years after the Taulliraju trip, it was back to Peru. This trip would be rather different however, as Taulliraju is in the popular and westernised Cordillera Blanca range, about thirty miles north of the more remote Cordillera Huayhuash that we knew was far less frequented by climbers and trekkers.

After several attempts from the north, Siula Chico was finally climbed in 1966 by a German team led by Manfred Sturm. They reached the summit by traversing from Siula Grande. Sturm had attempted the mountain previously by the same route but had retreated just below the summit when a huge cornice broke and a climber was killed. The 1966 team achieved success against the odds. With an untypical but rather endearing break from German efficiency Sturm's team arrived at Base Camp to find that they had three donkey-loads of beer but had somehow overlooked gasoline for their stoves. But by a curious coincidence the nearby Austrian Jirishanka team had excess of gasoline but no beer and thus a mutually beneficial swap was possible. Whether Sturm's group could have succeeded on beer alone remains open to debate! Certainly central European exactitude took on a new light after this incident.

The Sturm ascent was the only one of Siula Chico I was able to trace. No one appeared to have even tried to climb the mountain from the west. However Crag Jones, who had been with us on Ak-su back in 1990, had been up to the foot of the face in 1987. He had lacked an experienced partner, so no attempt was made, but he did confirm it looked exciting and provided detailed photographs taken from directly below.

From all the information I had managed to glean it looked to be a seriously inspirational objective; a very steep rock buttress with a smattering of fairly continuous ice streaks. I could feel a sense of excitement and anticipation arising – an essential pre-trip sensation.

After the experiences on Changabang I was keener than ever to stick with completely independent teams of two. Mike Morrison wished to visit Peru again and he teamed up with a friend of his from Bristol, Dave Walker, who was looking forward to what would be his first mountaineering trip outside Europe. Mike and Dave were just keen to explore and climb whatever took their fancy around the upper reaches of the glacier, leaving me, and whoever I chose to climb with, to concentrate on Siula Chico. This was perfect in that, after Changabang, I had vowed that I would never again end up with two teams going for the same objective.

It was down to me to find a partner. Initially Andy Cave was keen to come but with wedding plans well advanced he finally decided to drop out. Steve Sustad and Pat Littlejohn were already booked up for other trips and, after much thought and discussion with Nicki, I decided to approach Simon Yates – he who was with Joe Simpson on nearby Siula Grande back in 1985 and whose photograph in the magazine *High* first attracted my attention to Siula Chico.

The Simpson/Yates climb on Siula Grande ended with an epic that has gone down in mountaineering folklore and after the recent successful film based on an equally successful book is now widely known and discussed. It was their first climb outside Europe and after an audacious first ascent of Siula Grande's West Face Joe broke his leg on the summit ridge. Simon then helped him down almost to the glacier when, in the dark, he mistakenly lowered him over a large ice cliff. Joe was hanging free and unable to climb up the rope which wasn't long enough to lower him down. Simon was being pulled off and eventually he had no alternative but to cut the rope. In the morning it was obvious that Joe had fallen into a huge, gaping crevasse. There was no response to Simon's shouts and he returned to Base Camp, only to be awoken three days later by Joe's shouts from somewhere in the boulder field outside. Joe had survived and crawled down! It was one of the most amazing mountaineering survival stories ever and one which, through his book, *Touching the Void,* launched his extremely successful writing career.

I had known Simon Yates vaguely for many years. He had a reputation as an experienced mountaineer and a man who was good company and easy to get on with. Steve Sustad, who had climbed with him in Pakistan the previous year, spoke very highly of him. I am always very wary about climbing with new partners on big routes, but I respect Steve's judgement on partners and I liked Simon, and his track record in all respects seemed to speak for itself.

But Simon was due to get married in the summer. He is also a man who, as a leader of commercial mountaineering trips, has a very full diary. It seemed unlikely that suggesting in January that he might like to come on a trip in May would produce a very positive response. In fact I do wonder if I would ever have bothered mentioning it to him if Steve Sustad and I hadn't ended up at his and Jane's engagement party, in the Old Dungeon Ghyll Hotel in Langdale. We were chatting generally when Simon asked me what I was up to expedition-wise.

'Siula Chico,' I explained. 'But Andy's had to drop out.' Although I had thought about it before the engagement party somehow it didn't seem the right place to raise the subject. It was almost as a tongue in cheek comment that I added, 'You know all about that area, are you keen?' The legendary Yates enthusiasm was immediately apparent. 'Hey, yes, that looks excellent. had that in mind for years, I'll have to speak to Jane.'

I presumed that he meant at some stage over the next few days and didn't really think that much more about it. It was then a bit of a surprise when a smiling Yates came up to me later in the evening.

'We're on. Just a few little things to sort out but it should be OK.'

I was impressed. Jane was clearly a most understanding lady. I sought her out to commend her pre-marital appreciation of the concept that a happy spouse equates to a happy relationship.

And so the team was complete. There would be four of us, Mike Morrison and Dave Walker climbing as one team, me and Simon as the other. We were from diverse areas of life: Mike an industrial heating installation contracts manager, Dave a computer wizard working on reducing noise vibration in aircraft engines, Simon a director of a newly formed adventure holiday company, and me, a taxman. If nothing else this mountaineering game appeals to a wide cross-section of society. In climbing terms though our professional lives had little relevance. We were all drawn together by the Cordillera Huayhuash and the tantalising image of the unclimbed West Face of Siula Chico.

A few weeks after the final team was agreed Mike was on the phone. 'What's this about El Niño and Peru? Have you seen the news?'

I certainly had. Peru rarely features on the UK news so something exceptional was clearly happening. The film clips showed five-metre waves of silt-laden water rushing down the main street of a small town, cars were being swept along and the more flimsy houses collapsing under the strain. El Niño's distortions to the normal weather pattern are caused by variations in sea temperatures which have created another problem for Peru. The warming of the offshore waters makes the fish, which like cooler waters, go deeper and out of reach of the fishermen's nets – a major catastrophe for the Peruvian people.

We also considered how it might affect the climbing. From what we could work out there had been prolonged spells of heavy precipitation which would have dumped a lot of snow in the mountains. But then one of the problems in Peru, in climbing terms, is that the climate seems to be warming up and the snow line has been rising. In the Cordillera Huayhuash, where the rock tends to be rotten, we really wanted plenty of snow and ice to hold it all together. With plenty of precipitation and a bit of freeze/thaw in the usually clear April/May days we reasoned that El Niño could actually be to our advantage.

The man at the desk at the Lima bus company spoke no English and our Spanish was poor. He appeared (not unlike the classic English traveller) to think it would be clearer if he shouted loudly. 'Cajatambo?' he screamed. And then, pointing vigorously at a grubby map on the wall, 'Oyun!'

This seemed odd. According to our map Oyun was in a different valley system miles away. No, we didn't want to go to Oyun. We wanted to go to Cajatambo – a town of 5000 people where we wanted to hire donkeys and start our two-day walk in. Fruitless exchanges at maximum volume saw little progress. We retired to consider the situation. It was true that the bus station sign said 'Oyun (Cajatambo)' but Simon was adamant that last time he was here he and Joe had just caught a straightforward bus service direct to Cajatambo and it took twelve hours. Eventually we gave up and boarded the night bus to Oyun feeling distinctly uncertain as to whether or not we were doing the right thing.

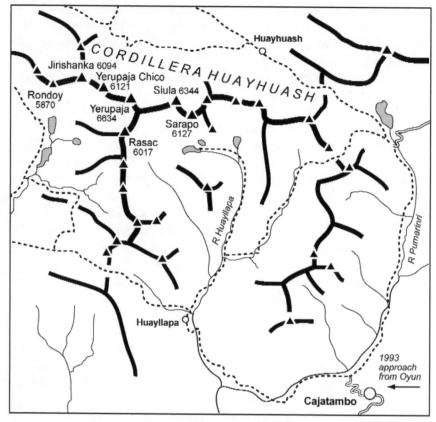

On climbing trips Mike Morrison always wears a watch with an inbuilt altimeter. This has caused him immense grief over the years in that overnight rises in altitude cause him deep concern that bad weather might be on the way. His climbing partners are always encouraging him to put it away, but referring to it seems to have become an addiction for him. At about 4am he nudged my arm.

'We are over 4000 metres!'

This did seem strange. Oyun was below 3000 metres and, according to our map, we should have followed the coast road and then turned up a valley leading straight to the town. There was no way we should be at over 4000 metres. The weather seemed fine and my initial reaction was that Mike's altimeter had malfunctioned and was again causing unnecessary distress. I glanced wearily out of the window. Our large coach was heading along a single-track dust road. In the first rays of dawn frost glistened on the short grass and baby llamas bounced energetically just below the road. Snow-covered mountains were visible with the snow line starting not that far above us. Simon was awake too.

'We didn't come this way last time,' he commented.

It all felt horribly wrong but there was little we could do about it but stay put and await developments. We were at least encouraged that a Peruvian family who seemed to be saying that they too were going to Cajatambo were still on board.

The road wound its way across the high plains and passed small but active mine-workings before dropping steeply with outrageously bus unfriendly hairpins, down to the town of Oyun. Our large modern bus looked most out of place in this environment.

Oyun was hot, dusty and uninspiring. There was no obvious transport to anywhere and certainly no bus with anything helpful like 'Cajatambo' written on it. We sat in a front room-style café with no windows, eating egg sandwiches and drinking a curious green liquid called Inca Cola.

Dave dug deep for his Spanish phrase book/dictionary as we prepared to quiz the proprietor about possible routes to Cajatambo. She and her daughter both wore blue bowler hats and dresses in numerous layers of brightly coloured fabric. They smelled quite strongly and Dave wondered how often they got round to changing the bottom layers. Unsurprisingly, they didn't speak a word of English.

Dave's phrase book was geared more to the requirements of the Costa Brava beach. It was not the most helpful publication. But we had nothing else and persevering was clearly in order. It felt rather stupid to be pointing at a map that showed no connecting road to Cajatambo and asking how to get there. Initial responses were as helpful as the map but tourists were clearly a novelty in Oyun and soon a small crowd had gathered to marvel at the lost gringos.

After several more egg sandwiches (we had difficulty asking for anything else) and endless cups of sickly Inca Cola, a short wiry character with obligatory black cowboy hat was shepherded towards us.

'Cajatambo,' he pronounced, indicating that we should follow him.

He turned out to be the driver of an ancient Chevrolet truck piled high with crates of bottled drink. In the back the Cajatambo family who were on the bus from Lima had already settled down between the crates. Their four-year-old snoozed, completely unfazed by the transfer from relatively luxurious bus to the back of a clearly unroadworthy truck. I still found it difficult to believe that this was the only way to a town of 5000 people. Whatever was going on? Surely there was a better way to Cajatambo?

'If there is we can't find it,' announced Simon pragmatically as we too squeezed into the back of the truck.

'This is my altitude record,' announced Dave some time later. There was no doubt about it, Mike's infamous altimeter watch recorded an altitude of 4700 metres. Despite being a fairly experienced mountaineer,

Dave had broken his previous altitude record by doing nothing more strenuous than sitting in the back of a truck. The truck appeared on its last legs, and had to stop once due to overheating, but it still had some life left in it. The dirt track had been relentlessly steep and, in places, spectacularly pitted. The climb up from Oyun had taken four hours without us meeting any other vehicles at all. I grew increasingly suspicious, nursed my altitude headache, and wondered what lay in store.

At one point we passed through what can only be described as a mining ghost settlement. In fact the track we were on appeared to be some kind of remnant from days when mining was a popular activity hereabouts. Road maintenance was clearly low on the agenda after the miners moved on and six hours into the journey everyone had to get out to help manhandle the truck through an axle-deep muddy section. The four-year-old loved it, but the grown-ups looked less exhilarated. Darkness fell and still we bounced onwards.

'So much for a twelve-hour bus ride from Lima.'

By 6pm the sun was going down and the temperature had dropped to the extent that we huddled together under the tarpaulin cover draped over the back of the truck. By 8pm we had been descending for a long time and the fumes under the tarpaulin were getting worse. I found it uncomfortable puking over the side; the sharp metal edge bashed unyieldingly into my ribs as I fought to avoid overbalancing whilst at the same time keeping an eye open for head-catching projections sticking out in the dark from the steep hillside.

It was a dishevelled version of my British civil servant self that arrived in Cajatambo. The others seemed not to have suffered so badly and looked relatively perky. The four-year-old in particular was very sprightly and kept jumping around, smiling and waving. I felt ill. Even so I could not help noticing that Cajatambo was a fairly big place. But, like Oyun, there was something strange about it. The central square, where we had stopped, had a wide concrete road along one side and I could just make out long straight roads stretching into the distance on either side of the square. There were quite a few people about but there was something missing. Vehicles. Why, in an age when the world is overrun with vehicles, were there none here, except for the truck that had brought us? I sat down to consider this on a rickety wooden bench outside the Hotel Cajatambo. The others manhandled our heavy unwieldy baggage, while I sat quietly taking in my surroundings and trying to regain my composure.

Our room was basic but had features which would, I felt, have made it Nicki-approved. Nicki's approval can be difficult to define but after ten years together I think I know it when I see it. Authentic old things are essential and it helps if a lot of effort went into them originally, they must also look well used but still be functional. The wallpaper here fell into this category. The designs were exactly the right size for the walls and it appeared that the pattern was at least partially hand-painted. But that was many years ago. Now most of the paper was missing and in two places doorways had been blocked up and the holes crudely mud-plastered over. Nicki's paper restoration skills could be put to good use here. I could imagine her enthusing over what a wonderful project it would be.

The floors too had that 'we've been here a very long time' look. Close inspection revealed that they were not your usual machine-sawn items, the boards varied considerably in thickness and width. They had been sawn and chiselled by hand and then worn smooth by a hundred years plus of hard wear. The panels in the door had the same appeal. Despite being covered in generations of paint it was still possible to see the chisel marks where they had been painstakingly prepared by hand. The room was bare, except for three single bed frames with mattresses and blankets lined up on each side. It had clearly faded from its former glory but had plenty of floor space and was ideal for our purposes.

But time was short on this trip and we were keen to leave Cajatambo the next day if at all possible. Somehow we had to organise some donkeys to carry our gear and an *arrero* (donkey-driver) to look after them.

'*Burro?*' asked Simon hesitantly.

The result was startlingly impressive. Within five minutes three black hatted, brown cloaked men were seated around the front table in the Hotel Cajatambo bar. So far so good.

But three hours later there had been little progress, if anything we had gone backwards. Only one potential *arrero* remained and he, Espinoza, was not exactly being over-co-operative. On the bright side, I was beginning to feel slightly better and the local school's English teacher had appeared on the scene to help with translation. Actually he was patently unable to speak fluent English but did seem to have a remarkable knowledge of things like Derby County football team. He also seemed keen to introduce us to his teenage girl pupils and force them to ask us English phrase book questions such as 'Are you married?' and 'How many children do you have?' All this was very interesting but it didn't help much as far as furthering the negotiations went. In fact Espinoza was proving to be a slippery character to deal with. He was either bloody thick or extremely astute. To this day I am not sure which it was. What I do know is that it seemed to be impossible to reach agreement with him.

He was a small wiry character and, not wishing to intimidate him too badly, we initially tried the softly, softly approach. This ended with Simon losing his temper and deciding that he had better leave before he hit the man. Mike and I persevered with Dave manning the dictionary and the

schoolteacher interjecting occasionally with the names of British foot-
ballers. The schoolgirls had long since gone home. By now we were trying
to explain that our latest offer included the Base Camp kitchen equipment
at the end of the trip. Mike, by far the best artist amongst us, produced
dinky little drawings of kettles, paraffin stoves and lanterns, whilst Dave
and I waved our arms frantically in an effort to emphasise what a
wonderful deal we were offering. A couple of times we thought we were
there. After all, we had actually accepted the rate that Espinoza was
asking, so how could we have failed? But then he would have second
thoughts, think of some extra problem and increase his price yet again.

We broke for the night in stormy mood, knowing by now that the few
arrerios around effectively formed a cartel and we were not going to get
a better deal by shopping around. It was either agree something in
Cajatambo or call off the trip.

By lunchtime the next day there was increasing local interest in our
negotiations. Heated exchanges must have been going on for at least
eight hours now and the proprietor of the hotel was looking pleased at the
amount of beer and coffee being consumed, both by us and the large
number of visitors. For, I think, the third time we seemed to be just about
there. Rates had been agreed for the donkeys, the *arrerio* and the Base Camp
guard (pilfering from camps is common in Peru) and Mike had just put the
finishing touches to yet another fine set of pictures of the kitchen items that
we would give Espinoza at the end. Despite an atmosphere of suspicion on
both sides, all this was being smoothly drawn into a contract when Espinoza
had yet another 'final' thought. Translation efforts proved difficult but with
the aid of a rather fine drawing from Espinoza all became clear. Grass was
the problem; he had forgotten to budget for grass for the donkeys.

Simon, who was back at the negotiating table, exploded: 'Grass! What
do you mean pay for the grass? The whole fucking hillside is covered in
grass!'

Simon was standing up, waving his arms and shouting. Espinoza
didn't need to speak English to get the gist of what was being said.

The lady proprietor of the hotel was physically imposing and clearly
feared and respected. Espinoza was small, if resilient. She leant across the
table and said something to him. Handshakes all round clinched the deal;
Espinoza signed on the dotted line. Nothing extra would be paid for grass
and the donkeys would be ready at 6am the following morning. It was
time to explore Cajatambo and do some shopping.

Cajatambo was rather like a wild west town. There were lots of people
about and almost all the men wore cowboy hats and the ladies colourful
multi-layered dresses and bowlers. There were plenty of horses saddled

up and ready to go and plenty of donkeys loaded up with all manner of goods. But no cars.

We wandered along to the outskirts of the town. Here a concrete archway spanned a short and incongruous section of dual carriageway. A little further and the mysterious lack of transport was explained. We couldn't understand how nobody we had spoken to, from the clerks at the Lima bus company to the proprietor of the Hotel Cajatambo, had failed to convey such a simple message to us. The road had gone. There was no other way to describe it. El Niño storms had simply swept away a bridge and a huge swathe of hillside. And this was just a small trickling tributary compared to the sections of deep gorge that Simon told us the road picked its way through lower down. Even here though the force of the water had plucked away far more than just the flood-prone land close to the river. Houses fifty yards back from the water's edge had been ripped in half and the remains hung precariously over the now deceptively meek and mellow trickle. We could only guess at how bad the damage was lower down. The reason for all our problems in getting to Cajatambo was immediately devastatingly clear. We returned to the town with a new respect for the world's weather phenomena.

The first day of the walk in was to the village of Huaylappa which, it turned out, was Espinoza's home village. The track rose steeply from Cajatambo zigzagging sharply up the hillside towards a 4000-metre col in the blunt ridge above the town. The corrugated tin roofs of Cajatambo glistened in the sun as we sweated our way up the track, Simon, Mike and Dave in front, me somewhere in the middle and Espinoza and the donkeys bringing up the rear. I was pleased to note that I was able to keep ahead of the donkeys but concerned that we might never see them again. With this in mind I sat on the flattish col, cursing my usual early expedition altitude headache and peering hopefully into the mist. My relief at seeing Espinoza and the donkeys appearing was promptly clouded by Espinoza apparently trying to re-open the food for the donkeys argument. I ran away down the far side of the col, wondering what other demands he would dream up whilst spending a couple of weeks as our Base Camp guard. It didn't bode well.

It was almost dark by the time we arrived in Huaylappa. The village was once fairly popular with westerners as an overnight stop on the 'round the Huayhuash' trek – a beautiful ten-day walk around the range which was popularised in various books of the 'hundred best treks in the world' type. The activities of the Shining Path stopped all that and by the attention that we received on arrival it was obvious that we were the first westerners here for some time. We were immediately surrounded by chattering children whose fingers were keen to explore everything we carried with us. Zips seemed particularly interesting to them and it was while we were fighting to maintain a balance between rudeness and control that Espinoza arrived.

Perhaps it was because he was on home ground or perhaps he was simply more relaxed now that we had left the strain of negotiations behind, either way he was suddenly the model of helpfulness. His neighbour was, it appeared, the village 'hotel' and we were more than welcome to stay there. He and his six children would help us with our luggage. And so in we all trooped to the mud hut hotel. The 'proprietor' and his wife and daughter were the model of politeness and helpfulness but it was difficult to see why this building was regarded as the hotel. There just wasn't anywhere to stay. Downstairs was one bare windowless room with a smooth concrete floor and upstairs was again one room, but beds at either end suggested this was where the family slept. The lady of the house appeared to be indicating that we should sleep in the family beds.

'And you?' asked Dave incredulously in his best phrase book Spanish. The lady pointed downstairs to the concrete floored room. We shuffled uncomfortably, their daughter was about nine years old. Kicking her out of her bed so that the premises could operate as an hotel didn't seem quite right. I didn't think my Tessa and Alec would appreciate such an arrangement.

But the lady repeated the gesture. It was clear that we were expected to sleep upstairs ... but on the floor or on the beds?

Dave, Mike and I positioned ourselves on the floor whilst Simon unpacked his sleeping bag on one of the beds.

'Feels very comfortable,' he said amidst our ribbing as to who his sleeping companion might turn out to be that night.

Meanwhile it seemed that dinner was being prepared in a pitch-black hut outside. It was a mystery to us as to why the kitchen should be 10 metres away from the house, but pleasant smells were spreading forth from a bubbling pot hanging over the flames of an open fire and we hung around expectantly in the dark, awaiting platefuls of something warm.

'Must go to the toilet,' said Dave doing his best to ask directions from the bemused family by means of sign language. He was directed to a wooden door in the mud wall surrounding the courtyard. The sound of expletives soon followed. Dave had not taken a torch and on stepping through the door he had bumped into something large and moving ... a donkey! It transpired that the 'toilet' was an area of land between the backs of the houses and a seventy-metre drop down into the river. Dave found the area to be uncomfortably squidgy and noted with horror that the donkeys liked to roll on their backs hereabouts. He wasn't gone for long.

Simon has been staring around intently. 'I think this is where I stayed with Joe,' he announced between mouthfuls of a difficult to pinpoint, but very pleasant, stew. Sure enough, after a serious session of arm-waving, the lady in charge remembered. I suppose it's not every day that a knackered westerner with a broken leg comes to stay. She made signs to indicate that he spent a lot of time asleep in the kitchen.

'Yes, that's right. Joe was pissed!' recalled Simon. 'We kept him drunk to take the pain away.'

A further thought struck him. His penknife! An added complication on the Joe and Simon epic was that they didn't have enough money to pay for a mule to carry Joe. Eventually Simon had to sell the penknife that he had used to cut the rope, an object which would doubtless have achieved cult status if he had managed to hang on to it. It was probably here somewhere in Huaylappa but our arm-waving communication techniques were simply not up to it. Sadly, Simon had to accept that it was not going to turn up.

The first day's walk from Cajatambo had been long and tiring; a steep 800-metre climb up to the col, a long gentle descent to below the level of Cajatambo and finally a further 500 metres of height gain to arrive at Huaylappa, at much the same altitude as we had started from.

The second day started more gently. The valleys radiating from the Huayhuash tend to be well cultivated in their lower reaches with broad well grazed grasslands higher up. This one was no exception and we made quick progress past the odd shepherds' hut. Simon knew exactly where we were going and what to watch out for.

'The dogs,' Simon was most insistent, 'watch out for the dogs.'

And so we did. There were plenty about around the shepherd's huts, and very friendly they were too! Simon couldn't believe it.

'This place has changed.'

It wouldn't be the last time on this trip that he would say this.

The last section to Base Camp was steeper but spectacular sharp-crested mountains began to pierce the sky. Feeling increasingly inspired, I managed to surpass my usual slowness and keep up with the others.
I recognised it immediately from a photograph in *Touching the Void*. There was no doubt about it, there was the distinctive rock that Joe lay beside at the end of his epic three-day crawl after he had been given up for dead. We had arrived at our Base Camp site.

It looked to be a very nice spot. A flat grassy area nestled next to a sparkling stream and the easily recognisable boulder looked to provide good bouldering if the urge should come over us. I adopted my 'early days at base camp' position of lying in the tent wondering when I might feel well enough to move. After all, we were at over 4000 metres, not far short of the altitude of Mont Blanc. Simon appeared not to be affected by such problems and enthusiastically talked about plans for the next day. He was keen to explore a ridge high above Base Camp and try to get a good view of the Siula peaks. In quieter moments he also talked about his feelings all those years ago when he woke in the middle of the night to the shouts of the friend he had given up for dead.

Mike and I had each read *Touching the Void* and been deeply moved by both Joe's and Simon's descriptions. But there is nothing like hearing it from the horse's mouth, so to speak. Later, when there were just the two of us, Mike expressed his thoughts out loud:

'Can you imagine it from Simon's point of view? Lying there cosily in your sleeping bag, upset over the horror of your climbing partner dying three days ago. All those thoughts which must have been going round in his mind. How should he explain it to Joe's parents? How would his friends react to him cutting the rope? Suddenly, the sound of faint screams from outside. He must have thought he was having a terrible nightmare. And then how did he feel when he realised it was for real? Imagine the awful realisation that you had abandoned your friend on the mountain when he was still alive!'

I shivered at the thought. Simon has had to take a fair amount of ribbing from his climbing friends over the years. It must have hurt sometimes, especially insensitive questions from people who have never been in such serious positions themselves and can never hope to fully understand. A few weeks before we left for Peru I had listened to him talking at the RGS in London. He said then that he would have done exactly the same things again, except that he wondered if he could have checked the crevasse more thoroughly to see if, by some miracle, Joe was still alive. He had gone as close to the edge as he dared and got no reply to his shouts but there was inevitably still a nagging doubt. Sitting around comfortably, well after the event, it is all very easy to say such things. One can only guess at how exhausted he felt at the time. He had been manhandling Joe down the mountain, had no food or drink for a couple of days and was suffering from exposure and frostbite. Finally, after the rope-cutting incident, he had spent a night in the open sitting on a steep snow slope. I remembered well how I had felt on Changabang. Probably I understood and respected Simon's judgement on Siula Grande better than most. There was no way that he could have done more than he did.

Mike and I were still discussing the subject when Simon wandered over and joined in the conversation. Simon reminded us that Joe arrived at Base Camp in the middle of the night when Simon and the donkeys were geared up to leave first thing the next morning. It was incredibly close, just a few hours longer and he would have arrived back to an empty and remote Base Camp. It was indeed the epic of a lifetime. I couldn't help but have recurring thoughts about it. Simon had mentioned it relatively little but was always happy to answer my probing questions about the whole incident. I hoped that I wasn't being too invasive and would be able to handle such an obviously traumatic set of memories in the same cool and collected manner.

The ridge crest above Base Camp was dry, dusty and at an altitude of over 5000 metres. My head hurt badly, but not enough to detract from the tremendous view of Siula Chico's West Face now towering over a minor peak, Sarapo Queste. Simon's photos from his last trip were, he admitted himself, 'just holiday snaps'. We had never been able to lay our hands on any really detailed photographs before we left England. Now though the upper part of the face could be seen to present a magnificent challenge. Head on, it looked to offer an extremely steep series of icy groove lines leading ultimately to an outrageously overhanging icicle-fringed amphi-theatre just below the summit. It looked very inspiring and we both couldn't wait to get going.

The approach from Base Camp was exactly the same as Simon had done with Joe thirteen years before.

'How the hell did he crawl down here?'

I groaned, falling over yet again on the razor-edged unstable boulders covering the glacier. The ground really was just about the most difficult walking country imaginable. Even upright on two legs I was having trouble, the thought of crawling, dragging a broken leg behind me, did not bear contemplation. Simon stared around him.

'I think it's got a bit worse over the years.'And then, almost as a sympathetic afterthought: 'But not that much worse.'

We looked around us for a few moments in silent contemplation of Joe's private agony. It was, I felt, the greatest unaided crawl in mountaineering history.

Simon kept staring at his and Joe's line on Siula Grande.

'The ice has all gone,' he marvelled, eyeing up the rocky lower slabs where his photographs from thirteen years ago showed glittering white, snow/ice slopes. Siula Chico too was not exactly as per the photographs I had seen. Above the bergschrund a 45-degree snow/ice slope formerly led to the start of the difficulties. Now bare rock slabs sported streaks of stone-pitted ice and an ominous band of overhangs, once hidden beneath the ice, now guarded the face.

Our observations on the way up had been mixed but the deep, crisp cold of the Peruvian night followed by a crystal clear dawn re-ignited our enthusiasm and sent us scampering across the frozen snow bowl to see if we could pinpoint the best way of getting to the foot of an obvious ice-choked diagonal ramp which looked to provide the best way up the first major steepening on the buttress.

'How about that yellow ramp?'

Simon was approaching from one side and felt sure that he had spotted a weakness in the overhangs immediately above the bergschrund. It looked promising from my position directly below too and I felt a healthy glow of optimism as I panted my way up the snow runnels beneath the face. It seemed that our predictions of the El Niño impact had been wrong, but perhaps the dry conditions really wouldn't matter after all.

The reality was depressing. Simon too looked rather taken aback. What from a distance had looked like a reasonably angled ramp giving access to a tongue of ice on the slabs above was in fact a leaning corner of appallingly disintegrating rock. There was a distinct lack of worthwhile cracks in the back and the right wall overhung considerably, whilst at the same time being peppered with precarious-looking blocks. The left wall lay back in a steep slab but was seriously exfoliating and steepened markedly at about twenty metres. It might be possible but on the other hand it might be an immense time-waster. I stared intently, trying to imagine how we could make quick progress up this unaccommodating feature. I was intrigued to see Simon's reaction. We had bumped into each other many times over the years and I knew of his reputation but this was the first time that we had actually climbed together. What would he make of this problem? He too was peering intently.

'Up and out to the left perhaps?'

He started to point gleefully to a very loose-looking line of holds that ran up to a thin veneer of ice. Clearly he wasn't intimidated in the slightest. I liked his attitude. A positive approach is a real boost in such situations. I sensed that we would climb well together.

But this was only a reconnaissance and a bit more ferreting about was definitely in order. However a fresh problem was developing. It was now 10.30am and the sun was striking the top of the face hundreds of metres above us. Small pieces of ice and little stones loosened by the sun were beginning to clatter down. Occasionally one would zoom past with a high pitched hum and thump into the frozen snow below.

Feeling slightly uncomfortable, I sneaked along leftwards beneath the overhanging rock wall. The next weakness had looked promising from a distance but close up it turned out to be a shattered overhanging crack which led out onto blank rock slabs. Further left, with the rockfall now increasing considerably, I stayed just long enough to note that the rock wall ended and an ice streak on the slabs above stretched all the way down to connect with the glacier. But it really did look too far to the left and would involve a couple of potentially difficult and time-consuming traverses across blank rock between ice streaks. At least it did allow a way through the initial overhangs. I stayed as long as I dared and scurried down to our little tent on the glacier. Simon was already there and we sat silently together, staring at the face and absorbing the possibilities.

Simon was the first to speak.

'Didn't like those rocks. What do you reckon?'

I too was feeling hesitant. It all seemed rather dangerous. The idea of being wiped out by falling rocks on the way there did not exactly appeal.

Simon was thinking out loud before I had a chance to answer.

'I think the left-hand line. We can climb up the ice streak and link up to the streaks farther right by penduluming across the rocky bits.'

I stared again at the face. The upper two-thirds of the line we intended to climb really did look excellent. From here I could see that the ice streaks were not continuous but were linked by short rocky sections and culminated in a fantastic icicle-fringed amphitheatre at the very top. It looked fairly safe if only we could somehow get above these lower slabs.

I agreed that the left-hand line looked the best of a series of bad options and we settled down to spend the day resting, acclimatising, eating and face watching.

As the sun's rays crept round onto the face volleys of stones and the clattering of falling ice increased in frequency. The sounds echoed menacingly around the small glacial cirque where we were camped. It was rarely possible to see exactly where the rock and ice was falling. There didn't seem to be one particular line down which most things fell and it seemed that the danger was fairly evenly spread. Not a good sign. We lay there soaking in the sounds of the mountain's defences whilst sheltering from the sun by spreading our sleeping bags out over the tent. By the end of the day we had decided that we could climb safely in the mornings, when the mountain was quiet and frozen. We would give the line a go.

I felt more relaxed once the decision had been made and we headed back down to Base Camp to eat and drink as much as possible and sort out food and equipment for the six days or so we reckoned the round trip from Base Camp would take.

Three days later we were back and ready to go. The weather was absolutely perfect.

Even on our chosen line the bergschrund presented a steep step. Simon took the first lead and I watched the ice shattering in the light of his head-torch as he fought his way up. It was 4.30am and the air was completely still. Suddenly a rushing noise signalled problems above. I could see that Simon had stopped climbing and was hunched over his axes. I could see nothing else but reasoned that I should be safe, protected by the steep wall of the bergschrund which sported an overhanging lip directly above me. As I watched, a curling white cascade sailed through the air in a spectacular arc and caught me head on. Being unable to move anywhere I stood miserably, feeling the forces increase as the flow built up. After what seemed an age the cascade of ice crystals eased and then stopped completely.

Simon sounded distinctly chirpy (I found out later that the ice fall had all but missed him) and was straining to continue.

'Yes, er, go for it.'

For some reason I struggled to sound enthusiastic. If the truth be known I was feeling rather intimidated and hesitant about the whole affair. It was not really a very serious incident but where had the ice come from, I wondered? There were no séracs above us and I could only assume that one of the uniquely Peruvian ice formations decorating the buttress had collapsed. Peru is infamous for hugely outrageous ice formations and I was uncomfortably aware that our objective was peppered with hanging ice brackets which stuck improbably to the steep rocky walls. Some of these were three metres wide and thirty metres long with huge damoclean icicles decorating the underside. They clearly weighed hundred of tons and I could think of one area in particular where we could well be exposed to them. There will always be an element of risk in greater range climbing but here I was beginning to feel a distinct sense of unease.

Simon disappeared and I followed, the exertion helping me to overcome my fears. Soon we had followed the ice streaks to their end at a huge overhanging rock wall which offered obvious safety from anything falling from above. The ice was hard and grey, completely different from the white snow/ice slopes shown in Simon's 1985 pictures. I cursed at the climatic changes as we tensioned and pendulumed from one ice streak to another. Thirteen years ago we would have been soloing at this point.

Simon too was looking rather disgruntled.

'Bloody rope manoeuvres take up too much time.'

I couldn't help but agree. By the time we reached the foot of a slanting ice gangway cutting through the overhanging walls the sun was beginning to peep onto the face and the first little stones, released from their nightly freeze, hummed past. I was grateful for the steep angle above us and watched, in a detached sort of way, as they bounced down the slopes we had just climbed. Our ramp line was protected from such nastiness and we turned to face the difficulties. It had looked relatively short from below but now we were here its true size was revealed. It would take at least three full rope-lengths of very steep ice climbing. Simon's eyes lit up.

'This is more like it.'

Again I had to agree. Objectively safe and difficult climbing is far more my cup of tea than scrabbling about on dangerously exposed slabs. I sat back to admire Simon's climbing. Initially all went well and progress was fast; soon though the angle steepened markedly and there appeared to be a ten-centimetre layer of loose snow stuck to the ice.

'Even steeper than it looks,' puffed Simon.

He was on 80-degree ice heading up towards an apparent cul-de-sac where icicle-fringed overhangs barred the way. Although he has large arms, the angle was clearly taking its toll. It would relieve the strain if he could clip himself into the ferrule of his ice-axe. I marvelled as he persevered without taking this simple option.

'Why don't you clip in?'

Simon turned and looked down at me. His surprise at my suggestion was openly visible.

'Would you?' he enquired.

'Definitely.'

A short ethical discussion ensued. It seemed a mildly ridiculous place to be having an exchange that can be a sensitive subject in Britain and first ascensionists on home ground are not regarded as having made an ethically pure ascent if they have 'given it clip'. I argued that Simon had two options. He could, if he wished, take off his 15-kilo rucksack, climb without clipping and then haul it up, or he could adopt the Fowler mountaineering ethic of anything goes as long as it doesn't involve bolts. With speed being important I had no hesitation in urging the latter.

Simon considered for a few moments before clipping a short loop into his ice-axe and sitting back to relax. I was amazed that, in all his previous exploits, he had never readily resorted to such techniques. Conversely, he was clearly surprised at my willingness to lower the ethical barriers. The scope for varying approaches to mountaineering is wide indeed.

With a routine 'clip as necessary' policy firmly established progress became more methodical. But by the time we reached the top of the ramp it was dark and the temperature had plummeted. We shivered together, tied onto a couple of ice screws on a 55-degree ice slope, and wondered exactly what to do next. Finding a bivi site was an urgent priority but the beams from our head torches revealed nothing but steep ground in all directions. Having studied the face closely through binoculars from the glacier below, we knew that the way was to traverse right to gain an icy groove line just right of the buttress crest, and we had identified a spot on the traverse which might provide a reasonable bivouac. With this in mind I headed off to the right, peering optimistically into the gloom. Soon the ice slope gave way to mixed ground with the overhanging buttress leaning out protectively overhead. I continued along an ice band leading to the right until it tapered to nothing. Above me a huge overhang of icicles, the underside of a monstrous ice bracket, clung to the rock face.

One good thing about these brackets is that the sun shining against the rock wall tends to melt the inner edge of the upper side with the result that, with a bit of work the tops tend to provide excellent, if potentially unstable, sleeping ledges. Presumably the process ends when the sun severs the grip of the ice and the whole lot collapses. As I pulled onto the top

of this particular specimen I noticed with alarm that there were substantial gaps between the rock and the ice in a couple of places. It would
provide a wonderful hanging balcony on which to spend the night but,
with the rock wall being completely crack-free, we would have to trust that
the whole lot would not be parting company in the night.

Simon came up and we assessed the pros and cons of our possible
bedroom.

'Very comfortable,' he observed.

'Those might add some interest.' I pointed up to some huge icicles
hanging from an ice boss five metres above us

We deliberated. A close inspection revealed that there were some areas
which appeared to be very well frozen to the wall. Also we could be pretty
sure that there wouldn't be any thawing in the night. But then presumably
the little avalanche of ice crystals as we crossed the bergschrund was the
remains of a similar feature which had partially collapsed at 5am or so.
Eventually we decided to go for it and carefully secured ourselves to ice
screws in the most permanent-looking pieces of ice that we could find
before snuggling down inside our sleeping bags.

I was tired and slept soundly. I abruptly returned to consciousness
when something hit my sleeping bag just next to my head. I felt a cold,
wet sensation against my ear and I was wide-awake immediately.

'Shit! That wasn't very nice.'

I fumbled around for my headtorch, studied the small icicle that had
woken me and thought of the much larger ones up there in the gloom. It
was perfectly calm and there was no obvious reason why this one should
have fallen down in the middle of the night. Simon said nothing. It later
transpired that he had been half-awake but had thought that I was groaning about his backside pushing me off the ledge!

It was difficult to get back to sleep. I lay awake intently aware of
my position. The night was crystal clear and a myriad stars brightened
the sky. Now and then a sharp crack from above or below would focus
attention on the dangers. Everything seemed OK but it really was impossible to say just how dangerous our position was. I didn't like it. I put my
helmet on, catnapped and clock-watched through the rest of the night.

Dawn broke to reveal another perfect day. Being on a West Face we
had no immediate need to worry about the sun's warming effect on our
bivouac ledge. I lay soaking in the view while Simon took charge of the
stove and applied himself to producing a rather unappetising but calorie-
laden breakfast of bland noodles. Such are the joys of mountain cuisine.

I am not sure what excuse we can make. Perhaps the previous day was
a bit too long, perhaps my unsettled night had something to do with it.
But for whatever reason we were late getting started and it was 8am before
we were under way again, creeping across ice brackets similar to the one

we had spent the night on. Simon, who had seemed remarkably calm about the likely longevity of our sleeping ledge, was making unhappy noises about these ones. I think we were both finding the situation rather wearing. Hard technical climbing is fine, uncomfortable bivouacs can be put up with, but the ever-present possibility of collapsing ice brackets was not quite so easy to live with or ignore.

Traversing for two pitches led us to the foot of a groove which our reconnaissance had identified in advance as the key to the central part of the route. There was a gap in the ice here and it was clear that very difficult rock climbing on poor rock would be necessary to gain the point where the ice started again. This in itself was not a problem but a few little stones clattering down brought it home to us that the groove was a funnel. Climbing it in the cold of the morning would largely avoid the danger but we were getting late. Also, two enormous ice brackets overhung the corner. We had spotted these through the binoculars but had judged their fall line to be just to one side. Now we were here it was obvious this assessment was overly optimistic. Morale dropped. We suddenly felt very small and vulnerable. There was little need for conversation. Sometimes a sixth sense comes into play. It just didn't feel 'right' to press on.

'Time to go down.'

I can't remember who actually voiced these thoughts first but no sooner had we started the descent than a ton or so of beautifully ornate ice chandelier collapsed without warning and swept down between us. It made us feel better about giving up our dream.

Awkward traverses back across the delicate ice brackets led to abseils down the ice ramp. The rock was so uniformly poor that we used ice anchors all the way. Midway down the ramp the rope stuck. The little piece of sticky tape wrapped round the end, which tells how long the rope is, must have somehow caught in the sling that we had tied through the eye of the screw. Try as we might, it would not budge. We both hung on the rope, maximising the stretch and the length we could retain, whilst Simon produced his penknife and suddenly we slumped onto the belays.

The rest of our descent was uneventful as we staggered down the glacier covered with the shifting, razor-sharp boulders that Joe had crawled down. He got up Siula Grande, we tried Siula Chico, failed and had slunk away. At least we were able to try. The other team were less lucky and were forced to abandon all efforts when Dave fell on the man-eating sharp-edged boulders of the moraine and gouged his knee.

Climbing is like that, a balance of judgement, ability and endurance. If we had continued we might have got up, but then we might have ended up in a worse state than Joe. We will never know. But success every time implies that one's objectives are not challenging enough. We enjoyed ourselves and lived to climb another day. These are the really important things.

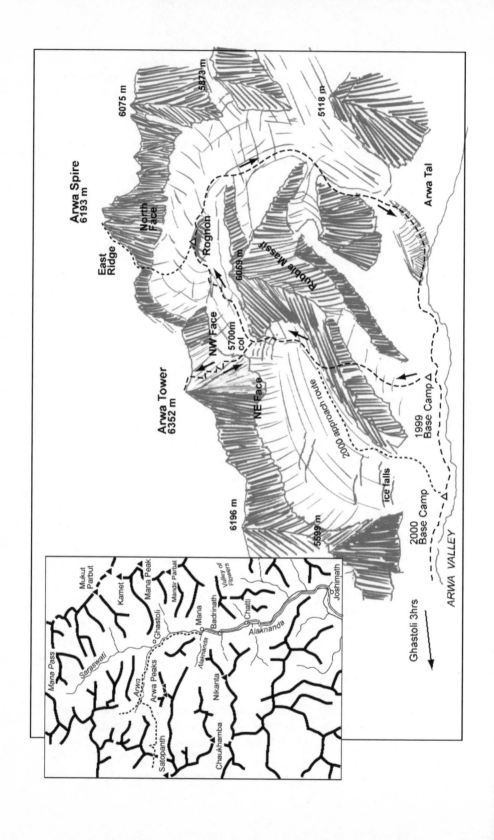

11

Arwa Tower – Yosemite in the Garhwal

*Harish Kapadia's tip – speedy passage through customs – bus ride to Joshimath –
the Sub District Magistrate's court room – continue to Mana – afternoon tea with the
border guards – Arwa Tower first ascent – failure and success on the Arwa Spire*

India was calling again. While the overall experience of Changabang
was not one I would care to repeat, it had certainly been a powerful and
challenging climb. There was no doubt that the innumerable spectacular
summits of the Garhwal exerted an irresistible pull and they seemed just
the right scale for the sort of climbing projects we were seeking. Steve
Sustad and I pooled our respective knowledge of the area but it was a
photograph in the 1998 *Alpine Journal* that sealed it for us. 'Probably
not been photographed before' the caption said. I peered more closely.
It showed a wild, ice-streaked, rocky spire which was beginning to give
me quite an urge. 'In the Arwa Valley, India' the text said. 'Photograph
by Harish Kapadia.' It was that man again. A promising sign. Harish
lives in Mumbai and has a commendable habit of exploring and
climbing in the rarely visited parts of the Indian Himalaya that also
attract the likes of Steve and me. It seemed that our paths were likely to
cross again.

But the Arwa Valley is a couple of days' walk north of the Hindu
holy temple at Badrinath in the Garhwal Himalaya. This area is close
to the Chinese border and as part of what the Indian authorities refer
to as the Inner Line access can be as big a challenge as the climb.
Westerners may not have visited this particular area since a British team
led by Frank Smythe were here in the 1930s. Expeditions to this part of
the world are only for those prepared to live with a fair amount of
bureaucratic uncertainty. There are, though, potential rewards that
to my mind outweigh the risks. Just about all the mountains in this area
are unclimbed. Harish's photograph showed two mind-boggling ones,
the Arwa Tower and the Arwa Spire, but it seemed probable that there
were other fine peaks nearby. And it looked as if it might just be possible
to climb one of them in a three-week trip. There was no doubt about it.
We simply had to go!

In theory the application procedure to climb in the Indian Himalaya is straightforward. The Indian Mountaineering Foundation (IMF) even has a web-site featuring a copy of the application form and giving detail about available peaks and the latest state of play on expeditions in progress. The uninitiated could easily be misled into thinking that the process might be simple and stress-free.

I was under no such illusions. The problem is that there does not appear to be any one individual who is the decision-taker. The IMF simply forwards applications to the Home Office and Defence Ministry who remain aloof, detached authorities that are virtually impossible to contact direct. With Arwa's Inner Line complication we feared the worst. Harish Kapadia, a fellow Alpine Club member, was also Vice-President of the IMF, so we hoped that judicious string-pulling and timely reminders would swing things in our favour.

Two weeks before departure we were still in the toils of IMF bureaucracy. 'Your application is with the Ministries.' 'We are told it is being progressed.' I was reduced to taking heart from Harish, who knows the system inside out and has been a real friend and ally to many visiting mountaineers. His thoughts were: 'If they are going to say no they usually say it early on.'

Our application had been in for six months. We could only keep our fingers crossed and get on with practical things like freighting gas, paying for air tickets and hoping it would all work out all right in the end. We were due to leave on 28 April 1999. On the 22nd the fax machine whirred and the magical permit arrived.

Steve and I were to be accompanied by my old friend Crag Jones, and the delightfully named Kenton Cool. Central casting could not have chosen a better appellation for a big-time mountaineer, and though he was yet to be regarded in this mould, he clearly had a great future. Kenton was a relative newcomer to our social scene. I knew him by his reputation as a talented rock climber but had only met him in person once a couple of years previously. He had been bum-shuffling around the floor of a London pub at the time. Curiously he seemed not to be drunk and a few questions revealed that he had recently fallen three metres on a slate climb in North Wales and badly broken both heels. The doctor's prognosis was gloomy and such a handicap would put most people down. Kenton though appeared cheerful and undeterred, speaking enthusiastically about past successes and positively about future projects. By 1999 he was beating doctors' predictions and was very much on his feet again earning a living doing roped access work from a base in the intense rock climbing centre of Sheffield. I hadn't seen him for a long time and had never been on a climbing trip with him before. But the vibes I had were good and I looked forward to getting to know him better.

Delhi was the usual combination of heat and uncertainty, bureaucratic hurdles and unforeseen charges which sent all four of us scurrying between various corners of the airport and the IMF office. We had learned much from the Payne/Clyma techniques of 1997. The bribe kitty was 2000 rupees lighter by the evening of our first day in Delhi but we and our equipment were ready to go. A minibus was due to collect us at 4am the next morning and all looked to be on course for the quickest transit through Delhi yet.

Steve stared at the large luxury bus outside the IMF building.'What the hell is this?' he enquired, aghast at the huge, TOURIST sticker emblazoned across the windscreen.

'Surely this can't be ours?' asked Crag, who, despite the early hour, was engrossed in a last minute repack. Knowing my penny-pinching approach to such matters, Crag was similarly amazed by these unexpectedly lavish transport arrangements.

I was shocked. The driver, who had now stirred from his night's sleep, was making moves to suggest that we should start loading up. I had taken a leaf from Roger Payne's book and pre-booked the transport from Britain. I thought that the £250 quoted was excessive but in the rush to get everything organised I had never got round to querying it.

Two hours later we were sitting at the roadside whilst our driver struggled to fix a problem. It seemed that air was leaking into the diesel. Meanwhile the others took great pleasure in pointing out to me the very cheap and efficient public buses which regularly roared past.

Our driver though was less ostentatious than his bus. Having got right down there into the problem, he eventually emerged covered in grime and sweating profusely. We were on the way again. But he was obviously far more used to catering for tourists craving creature comforts than groups of smelly mountaineers. The tea shops he chose to stop at were posh in the extreme. At one there was even a sign imploring undesirables to keep away. Steve posed by the sign looking as 'undesirable' as possible, while my requests that the driver got a move on and stopped at less pretentious places met with blank looks of incomprehension.

Yet again we were on the Joshimath road and the idea was that we would save time by driving the eighteen hours to the town, non-stop. By nightfall though we were only at Rishikesh where the Himalayan foothills start and the Ganges disgorges itself onto the Indian plains. Our driver stopped. There had been several more involuntary stops but this one appeared to be intentional. It seemed that he was suggesting that we stay the night at an expensive hotel owned by a friend of his.

We needed a hill permit to go further but we didn't have one. The permit office did not open until 10.30 next morning. Over-nighting at Rishikesh was unavoidable – another late point scored in extra time by Indian bureaucracy.

Eventually it was 1pm before we left Rishikesh and thirty breakdown-ridden hours later we arrived at Joshimath. Ironically we then felt obliged to give our driver a substantial tip as a vote of thanks for him regularly demonstrating his mechanical skills and responding positively to our pleadings that he blatantly disregard a rule which apparently forbade night driving for buses on this stretch of road.

The first thing to do in Joshimath was for Steve and I to try and sort out the problem of Brendan Murphy's death certificate.

After the Changabang accident in 1997 Brendan's death had been reported to the authorities by Roger Payne. However no death certificate had been issued and this meant that it had not been possible to finalise his estate. Since then Brendan's parents had suffered hugely at the hands of indecisive officials. They had got as far as discovering that it was the responsibility of the Sub District Magistrate (SDM) at Joshimath to issue the certificate but it appeared that this official had refused to do so and was being as unreasonable as he possibly could be. The family's solicitor in Delhi had sent two advocates all the way to Joshimath and when this had failed to achieve the desired outcome they even served a writ on the magistrate himself. In response to this the SDM responded that he could not issue a death certificate without having viewed the site of the fatality in the company of those who had witnessed the death. Upon being advised that the body was in a remote area that he would not be able to get to, and it couldn't be viewed anyway because it was buried under thousands of tons of ice, he suggested that a possible solution was for Andy Cave, Steve and I to come out from England and arrange a visit by helicopter. In an effort to bypass such an expensive and pointless exercise, Steve, Andy and I had sworn affidavits that we had witnessed the death which were sent to the solicitors in Delhi, but to no avail.

It was thus with a sense of trepidation that Steve and I approached the Magistrate's offices and awaited our turn to meet the man who had proved so difficult to deal with.

We were accompanied to court by Nazzum, our liaison officer. Nazzum was an abbreviation for something more complicated which I always felt embarrassed at not remembering. But this didn't seem to worry him and he was a likeable chap who spoke English well and had already proved himself willing to argue our corner during the delays on our bus journey. So we were hopeful that he would now be able to guide us through the legal obfuscation ahead. For some odd reason we were allowed to read the official file before meeting the SDM. None of the affidavits we had signed in England were in it. In fact, according to the file, nothing of significance had happened since Roger's initial report.

The court room was surprisingly plush and formal. The SDM sat in a huge, high-back chair on a raised platform, whilst the three of us cowered meekly in the front row of perhaps fifty seats facing the bench. The hearing started badly as the new Magistrate, who had been recently appointed and seemed a very sensible character, pointed to the paucity of information on his file and refused to do anything. After an hour of negative-sounding exchanges in Hindi we were reduced to pleading via Nazzum and discreetly fingering the bribe wad.

Nazzum was on a £50 bonus if he could swing this for us. After a painfully long time he suddenly stood up, turned his back to the magistrate and addressed us.

'OK, we go.'

He was moving as if to leave. This was an unwelcome development. We didn't have a clue what had happened. What were we to tell Brendan's parents? That we gave up and just walked out? But we were being almost forcibly removed from the court room. More, apparently heated, exchanges occurred with court officials before our liaison officer stomped off.

'Bloody officials,' he growled in his best English.

Thirty minutes later he was back with three pieces of flimsy paper.

'Sign these,' he instructed.

We dutifully read them through. The first two were affidavits of some kind, very brief and simplistic compared to what we had signed in England but they were ready franked with the swearing charge of 20 rupees each, a total of just over 50p. This compared rather favourably with the cost of £40 each in Britain.

The third was typed erratically on scruffy, unheaded paper. I looked at it quizzically.

'The certificate,' explained Nazzum.

As a simplistic statement rather than a formal certificate it wasn't exactly what we had been expecting. It was worded in rather fractured English which was, apparently, a direct translation of a standard Joshimath death certificate. But, most importantly, it appeared that the Sub-District Magistrate was prepared to stamp and sign it. We left clutching this all-important piece of paper. It subsequently turned out to be acceptable to the UK authorities but at the time it seemed a slightly hollow victory at the end of such long drawn out, expensive and distressing efforts by Brendan's parents.

'Be careful,' whispered Steve. 'I don't want to go through this again.'

At Joshimath our Changabang approach of two years earlier went up a valley to the east, but the road to the Arwa Valley headed north towards the border. It was steep and spectacular but tarmacked and, during the summer, much frequented by Indian tourists and pilgrims heading for the Hindu temple at Badrinath, four miles short of the road-head at the summer village of Mana. Some of our fellow travellers were very interesting. At one stage we assisted two pilgrims in a tiny Suzuki that had stalled on an incredibly steep hill. Crag Jones taking the wheel. The death potential from uncontrollably rolling back looked as if it could be high, a possibility reinforced by the large crowd that gathered. Quite what they were all hoping to see was worrying, but it was to great applause that, with the tiny engine screaming and everyone else pushing, he finally overcame the steep section and handed the vehicle back to the two occupants. The crowd melted away looking disappointed. Remarkably they appeared to make it without further assistance and we saw them in Badrinath later in the day.

The policeman at the roadhead village of Mana was polite but firm.

'Very sorry, your porters do not have Inner Line permits. You must get permission from the Sub-District Magistrate in Joshimath.'

Not him again! It would take a whole day to get down to Joshimath and back.

'Can't I speak to him on the telephone?' I pointed at the large satellite dish outside his tiny checkpoint.

'Telephone is not working, sir.'

Things were not looking good. I was uncomfortably aware that we were paying twenty porters to sit around doing nothing. Our finances couldn't stand very much of this. The fact that the porters only carried three days' rations and seemed to have already consumed most of one day's didn't help.

Nazzum took up the argument in Hindi and, at length, indicated that a compromise was in the air.

'He will come down to Badrinath and telephone from there.'

Badrinath is one hour down from Mana and by late afternoon contact had been made with both the Sub-District Magistrate and the District Magistrate. Such a serious problem clearly demanded authority from the highest level! Somehow, in that delightfully Indian way, a decision was made with no one individual apparently being responsible for it. We would be allowed to continue as long as the porters all signed their names. Most of them couldn't write but this minor technicality was overcome by the policeman asking them their names and writing down the response. A list was prepared and everyone was happy. We had the green light to continue. But another day in our tight schedule had been wasted.

Beyond Mana an army road continued for a couple of miles towards the army outpost of Ghastoli. Here a cluster of ghastly bland buildings huddled at 4000 metres, the occupants apparently charged with defending India against any invasion from China, about ten miles to the north.

As we approached an Indian officer came out and invited us in for tea. It was cold in the buildings but after about fifteen minutes huddled round a small and very dangerous-looking stove, tea was served and there was a stirring amongst what I had taken to be a pile of sleeping bags on a bunk bed.

'You must meet our new camp commander,' announced our host.

An unshaven face, largely obscured by a hairy woollen balaclava with a large bobble on top, peered out from the sleeping bag.

It transpired that our host was the old commander who was off down to Badrinath the next day. He was so overjoyed at completing his six-month stint at Ghastoli that he was throwing this impromptu afternoon tea party. The new man did not look so enamoured. He never emerged completely from his sleeping bag but sat up and stuck out a hand to accept his tea before pouring forth with a long tirade about how this was a compulsory posting and one that he, as a man from the oppressively hot south of India, found far from appealing.

It seemed that the Chinese had a similar set-up on their side of the border. There was regular radio contact between them and an arrangement in place whereby soldiers from the two sides visited the border col to proudly claim control on alternate days.

The commander's main responsibility seemed to be to make sure this happened. Whether it would ever be necessary for him to get out of bed seemed unclear.

As we said our goodbyes I noted a headstone commemorating two Indian solders who died here.

'From boredom I expect,' commented Steve.

The old commander waved enthusiastically as we turned to head up the Arwa Valley.

The layout of the Arwa Valley was not as clear-cut as I had hoped. In retrospect, we put so much effort into getting a permit from the authorities that we had not focused sufficiently on finding a bit more out about the topography of the area. Our maps showed that Arwa Tal (Arwa Lake) was the obvious place to have a Base Camp – but where was it? In fact, where were the mountains we had come to climb? Naively, I had expected them to be obvious, rearing up in their full splendour above the Arwa Valley – the Valley of the Ghosts in Hindu mythology. Persistent low mist didn't exactly help but in a sudden clearing we could see a spectacular summit poking up over the bounding ridge. It didn't look like either of the peaks we had seen photos of and we would have to cross the ridge to get to it. This was a serious problem; if the ridge was too difficult or dangerous on the far side we could fail without even reaching the mountain.

We decided to press on up the valley but our two teams of two had somehow become separated.

Crag and Kenton were with the main group of porters who refused to continue, thereby leaving them no alternative but to stop at the only passable Base Camp site they could find. Meanwhile Steve and I, with a small group of porters, got ahead and out of contact with the others. It was delightfully disorganised. Tempers became frayed and it was perhaps something of a miracle that the day ended with all of us and all of the gear in the same place. All the porters now refused to continue and there was nothing for it but to pay them off and make the best of a bad job at Crag and Kenton's Base Camp site.

Our maps were clearly inaccurate and we had no idea of our exact whereabouts, or those of the mountains we had come to climb.

'What is this peak?'

Steve and I were standing on the ridge separating the Arwa Valley from the summit that we had glimpsed earlier. To the east the pyramidal hulk of Kamet (7756m) was now prominent, with the prow of Mana Peak (7274m), its assertive satellite, looked less inspiring from this viewpoint. Much to our relief the descent on the far side of our ridge didn't look too bad. I had feared that we might be heading for a boring peak capped with an interesting summit but ahead of us was a mind-blowing mountain that dropped sheer to the unnamed snow-covered glacier below us. It bore no relation to either of Harish's photographs but whatever it was, it was the one for us. Somehow we convinced ourselves that it must be the Arwa Spire, viewed from a new direction. Retreating to Base Camp we formed a plan of action. Things were looking up after all.

It took us two days to get from Base Camp to a relaxingly flat col at the foot of the North Buttress of what we were ultimately to conclude was in fact the Arwa Tower. It was indeed a superb, impregnable peak, possibly the finest-looking unclimbed peak that I had come across. Above us the buttress soared to a forepeak, whilst to its right the North-West Face, steeply slabby and smooth, was seamed with snow/ice streaks that offered hopes of rapid progress and looked an enticingly adventurous line. There were, however, several blank-looking sections – this peak was not going to give up her virginity easily.

Crag and Kenton were also on the col. We had by now sorted out the location of the two peaks that we had come to climb and they were off to attempt the Arwa Spire which had previously been out of sight on the far side of the col. This too looked equally inspirational with three soaring buttresses on its north face and a narrow summit crest. Yet somehow our peak looked the more spire-like, while theirs, with its impressive castellations, was a more of a tower that a spire.

The weather was perfect but ground conditions were prompting considerable comment.

'What's going on here?'

Steve was voluble in his disapproval. Never before had any of us come across glacier conditions quite like this. The surface layer was a 10 centimetres thick plate of ice but every few steps this would collapse and we would fall into a bottomless sea of sugary snow. The sensation was not unlike what I imagine it would be like to fall through the surface of a frozen lake. The energy expenditure required to get back on to the hard surface was indescribable. Later in the trip we were only able to make progress by crawling on the surface, towing our heavy sacks behind. I have never encountered such conditions before or since and have no idea what causes them.

Faced with such pleasures, Crag and Kenton made the wise decision to stay put until the morning, whilst Steve and I opted to crawl, fall and stagger our way across the short distance that separated us from the foot of the North-West Face which started to look increasingly challenging the closer we got.

One good thing about the vast blank rock walls at the foot of the face was the minimal scope for disagreement over where to start. The north spur bounding the left edge provided the only feasible possibility, but not an easy one, as we were soon to find out.

A few unremarkable pitches led to an impass. While the rock was excellent, we had taken the advance view that this was likely to be a mixed route and were therefore wearing plastic double boots.

'The crack has run out.'

Steve was sounding uncharacteristically negative. We were less than five pitches up and he was climbing a horribly thin-looking crack – or rather he had been but had now ground to a halt.

The sun was shining obliquely across the face and I was feeling comfortably warm and relaxed and well able to offer the sort of moral support that stretched leaders find so completely useless.

'How about traversing to that bit of snow out to your left?' I suggested helpfully.

Unrepeatable rudeness, indeed lurid oaths, came from above as I continued to happily soak up the Himalayan rays. Soon blank granite in all directions prompted a fresh assessment of the situation.

'I'll see if I can get a good peg in and then tension across.'

There was a sound of heavy pounding as I lay back once more.

'Ahggh!'

The air was suddenly full of a falling body. There was a thump, followed by silence and then a string of obscenities.

'Effing peg opened up the effing crack' was the jist of the communiqué. He had been held on a nut runner wedged in a crack three metres below him.

I murmured sympathies whilst noting that in half an hour I would be in the shade and the temperature would plummet. This was a seriously uncomfortable thought which made me relieved to see Steve get quickly back to the end of the crack.

'I'm going to tension again.'

It all looked horribly precarious. I felt glad to have the soft option of simply holding the rope. Disturbingly, I noted that Steve had left his rucksack hanging on the tension point. A problem for me to deal with at some stage, although in the circumstances I could hardly complain.

Much scraping and grunting started to come from above, interspersed with the occasional, 'Watch me.' It was clearly a desperate pitch and following it with the security of a rope I used my usual Himalayan excuse of heavy sack (two in this case) and the need for speed to throw any ethical consideration to the wind.

'Pull!' I shouted unashamedly as I dangled on the rope, gaining even more respect for Steve's efforts.

'A fine achievement, Stephen. A pleasure to second you.'

We shook hands because that's what the English do in such situations. And Steve, though an American, has lived in Britain for so long, that he has by now adopted these quaint customs.

He was his usual calm and philosophical self. 'Your pitch looks nice, too,' he said.

We almost always stick to alternate leads on long climbs. Sometimes Steve will take the lead out of turn on aid pitches and I on mixed sections but by and large we are of much the same ability and it suits our style to swing the leads.

The pitch that Steve was pointing to looked to be a short but vicious and unprotected wide crack which led to what appeared to be a ledge of some kind. I was feeling tired but, try as I might, it was difficult to characterise it as an obvious aid pitch and hand over to Steve. We were now 200 metres up the face and the scenery was becoming very grand. Below us to our right was a fabulous plaque of peerless rock with no ledge in sight. It was a sort of huge Himalayan Etive Slabs or Glacier Point Apron but so blank that I made a mental note to keep well away from it if we decided to abseil back down the face on our descent.

It was getting late now and Steve's belay was a foothold on a steep slab. Unplanned Himalayan bivouacs are invariably cold and unpleasant, they can easily result in rapid erosion of willpower and ignominious retreat. With such thoughts in mind and the lure of a ledge not far ahead, an extra special effort was called for. I therefore thrashed upwards, in the gathering gloom, in an amusing but ungainly manner.

'It was a pleasure to see you move so gracefully,' quipped Steve with barely veiled relish after my indifference to his struggles.

It perhaps says a lot about Himalayan climbing that it is a real pleasure when a potentially atrocious night is suddenly replaced with the relative luxury of a ledge to lie on. In fact, this one was not quite five-star accommodation but we could at least lie down end to end. I snuggled into a Gore-Tex bivouac bag, whilst Steve managed to half erect the tent and began the evening's cooking efforts.

Our food requirements had arguably not been attended to thoroughly enough before leaving the UK. On Changabang, our last expedition together, we had existed primarily on noodles and a superfluity of mashed potato. It was not exactly the world's most interesting or varied diet but Steve, who is more of an expert than I in these matters, had assured me that it contained just about all the nutrients we might need. As we survived for near on a fortnight on it, I could only assume that he was correct and so, there had been no need for complex discussions about dietary requirements for this trip. Mashed potato and noodles would be fine. But we had hit a problem. Try as we might, we couldn't find any dehydrated potato in Delhi. Perhaps we had brought it out from England last time? In true disorganised fashion neither of us could remember. On an expedition to Cerro Kishtwar back in 1993, we had used baby food as one of our staple courses. That had worked well then and so the decision was made. Alternate nights of noodles and Indian baby food it would be.

Over the years we have climbed together Steve has increasingly recognised what Nicki has always told him. I appear not to be suited to work in the kitchen or any task to do with the preparation of food. My

mealtime responsibilities in the mountains now usually stretch only to
snow collection and melting, whilst Steve takes on technical jobs such as
hydrating noodles and mixing baby powder.

And so I was able to lie in my sleeping bag and marvel at the stars
whilst Steve laboured over the stove and produced a truly disgusting
meal of lurid orange peach-flavoured baby food. I chewed the powdery
lumps thoughtfully, trying to assure myself that they were packed full of
nutrients that would see me bursting with energy in the morning.

Up above us the rock looked steep and blank. With hot weather and
rock boots it would give excellent rock climbing but the morning dawned
with bleak grey sky and gentle snowflakes. Also our heavy sacks, big boots
and ice climbing gear were clearly more suited to any ice streaks we could
find. Steve had actually brought his rock boots along but the weather
conditions and ground ahead convinced him that they would no longer
be required. Ever conscious of surplus weight, he had tied them together
and, thrown them down to be picked up from the foot of the face on our
way down. Needless to say, they were never seen again.

Our appealing snow/ice streaks, as seen from the start, proved to be
illusory. The rock hereabouts was smooth sparsely featured granite. It
rapidly became clear that what looked to be fairly substantial snow/ice
lines tended to be powder snow clinging to slight easings of the angle. My
crampon points scratched and grated. I felt distinctly insecure.

'Can't you get any protection in?'

I obviously looked as insecure as I felt. Or was it just that Steve was
noting the long swing onto blank rock that he was facing if he should
slip? We persevered. Patches of ice occasionally provided security, by
way of solid ice screws, but the rock was notably blank and the climbing
unsettling and time-consuming. I was also very aware that we were moving
out above smooth blank walls which I had already noted and it might be
extremely difficult to abseil directly down. The sense of commitment was
slowly but inexorably building up.

As the hours ticked by I began to wonder where we might spend
the night. A repeat of the previous night's relative luxury looked unlikely.
I must be getting old. I didn't remember feeling this concern ten years
ago. Then I would just climb and trust that when dusk was approaching
we would be able to cut a bum-width step in the ice and hold ourselves
in place with a length of rope stretched taut between ice screws on either
side. Perhaps, I considered, that was the problem. On this kind of ground
there was no guarantee that we would be able to find a big enough
patch of thick ice and the thought of spending the night standing on a
collapsing step in three-inch-thick powder snow with minimal belays did
not appeal.

By late afternoon we were about two-thirds of the way up the face, but the conditions remained much the same. A couple of particularly exciting pitches up very thin ice streaks had necessitated sack-hauling again but we had now reached an impasse with no obvious way around it.

'Take care, Mick. Belays aren't very good.'

Reluctantly my eyes were drawn to the three tied off ice screws that Steve was attached to. Half of their length was protruding from the ice. Backed up by the picks of his axes they might hold a fall but they hardly inspired confidence.

The impasse was a twenty-metre exfoliating rock slab with an occasional smear of transparent ice. I teetered up on fragile edges, the points of my crampons grating unnervingly. Pegs behind insecure exfoliating flakes did not encourage positive thinking.

A bolt would solve the problem but Steve and I have strong views on such things. Bolts can solve almost any protection problem. They do not require any weakness in the rock or any skill to place. They destroy the traditional challenge of mountaineering. Once, after completing the first ascent of the Golden Pillar of Spantik in Pakistan, with Victor Saunders, a continental team actually contacted Victor and asked him if we minded them climbing the route with bolts. Perhaps their misgivings sum up the sensitivities on the subject.

Either way, here on the Arwa Tower, we had no bolts and no intention of using any.

It was one of those pitches where the worry-factor increases as height is gained. All too soon a judgement call was demanded on whether to retreat in relative safety or push on boldly via protectionless climbing on small flakes. It wasn't too far to go to a snowy band, but a glance around revealed no easier possibilities for making progress. I considered taking off my crampons but in the end opted for teetering upwards feeling the increasing bite, not of crampon points, but of a tense yet controlled concern. Yet I was determined and I felt I was climbing well ... all the same it was a hard pitch in a very serious position.

Pulling out onto the snow band, a real change in the conditions was heralded. We were approaching the upper bowl of the face and I could only assume that the wind howling over the crest and the lower temperatures at this altitude were responsible for the sudden change to serious amounts of powder snow. It was getting late and I was feeling exhausted as Steve came up and headed off into the gathering gloom. The angle averaged perhaps 60 degrees, with numerous vertical rock steps. Protection was difficult to find and there was still no obvious place to spend the night.

By the time Steve had belayed and brought me up there was nothing for it but to bivouac where we were. Overhangs above looked as if they might provide some shelter but the absence of any ledge promised some interest. I hung forlornly in a shallow scoop in the powdery snow. Steve had somehow managed to excavate a better-looking ledge and set about preparing lukewarm baby food. Meanwhile I felt incredibly tired and struggled not to retch while contemplating the gently falling snow and increasingly poor visibility. I was thankful that we were high enough on the face to be above any dangerous spindrift avalanches.

There was a time when I would have been deeply concerned at the onset of a spell of bad weather but years of doing this kind of thing have changed the old feeling of rising panic to one of resigned acceptance. After all, it would be naive to expect the weather gods to provide absolutely perfect weather for the full duration of something like a seven-day climb.

We were gaining height and, through gaps in the cloud, we could see over the lower peaks to the north and on to the Tibetan plateau beyond. To the north-west in particular exciting unclimbed objectives were coming into view. Our rudimentary map gave only a vague idea of what they were but it was clear that there will be plenty of potential in this part of the Himalaya for a few generations yet.

Things had improved slightly by the morning. I was feeling a bit brighter and up above us the sun intermittently caught the jagged crest marking the top of the face. Out to the west the snowy bulk of Chaukhamba (7138m) was now dominating the view beyond the Arwa Spire, with the more rocky Satopanth (7075m) further north and interesting spectacular objectives between the two.

We ploughed on – literally. Even near vertical pitches were plastered with a deep layer of useless powder snow. The climbing was precariously time-consuming and it was not until late afternoon that we broke through the final difficulties onto the crest. I had long anticipated this moment and hoped that from here it would be an enjoyable scramble to the summit. It was then with some dismay we saw that, although it was probably less than 100 metres vertically to the highest point, the ridge was a complex knife-edge of overhanging towers. Some of them looked perversely blank and holdless. We were on an unclimbed mountain however, so the summit was a pressing preoccupation rather than a merely desirable finale, as it had been on Taweche and Changabang.

The view on the far side was magnificent. Nilkanth rose spectacularly to the south and much farther to the south-east we could even pick out our line of two years earlier on Changabang's North Face. By nightfall we had made little progress but we had at least managed to cut a ledge in a small ice shelf and were able to spend our first night together inside the tent since we started on the face. A quarter of the floor space hung off the ledge but with sleeping mats down it was easy to forget such minor problems. We slept soundly.

Next day, after a supposedly fortifying breakfast of tea and a small muesli portion, we considered what to do next.

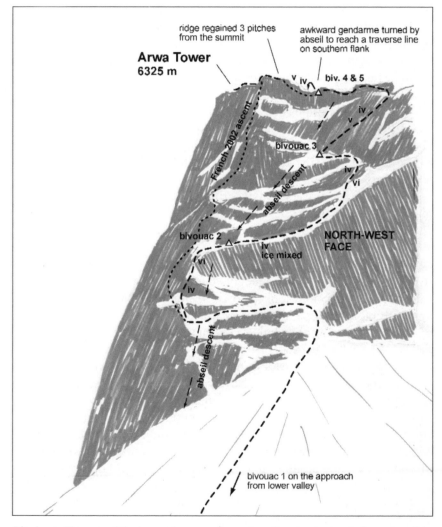

Editor's note: The names of the Arwa peaks may confuse as Arwa Tower is spire-shaped whereas Arwa Spire resembles three-towers. Inspired by the Fowler/Sustad ascent of the Tower and the 2001 ascent of the Spire, a French GMHM party made a number of climbs in the area including a new line (marked above – dotted line) left of the Fowler/Sustad route. Called 'Pilier Guilhem Chaffiol', this was done alpine-style on May 14-16, 2002 by Dimitry Munoz, Grégory Muffat Joly, Laurent Miston and Antoine de Choudens. The climb gave 14 pitches of fine quality free rock-climbing (F6b) with no bolts and pitons only used at the stances. See: *AAJ* 77 pp 94-99.

'Perhaps we could abseil down here.'

Steve was standing on the knife-edge crest of the ridge at a point where the way ahead was barred by an intimidatingly crackless tower.

'Mmmmmm.'

We both stared thoughtfully down the far side of the ridge. A twenty-five-metre free abseil would place us on a steep snow/ice slope that we might be able to traverse and then regain the ridge beyond the tower. There was still the slight problem of how to reverse this manoeuvre on the way back. Climbing up ropes, as I have already noted, is my least favourite mountaineering activity. Here, though, we seemed to have no alternative but to commit ourselves if we were to stand a chance of reaching the summit. Leaving our bivouac equipment behind and one of our two ropes in place, we slid down and started our summit bid.

My level of optimism was not high. It was one of those situations where I think we both felt that the weather and/or the apparent difficulty ahead were likely to defeat us. But we judged that it was not dangerous to continue and, having got so far, we felt that we owed it to ourselves to give it a go.

The snow/ice traverse was horrible. Rotten snow lying on hard ice made for difficult going. Steve then managed a desperate pitch on powder-covered rock and suddenly we were back on the crest.

'What do you think?'

It was difficult to suppress my growing elation. Neither of us could really believe that three rope-lengths had changed the outlook so much. What, from below, had looked to be an impregnable final section now appeared passable. Even the weather was brightening up with the odd ray of sunshine piercing the cloud. The summit spire was visible only fifty metres away, split by a short chimney.

This provided a satisfying final tussle so that it was then almost with a sense of surprise and disbelief that we were able to sit astride the summit knife-edge, marvel at the intermittent view, take stock of the situation and contemplate what had driven us to focus so much time and effort in reaching such a place. The pleasure and satisfaction in reaching a challenging unclimbed summit is difficult to describe. All those months of preparation and all those pitches of hard technical climbing somehow get formed into the moment. The end is a truly euphoric sensation. We both wallowed in our success unashamedly as we sat astride the top soaking it all in.

The descent was straightforward apart from the final exhausting haul up the abseil rope, using small prusiking clamps. Back in the tent our conversation turned to more everyday things. Steve enthused about the mass market potential of a porch that he had designed, whilst I enjoyed shocking him with civil servant tales from the Shares Valuation Division. Our climbing aspirations are very similar, our ways of earning a living sharply contrasting.

It was time to return to our other lives.

A day of abseiling back to the foot of the face led to the awful realisation that the slope we had used to approach was now too avalanche-prone to descend. There was nothing for it but to drop down the other side of the col and follow a long circuitous route to the north beneath the North Face of Arwa Spire which was getting on for twice as long as a direct route. It would also involve descending a long glacier that would probably have the awful surface conditions that we had encountered earlier.

I have a lasting memory of the two of us struggling along in the hot still air beneath the towering North Face of the Arwa Spire. We were both revelling in our success and cursing the conditions in equal measure. The sound of puffing, grunting and swearing rent the air as one or the other of us fell through the icy crust into the bottomless sugary snow beneath. At one point there was a long section where both of us were reduced to crawling on all fours and spreading the weight by towing our rucksacks on short lengths of rope.

'Wonder if they made it?' pronounced Steve, staring up at the Arwa Spire as we lay there on our backs during yet another rest break. Stopping was bliss and with such an inspiring view we had every excuse. 'Might have to come back if they haven't,' he added.

I stared at the face. It did look good – but somehow I felt we had been to this area now. And in a world so full of objectives it has to be something special to draw me back a second time. I did once do this, on Cerro Kishtwar in the Indian Kishtwar Himalaya and on that second occasion we enjoyed a superb trip in which Steve and I succeeded where I had failed before. But somehow going back, even though we enjoyed success, was an anticlimax. The pleasure of these trips is not only the climbing challenge but also the exploratory enjoyment of visiting new places. All the same, the Arwa Spire did look very good indeed and rules are made to be broken.

It transpired that illness and poor conditions led Crag and Kenton to retreat well short of the top. Ultimately, of our team of four, only Kenton returned, in 2000, when he, together with Al Powell, Ian Parnell, Pete and Andy Benson, was successful in climbing the Spire via the East Ridge. And in 2002, Bruno Hasler, Stephan Harvey and Roger Schali, three Swiss guides, inspired by our photographs, completed two stunning lines on the North Face.

So we lost the Arwa Spire. But you can't win them all!

12

Filming on the Lofoten Islands
with Dr Death

It was just before the Arwa trip that Richard Else, the documentary film-maker, contacted me again. Another climbing series was afoot.

'I need someone with a proper job to spend a week climbing in the Lofoten Islands. Being a tax man is classed as a proper job so we want you.'

The Lofoten Islands are off the Norwegian coast, well inside the Arctic Circle. They are renowned for dodgy weather, exceptional climbs, expensive beer and vast tracts of unexplored rock. As an area that had been on my list of interesting places to visit for many years, I simply had to go.

The idea was to produce a thirty-minute film about two people with 'proper' jobs meeting for the first time and then climbing a new route together. It rather struck me that climbing a new route at the best of times can be a challenging affair; to do a worthwhile one for the cameras in a distant and meteorologically challenged chain of islands with someone I'd never met before sounded remarkably optimistic. But Richard was keen.

'It's a fantastic place,' he enthused.

'We'll spend a day or so finding a suitable route and then we'll have the rest of the week for you and Mark to climb it.'

'Mark?' I enquired. Who was this climbing partner that I had been chosen to team up with for the week? A 'Mark' with a 'proper job'. I contemplated for a moment before Richard enlightened me.

'Garth. Doctor Death ... Mark Garthwaite.'

The clouds parted. Dr Mark Garthwaite, Glasgow GP, drugs clinic guru and Scottish master climber. I knew him by reputation – he had just made the first ascent of one of the steepest winter routes in Scotland – but I could not recall ever having met him in person. I did, however, know that he was a mega keen activist whose rock climbing ability far out-stripped my own. This could be embarrassing.

Although not having the conventional doctor look, the tall, fit looking, shaven-headed man sporting an earring and ambling around the check-in desk could be none other than Dr Garthwaite himself. He shook my hand vigorously and engaged me in animated conversation as we moved through to meet the film crew in the transit lounge. They were on their way from the Czech Republic where they had been filming Andy Cave and rock climbing hotshot Leo Houlding in action on the sandstone towers there. Many of the team were familiar from the Scottish ice climbing film: Brian Hall, John Whittle, Cubby, Keith Partridge, the cameraman and, of course, Richard himself. It seemed that the only two people who didn't know each other were the two who would be climbing together!

Hemmingsvaer is a quaint fishing village on a small island just off the main Lofoten Island of Austvagoy. It was here, in modernised versions of the traditional *rorbu* (fisherman's huts), that we were to be based. The overwhelming first impression was one of fish. There was obviously superb rock climbing around but the fish took precedence. They seemed to be everywhere – from hanging on huge drying racks to dangling from the ceilings of the café. The whole place had an underlying odour of fish.

Other first impressions were the fantastic night light inside the Arctic Circle and the superb road system. The population of the Lofoten Islands is sparse to say the least but the road from Svolvaer to Hemmingsvaer passed through a long tunnel and across a modern bridge to the small island that sported the small village of Hemmingsvaer and nothing much else.

Remarkably the temperature was close to 30°C and Richard was, understandably, keen to take advantage and get the filming under way. The first problem was what to climb. Various members of the team had been here before but specific ideas were a bit thin on the ground. It was clear that a day of reconnaissance was called for. Fortunately, climbers weren't required for reconnaissance purposes and so Mark and I were allowed out to play and 'get to know each other'.

The Priest is a magnificent 350-metre roadside crag with a classic climb, Vestpillaren (West Pillar), up the right-hand side. By the time we reached the top I knew that my suspicions were correct. Dr Mark Garthwaite was disturbingly fast and competent. He also spoke with a fast Glasgow lilt that I found difficult to keep up with. The possibilities for poor communication and me demonstrating my relative incompetence on the crag began to look decidedly high.

Meanwhile the route-finding team rejected my suggestion of a modest but spectacular crack line and focused on a wild-looking unclimbed line up the front face of the Priest. A blank section at 100 metres looked likely to to make the Fowler body gibber, squeal and dangle. Before we left the crag that evening I calculated how the leads might work out, inking in Dr Death for the pitch with the blank section.

My plan was to put in a long second pitch that would position me just below the blank section and in an ideal position to watch the master in action. In reality there was a slight technical error. I struggled rather inelegantly up to ten metres below the blank section, only to find that my intended belay ledge was simply a bare rock ledge with nothing solid to belay on. This was tricky. If I pressed on I might end up committed on the blank bit myself, but if I retreated too far Garth might find a belay just below it and decide it was best to belay there. For a moment I contemplated whether or not to make the best of a bad job and belay where I was. Visions of belays failing and climbers gracefully plummeting to their deaths on national television brought me back to my senses. At risk of causing general confusion in the TV-watching public, I lowered and down climbed ten metres or so and belayed in a tangle of ropes stretching up to my high point. Garth, I was pleased to see, was positively straining to get up onto the more testing ground ahead. A very hard-looking unprotected wall that I hadn't noticed from below gave access to a short groove below the blank section.

'Excellent runners,' came from above.

Things were looking up. He's going to go for it, I thought.

And then it rained. It had been threatening for some time but now the drops were heavier; the rock darkened and quickly became greasy. Garth stopped. 'I'll belay here,' floated down from above.

This was bad news. Firstly the temperature, which had been very reasonable when we set out, had dropped dramatically. Jackets tied around waists and the like had been deemed unsightly and so my goosepimples were looking increasingly impressive. Despite this it seemed that I was now required to look vaguely competent seconding a pitch which was now damp and, even when dry, clearly gave very difficult climbing on tiny holds. Worst of all was the fact that Garth had belayed just below the really blank section. There was no way I could squeeze another belay in. It was going to be my lead after all.

But rain had clearly stopped play for the day and, shivering memorably, we abseiled off to retreat to the joys of an evening in Hemmingsvaer bars.

Beer was frighteningly expensive but the cuisine interesting. Experimenting with meals of whale meat slowed down some of the team but the arrival of a drunken group of biking ladies from Narvik revived spirits and led to an invite to a party in the next village. This was all very tempting but Richard, perhaps understandably, seemed to feel that such activities might not be conducive to an early start. Garth and I opted for the boring 'proper job' option but retired badly torn between the joys of a serious Lofoten evening and the need to put in a creditable performance the following morning. Such are the strains of filming.

It was not raining the next day and by the time we were in position (and the spider's web of ropes had been moved out of camera view) the rock had dried out quite nicely. The blank section hadn't grown any more holds though.

I edged up gingerly above the belay. To begin with there was a good crack and I was determined to fix plenty of secure protection in an effort to boost my confidence. I felt very hesitant and dithery, fiddling good wires in place and then removing them and trying again in the hope of getting even better placements. Keith, the cameraman, hung just above me zooming in on every detail. Dr Death, noting my enthusiasm for protection as opposed to upward movement, recognised a hesitating man and did his best to offer encouragement from below.

A couple of forays above the point where the crack petered out revealed that the blank section was only three metres or so and looked to end with a square-cut finger edge just below another thin crack line and more runners. It was getting to the stage where I couldn't physically fit any more protection into the crack. Also, everyone was poised for action. We had reached the point where something had to happen. I had a sudden and unwelcome image of audiences at home laughing at my indecision.

'Go for it,' purred Dr Death seductively.

I moved cautiously out beyond my last runner. The smooth granite was peppered with little scoops but all seemed equally unhelpful and insecure. Somehow I couldn't prevent myself trying out one scoop, rejecting it, dithering and then returning to the self same one that I had already rejected. A sure sign of a hesitant climber in action! I could feel Keith's lens burning into my face, trying to tease out every muscle of concern. But soon I was committed, there was no way I could get back; upwards was the only way out. What I would like to say is something along the lines that my focus and commitment lifted my ability to a higher level and enabled me to float gracefully over the difficulty. In fact I quickly became aware that I was stuck. Despite my high-friction-soled rock boots my feet seemed not to want to stick to the tiny depressions. I moved my weight uncomfortably from one sliding foot to the other before deciding that the best solution was a controlled lunge for the tantalisingly out of reach finger edge. With the benefit of seeing a replay I can confirm that I was nearly there – but in the act of stretching upwards my foot slipped and with a (though I say it myself) very fine scream I scraped painfully down the slab, penduluming directly into Dr Death who, in the circumstances, did a very fine job of carrying on smiling at the camera.

A second attempt ended with similar but even more painful results. Somehow I managed to catch my elbow which swelled up alarmingly. My GP belayer, was most interested and offered various helpful suggestions, the best one by far being to abseil off and drink beer with the swollen bit immersed in an ice bucket. Fortunately it was just about the end of the day and, with this suggestion being director-approved, we were soon ensconced in the bar with my problem area immersed in a nastily flowery bowl overflowing with ice. Merriment levels were high (me excluded) but with the next day in mind my personal challenge was moderate alcohol intake whilst maximising elbow immersion.

By the following morning it was clear that the Doctor's advice had been remarkably sound. My arm, though curiously coloured, was more or less back to its normal size. The long jumar back up to our high point could proceed. Filming, I contemplated, tends to involve at least as much time hanging about on ropes (and removing them from the camera's view) as actually climbing. But at length everyone was in the right position and it was time for me to perform again. Bridge up the shallow groove, place even more protection – out onto the blank section and then … Yes! I was there! It all seemed so easy when it worked. Above me now was a superb crack that I romped up to a fine belay below a roof. Dr Garthwaite seconded the pitch with sickening ease, despite carrying a small rucksack, but my feeling of satisfaction remained strong and enduring. It's good to find something difficult but succeed in the end. The fact that others might find it easy is largely irrelevant. It's the personal satisfaction that counts.

'Excellent,' announced Director Else that evening.

The ingredients of uncertainty, screaming plummets, injury and eventual success were clearly to his liking.

'Tomorrow we can do the long shots.'

'Sorry?' I knew exactly what he meant but somehow in my euphoria, I had overlooked his enthusiasm for replays from various 'interesting' positions. Another sleepless night lay ahead.

In fact all went remarkably smoothly; no more graceful plummets or blood-curdling screams. Richard must have been quite disappointed.

We spent the following days performing for the cameras on glorious sun drenched rock. The higher we got the more complex and time-consuming the filming arrangements became. Three hundred and fifty metres is a long way up to sort out access ropes and sound cables, not to mention a long way for the performers to jumar to work every day. But the weather was wonderfully kind and we finished a day early.

Sod's law though dictated that it would rain on the one day that we had to ourselves. Dr Garthwaite and I had a fine-looking objective on the magnificent peak of Vagakallen in mind but the end result was an excellent grovel with Keith Partridge, the cameraman, up the famous, albeit rain-drenched, pinnacle of Svolvaergeita (the Svolvaer Goat) overlooking the town of Svolvaer. Modestly graded it might be, but in the conditions it was challenging enough to be most memorable – which is, of course, the most important factor.

Being paid to go climbing has to be good news but the time inevitably bites into my holiday entitlement. Also, despite the presence of a safety team, my track record so far suggests that it is a lot more dangerous than just climbing for fun! In thirty-one years of climbing I can boast of one injury, an ice-axe in the elbow, whereas in less than two weeks of filming time I have managed to plummet into the ground, break a rib, batter my elbow and land on my partner. Dangerous business this performing!

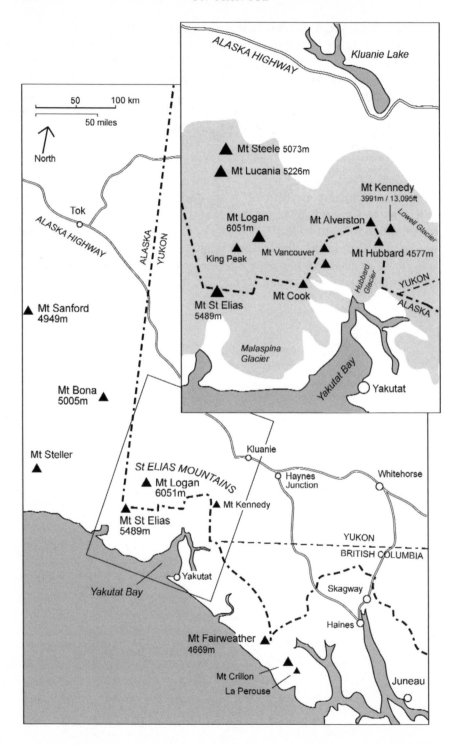

13

Mount Kennedy

Finding a good short duration target – North American possibilities –
flying in from Yakutat – considering the options – on the North Buttress –
– return from the Cathedral Glacier – the death of Kurt Gloyer

My mind was running on the Kokshaal Too range in Kyrgyzstan. Then the spectacular peaks of inner China were becoming increasingly accessible. And what about Patagonia? I had never been there either. An Antarctica project was bubbling too. I was rather aware that the Arwa trip had run a week over my three-week allowance and, as the Lofoten filming had also taken up valuable time, it might be best to look for a more accessible target so I could redress the time away balance in 2000.

I asked around and it was on one of my Tuesday evenings out in the Peak District that the next plan fell into shape. Paul Ramsden, one of my regular climbing partners since I escaped London for the East Midlands in 1992, started to seriously interest me in the prospect of North America.

I had always viewed places like Alaska as lacking ethnic interest and therefore offering a less attractive package than some of the other areas I had in mind. But Paul had been there and brought a book along to show me. As we sat in a very pleasant Peak District pub, he was waving it about with increasing excitement.

'You asked about Alaska, look at all these lines!'

I struggled to focus on the photographs. They all looked to be of alarmingly steep mountains. It had been a testing evening at the infamous Eastwood Rocks, where the slimy and depressingly undergraded gritstone cracks had spat me out with even greater ease than usual. I was nursing my flattened ego and bleeding hands but it had to be said that these photographs were giving me quite an urge. Meanwhile, Paul was moving on to the finer detail.

'You'd love it. Only a day from the UK to base, wonderful lines, nice and cold. Lots of snow.'

'And the downside?'

'Well the weather might not be too good. Geoff Hornby had four metres of snow in twenty-three days last year. But at least he got there.

I've heard of some people who don't even get a good enough weather window to fly in.'

This suddenly wasn't sounding so good to a civil servant with limited holidays. We ordered more beer and the conversation moved onto the usual problem of where our group should climb the following Tuesday evening.

But the photographs had unsettled me. I'd never even been to North America, let alone climbed on the mountains of Yukon and Alaska. Adopting the attitude that the weather might be bad so I'll never go didn't really sit very comfortably with my underlying keenness for climbing in new areas. There was no doubt about it, I would have to go for it and risk the weather. But who with and what exactly should we try?

The first question was easily solved. Andy Cave had not climbed in this part of the world either and was quick to show his whippet-like enthusiasm for anything that looked remotely inspirational. Andy is one of those sickening people who excels at just about every facet of climbing: desperate traditional climbs, 8a sport routes, new winter routes in Scotland, Himalayan first ascents – he's done them all. And he's an incredibly nice bloke too, as I had discovered on Changabang.

I recall meeting him when Nanda, Nicki's dog, ate his sandwiches when he was preparing to climb in North Wales and again when he was training for his British Mountaineering Council guide's test. It was a foul Scottish winter day and a hail-laden gale blasted a group of us mercilessly on the desolate expanse of the Cairngorm plateau. I got my compass out but Andy modestly said that he'd like to try and test his navigation skills as good training for his forthcoming guide's test. The fact that I was fumbling badly and it is very important to get the bearing just right may have had something to do with it too, but Andy was far too polite to say so. Later in the day Noel Craine and I completed Tom Patey's classic Scorpion in the dark and proved Andy's judgement correct by mistakenly following the wrong end of the compass needle for thirty minutes. Why *does* the red end have to point north? It seemed illogical to me – surely the compass was invented in the northern hemisphere and red denotes heat which should be to the south? The white end conversely surely points to the cold areas in the north? Mind you, to eliminate confusion for people like me they should just place a bloody great 'N' on the relevant end of the needle.

Anyway eventually Noel and I found our way round the top of Shelterstone and latched onto the tail of another group heading back across the plateau to an event at Glenmore Lodge that night where our incompetence was relayed gleefully to Andy amidst much hilarity.

So despite my inability to control dogs or compasses he was still keen for us to climb together on some 'yet to be identified' project in the wastes of the Canadian/Alaska borders.

We were starting from scratch and after an unproductive round of library research we were reduced to a series of pleading e-mails to well known North American activists. Andy and I considered the results together. People had been amazingly helpful.

What about the North Face of Devil's Thumb? Randy's been there twice and the weather was terrible. A couple of Canadian kids sat in there last year for about two months and it never froze.

That one didn't sound very hopeful. We moved on to the next.

You could aim for a line on the East Face of Moose's Tooth and find it too dry – without ice. Some guys get lucky their first time out [in Alaska], others spend a lot of their time and money before tasting a morsel of success. How lucky do you feel?

Andy and I contemplated these messages and the photographs that we had managed to get hold of. One in particular grabbed our attention; Bradford Washburn's of the north side of Mount Kennedy.

Kennedy is in the St Elias Range just on the Canadian side of the border. When it was named, after the recently assassinated president, in January 1965, it was the highest unclimbed peak in North America and Senator Bobby Kennedy, JFK's younger brother, although not a mountaineer, promptly expressed an interest in climbing it. With assistance from the National Geographic Society an expedition was organised and in March 1965 Bobby Kennedy became the first non-mountaineer ever to make the first ascent of a major North American mountain. The ethics were questionable but it is amazing what can be arranged if you carry enough influence! The Bobby Kennedy team had climbed from the south side but it was the tremendous 1800-metre high north side which attracted our attention. The North Buttress had been climbed twice before, once in 1968 and again in 1977, both ascents using siege tactics. A couple of alpine-style attempts had also been made. It was an obvious alpine-style objective and when we heard a rumour that the chirpy and ubiquitous Andy Kirkpatrick, a mountaineer of growing reputation, had been toying with the same idea, this helped to focus our decision. Mount Kennedy it would be.

It was the face to the right of the spur that was to become our prime objective. Sporting 900 metres of hard mixed ground, followed by 900 metres of easier terrain, it looked to be a superb challenge, albeit possibly threatened by a menacing-looking line of séracs. Four years previously two US climbers, Jack Tackle and Jack Roberts, had spent nine days forcing a route to within 500 metres of the summit before a dropped crampon and bad weather stopped play. They had covered the difficult ground but the face itself was still unclimbed.

Duncan Tunstall and Chris Pasteur, two old friends of mine, were keen to join us and so we were set as a team of four. In line with the strict post-Changabang way of doing things, Duncan and Chris would ski tour and climb various objectives that took their fancy, whilst Andy and I would be left to focus on Kennedy's North Face.

Yakutat (population 600) nestles on the South Alaska coastline and is apparently the smallest community in America to be served by a daily scheduled air service. It is also interesting in that it is not connected to the main North American road network and there are only twenty-seven miles of road for the inhabitants to drive around on. This means that priorities are rather different. Cars, for example, are generally not felt to be some-thing worth investing great amounts of money in.

Kurt Gloyer, who was to fly us in to the mountain, owned an amazingly tatty specimen which was fortunate really because he was not the slightest bit concerned when, at the end of the trip, after an ill-advised drinking session with locals, I was sick in it. He did though have a light plane which was his pride and joy and which he would regularly use to take his eleven-year-old daughter to the cinema in the Alaskan capital of Juneau, well over an hour's flight away.

Apart from drinking, fishing, surfing and love-making, all of which seemed very popular, there didn't seem to be a lot to do in Yakutat.

'It's why I moved here. What else do you need in life?' said Kurt.

But, much as Kurt couldn't really comprehend it, we were here for the mountaineering.

First impressions of Mount Kennedy were memorable. Andy was in full optimistic mode. 'Not as steep as I'd expected. Looks fine.' I just fought to overcome my feeling of nausea as Kurt circled tightly in his final approach to the landing. Perhaps it was the angle of the plane, but the glimpses that I was getting from my side didn't sit comfortably with Andy's assessment at all. It looked horrific. But my priority was to take some photographs and not be sick. I pointed the camera in vaguely the right direction and tried hard to ignore the sensation of being on a wild fair-ground ride.

The plane could only take two passengers at a time so it was an hour and a half later that Duncan and Chris joined us. By then I felt well enough to join half-heartedly in the collective ooh's and aah's and camera clicks. It did look very fine, but I couldn't help but notice the séracs overlooking the right-hand side of the face. Perhaps I'm getting old. My wife tells me that I worry more than I used to. I'm sure that I wouldn't have focused on such things twenty years ago, but now I found the binoculars trained, not on the technical joys of the climbing, but on the steely blue ice walls forming the lower edge of the summit ice field. I noticed that Andy too seemed to be paying close attention to such things.

As Kurt took off we stared first at the receding shape of the plane and then the cold wall of Kennedy's huge North Face. No one said a word until the sound of the plane had completely disappeared into the vastness. The arrangement was a pick-up in three weeks or as soon as we radioed which, because of the radio shadow behind Kennedy, would only be possible from the summit. I wondered when we would see Kurt again. It suddenly felt very quiet and very lonely. Exactly as I remembered Paul Ramsden telling me it would.

The lines on the face were not as obvious as we had expected. We spied several possible connecting streaks of ice towards the right-hand side but they were definitely in the fall zone of the séracs. Perhaps it was the all-concealing smattering of snow but, despite a detailed topo from the ever helpful Jack Tackle, it took us some time to work out the exact line taken by him and Jack Roberts. Even peering through the binoculars, it was impossible to decide whether or not it was ice or powder snow stuck to rock on their line. The line itself seemed to be just out of the fall line of the séracs, but a semi-permanent thundering cloud of spindrift brought it sharply home to us that it was the main, albeit shallow, funnel draining snowfall from the 900 metres upper face.

We decided that we had enough excuses to sit back and adopt that wonderfully sensible middle-aged approach of sitting back, eating, drinking and – observing.

Observing too much can be a bad idea. Inevitably we observed spindrift. Lots of it. Lying in nice warm sleeping bags on the glacier it was easy to talk ourselves out of anything too masochistic. With regular spindrift and temperatures in the shade plunging to –25°C, the chance of freezing solid on a hanging bivouac looked high. The tone of our conversations moved steadily away from Andy's initial optimism.

'Don't fancy getting flushed off by that lot.'

'Looks much safer on the North Buttress.'

'Brilliant line too.'

We did try skinning up the glacier to look at the face from different angles, but it didn't change anything. There was no doubt about it, we had subtly changed objectives. We would go for an alpine-style attempt on the North Buttress.

No sooner had the decision been made than the sun came out and, having heard plenty of St Elias weather horror stories, we felt obliged to stir ourselves into action.

The buttress did look an excellent climb though it was very difficult to say how hard it might be. From the glacier the first two thirds looked OK, but in the upper third mixed buttresses could be seen to block progress. We had the first ascensionists' report which referred to A3 aid climbing and included a disturbing photograph of someone aiding up a decidedly blank-looking wall. Clearly we would need to carry a fair amount of technical gear to stand a chance of coping with this.

With more or less continuous daylight and an obvious bivi spot after 300 metres, an early morning start somehow didn't seem very necessary. Relishing in the luxury of being able to leave our headtorches behind, we relaxed over a leisurely breakfast of fried halibut and it wasn't until around midday that we felt obliged to haul our bursting stomachs towards the toe of the buttress.

One of the good things about steep lines is that fresh snow tends to slide off rather than accumulate. Even better, the polishing effect of frequent snow slides tends to create streaks of squeaky white ice – perfect for climbing on. Andy and I wavered up the lower slopes, picking out the 'squeaky' lines wherever possible. Though the weather was perfect and the climbing easy, it was unsettling to have heavy waves of spindrift engulfing us every now and then. We made quick progress, trying not to think how the spindrift might look if it started to snow.

Gaining height brought home the scale and spectacular remoteness of the St Elias Range. Below us the Kennedy Glacier presented a flat white expanse, perhaps three kilometres wide, which wound its way majestically down to the Lowell Glacier, ultimately emptying into the Alsek River and the sea south of Yakutat Bay. In a way, despite the ease of access, it seemed more remote than the Himalaya. Walking out with all our equipment was definitely not on. Even just carrying survival gear, it would be a testing effort to get out to the Alaskan Highway, which would be not much use for getting back to Yakutat. Walking to Yakutat from Kennedy would involve 100 kilometres of crevassed glacier, ice bloc-ridden inlets and mosquito-ravaged bogs. There was no doubt about it, we were dependent on Kurt Gloyer to pick us up. It was a new and slightly uncomfortable feeling to be so dependant on someone else.

I suppose we should have been getting a move on, but good weather, scenic views and an idyllic safe bivouac site on a projecting crest prompted a relaxed approach and a short day.

This amiable weather did not persist however and by mid-afternoon on day two we were experiencing full Yukon conditions.

Although our chosen line primarily followed the crest, it was quite a broad crest and we tended to veer backwards and forwards between subsidiary ribs. It was whilst making one of these rising traverses that the occasional gentle flurries of snow built up into something more substantial. With getting on for 1500 metres of mountain above us, it was perhaps unsurprising that the intermittent clouds of spindrift soon developed into roaring snow slides. To make matters worse the slope was not of a good consistency for reliable ice screws and communication was near impossible. In this manner an uncomfortably dangerous situation had developed and another short day was called for.

The rib on the right gave a ray of hope, but this Yukon snowfall was something else. Even the crests of the buttress were mercilessly raked by the ongoing deluge of spindrift.

'Glad we're not on the face,' said Andy in philosophical mode.

'Mmmm …' Somehow my mumbled response didn't sound so calm. 'Perhaps head for that one?'

I pointed hesitantly through the mist to an indistinct rib, adorned with a fragile cornice. It appeared to stand sufficiently proud of the slope to escape the worst of the spindrift waves. It took half an hour of wallowing against the flow before Andy was somewhere near it.

'Am I in the right place?'

This didn't sound good. Much cursing and excavating was followed by a welcome call for me to climb.

The sensation on reaching Andy's powdery perch was memorable. It felt like sitting on a small island in the middle of a raging river. All was safe for the moment but added interest was guaranteed if the spindrift rivers rose much more. We looked glumly at each other.

'Can't just stand here. Best get the tent up.'

The softest and most fragile snow edges tend to have good ice somewhere deep down inside. This one seemed to defy normal characteristics, it appeared to be simply powder snow resting on granulated snow. Reliable belays were distressingly non-existent.

'The ice screw I put in up there isn't bad,' announced Andy, pointing at a screw six metres above and three metres to one side.

I silently imagined the two of us fighting claustrophobic fabric whilst ensconced in a tent penduluming off the crest and being battered by snow slides.

'Perhaps a couple more would be nice?'

And so with snow still falling (where does it all come from in Yukon?)

the two of us squeezed into our little tent secured by a selection of ice screws well above us and way to one side. Within minutes the snow had completely blocked the entrance and the tent had merged into the profile of the crest.

We had a radio with us but this was not much use as contact with the outside world was impossible. Also, after twenty-four hours there was little in the way of exciting news to report to the boys at Base Camp. Our exchanges were becoming a trifle banal.

'Base Camp here. What's it like up there? Over.'

'Snowing. How about down there? Over.'

'About a metre now. What are your plans? Over.'

'More reading. Over and out.'

I had chosen light-hearted reading. My children having become avid Harry Potter fans, I relished the opportunity to catch up on Harry's latest adventures, my aim being to become fully versed on Hogwart's tittle-tattle so that I could hold my own with them. I lay engrossed. Andy, himself a former coal-miner, had chosen reading matter designed to further his thesis on mining dialects. Somehow he seemed to find it difficult to concentrate, although perhaps this was less to do with his choice of reading, more with the fact that his head was at the mountain end and in close proximity to the constant roar of spindrift avalanches. A particularly loud roar, followed by a severe pummelling of the fabric at his end, was enough to make him look uncharacteristically uneasy.

'Not very pleasant, Mick.'

I mumbled agreement, whilst trying to concentrate harder on Harry.

By the morning of day three Andy and I were tiring of inactivity by the time we made our morning radio call.

'Tent excavation under way.'

Deep down inside though I didn't feel quite so positive. The tent had the appearance of having been sucked into the bowels of the mountain. In clearings in the cloud Duncan and Chris had failed to spot us through their binoculars, even though we were not that far up and in direct line of sight from Base Camp. In terms of progress everything would hinge on how much snow was lying on the snow slopes we would have to cross. The weather was still not at its best. Cloud hung thick and persistent above us and the air was heavy with blowing snow.

We waded off our protected little ridge crest and back into action. Invisible granite slabs grated unnervingly against crampon points but our guarded optimism proved correct in that the angle was such that most of the new snow had simply slipped off the face.

The ground wasn't technically difficult but we were worried about the slopes above – pregnant with unstable snow – and thus took great care to belay securely. Despite this, we soon got into a good rhythm and by late afternoon we were halfway up the face. More importantly, the skies had cleared. A glorious panoramic view had opened up. Any doubts we had over the wisdom of continuing evaporated. Pinnacle Peak now soared spectacularly above an intervening ridge and we could see obliquely across the North-West Face onto the huge Kennedy ice shelf slanting up towards Mount Alverstone. Another fine snow crest, with big overhangs below, made for a spectacular bivouac. The atmosphere had totally changed. Smiles came readily – we were in with a chance. The obvious crux of the line was still above us but that was just some technical climbing, whereas success on this climb seemed to hinge more on conditions and judgement.

Aid climbing is definitely not my forte, so we were working on the basis that we would be able to find interlinking ice streaks and avoid time-consuming aid pitches. (It's amazing how optimistic it is possible to be when viewing from a position of comfort.) Now we had our noses up against the problem, the lines that we had spotted through binoculars from Base Camp were far from obvious. In fact we couldn't see them at all. We studied the old Washburn photograph that we had brought with us. Creases had appeared in all the wrong places and these made it almost impossible to pinpoint our exact position.

'Perhaps we're just here? Ought we to be over to the right a bit?'

Andy pointed at a vague couloir, almost entirely obliterated by a crease. Our on the spot assessment didn't add much, although there was certainly a line of sorts up to our right and few other options.

Everything looks more difficult when viewed from below. This generalisation certainly applied to the feature that we were now looking at. The weather was worsening. By the time we reached the steepening, spindrift was pouring over an overhang ten metres above, spraying out and catching us squarely in a fine mist. At least it was intermittent.

One of the good things about climbing with Andy is that he is equally at home on rock and ice. Regardless of the terrain, he can be put in the lead whenever there is a hint of any kind of difficulty. I recalled a rock climbing evening at Stoney Middleton in the Peak District when he had surged up an E5 in the rain, leaving me to attempt to second but ending up dangling in front of an appreciative audience. No audience here and at least I climbed comfortable in the knowledge that I had this secret weapon to tackle any really nasty bits that we might come across.

We were leading alternate pitches and the first pitch on this steeper ground was mine. Soon I was thrashing in an acute-angled, slanting groove.

The spindrift had swept the loose snow away leaving squeaky white ice but it was right at the back and my sack kept forcing me out.

'This is better,' I grunted, energetically warming to the task.

By dint of more brute strength than skill I scraped the sack up the groove, emerged on a small ledge with a good belay and sat down to bring Andy up. I suppose I should have expected it to be a bad-for-the-ego experience but it would have been nice if he had looked just a little bit more stretched.

Impressively, voluminous flakes now fell quietly from a bleak grey sky. In tune with the weather, the rock changed from golden granite to slate grey dolerite. At least we knew that the dolerite only appeared on the top third of the route. And once through this section we knew there were only 500 metres of ice slopes to the summit. But it was somewhere here that Jack Tackle and Jack Roberts had turned back in 1996. They had completed the technically difficult climbing and veered left to the point where we now were and then ground to a halt when the weather became really bad. They must have been gutted not to stand on the summit after nine days of effort. It was a sobering thought for us to know that it took them two full days and thirty-six full-length sixty-metre abseils to get back down. The summit and a possible walking descent on the far side looked increasingly appealing. But even the upwards path of ever versatile coal miner Cave had ground to a halt. Bad news indeed.

A sudden clearing of the skies revealed the Cave body poised precariously.

'I'm in the wrong place. Should be over there,' he yelled.

It did all look horribly insecure. Crampons scraping unnervingly Andy started to curse, down climb and traverse, whilst I soaked up the sun's rays. It was as if our fortunes had turned – what a few minutes earlier had seemed desperate had changed to distinctly possible.

The sky was now completely clear and the views again stunning. I sat back clicking away with the camera whilst Andy inched himself out to the base of the summit icefield.[1]

Soon we had found a spot where we could pitch the tent. Admittedly one-third of the floor space hung off the ledge we hacked out and I lost the toss and got the outside position. But it seemed to matter little in the face

---

[1] Mt. Kennedy's 1800m North Buttress was first climbed by Dave Seidman and Todd Thomson, supported by Phil Koch and Joe Faint, on July 29 1966 after a month of attempts, fixing rope, and with three camps. They retreated down their own equipped route and were helicoptered out when their ski plane pilot considered landing too risky. The climb was repeated in similar style in 1977 (but with a seven-day walk in and out from the Alaska Highway) by Terry Boley, Jack Lewis, Alan Millar, David Stevenson and Scott Baker – again retreating down the route of ascent. In 1997 the harder North-West Face was climbed (alpine style) to a junction with the North Ridge c.500m below the summit by Jack Tackle and Jack Roberts. Having lost a crampon and running short of food they made a hazaradous (spindrift inundated) retreat down a line between the two routes. Source: *AAJ*s 52 and 71.

of the sun streaming through the door and the possibility of the summit the next day. We lay there chatting contentedly as the sun dropped in the sky and the steely cold of the night tightened its grip.

The morning dawned clear but of course the sun doesn't really set in this part of the world; best to say that remarkably clear weather continued as we emerged into the crystal clear and frigidly cold morning air. Rare conditions indeed. Soaking in the scenery, we alternately led along a narrow connecting crest and finally moved together up the easing angle to the summit snow cone. This was our sixth day out from Base Camp.

It was a great feeling to stand there in perfect weather on the summit of such a demanding mountain. A cloud layer covered the sea but summits in all directions stood proud. It was a sobering thought that there might not be anyone at all within forty or fifty miles. For ease of access, combined with remoteness and solitude it's difficult to beat this part of the world.

Andy was on the radio trying to reach Kurt in Yakutat. We had been assured that it would be possible to make radio contact from the summit. But if we couldn't our only sensible option was to descend the way we had come up. I didn't fancy that very much.

'Hello. Hello, Kurt. We're on top … Can you pick us up from the Lower Cathedral Glacier at 5pm tomorrow?'

'No problem. See you there.'

All confirmed then. All we had to do was get down to the Cathedral Glacier and then navigate our way down its vast upper reaches to a flat pick-up point. As to the exact location of this we knew nothing, except that Kurt had described it as 'just below the big icefall'.

We stared together at the vast pristine glacial landscape and glanced anxiously at the few clouds dotting the sky. Bad visibility was definitely something we could do without.

'Perhaps you should take a bearing,' commented Andy passing me the compass with a huge grin on his face.

The next evening we were back in Yakutat Jack's Bar drinking to Geoff Hornby's four metres of snow and twenty-three days inactivity the previous year.[2] The experience had ended as abruptly as it had begun. The total time away from home was just two weeks! And, as an extra bonus, I was fully clued up on Harry Potter's latest adventures.

---

[2] Fowler and Cave were picked up on the Cathedral Glacier as planned after which Gloyer returned to the start point to pick up Pasteur and Tunstall.

POSTCRIPT

In July 2001 Bill Pilling and Andy Selters completed the second alpine-style ascent of the North Buttress of Mount Kennedy. Bad weather pinned them down on their descent but during the first break in the clouds for days Kurt Gloyer, true to form, had flown in to the Upper Cathedral Glacier to try and get them off. On take off the plane fell into a huge crevasse, killing Kurt and injuring Pilling and Selters who were rescued the following day by a combined military/coastguard/ranger effort.

I shall remember Kurt as an immensely likeable, easy to talk to character. He was well known to St. Elias climbers as someone who was prepared to stretch the limits in terms of flying conditions and suitable landing spots. As such he was very much both a personal friend and a climbers' friend. It was a sad loss.

14

The Elephant's Trunk of Etratat

*Something for the French weekend – two climbs and one fall –
admiring the crab collectors – grappling with the Trunk –
the Pauls get scraped – apprehended by the Gendarmerie*

Memorable climbing doesn't have to take place in distant spots. The lengthy UK coastline has almost unlimited scope for adventure climbing and France too has some decidedly interesting sea cliffs, easily reachable in a weekend from England. One recent trip in particular sums up all that I find attractive about such exploits. The cliffs in question had been in my mind for many years before I got round to telephoning Mike Morrison and taking the idea further.

'Guess what. It's white. It's French. It's long and thin and it hangs down into the sea. What do you think?'

'Sorry?' Mike sounded uncharacteristically taken aback.

'It's at Etratat.' I explained ... 'The Elephant's Trunk.'

'What?'

Mike was not getting the drift. A bit more detail was obviously called for.

The Elephant's Trunk is a 100-metre-high slender chalk arch near the town of Etratat on the Normandy coast. I had been vaguely aware of its existence for many years but a 1999 eclipse-hunting family holiday sealed my urge to climb it. It was the children's fault really.

'Why haven't you climbed this?' they had enquired, apparently incredulous that I called myself a climber and yet had somehow over-looked such an obviously enticing objective. There was no easy answer to their question. Etratat is not far from Le Havre and is within easy weekend striking distance of Britain. And the arch, not to mention a rather fine sea stack, really did call out for attention.

True to form, Mike was keen. So were two of my East Midlands climbing friends, Paul Eastwood and Paul Ramsden. An old friend from Scottish weekending days, Jon Lincoln, now living the life of an EEC bureaucrat in Brussels, decided that he too could not miss out and arranged to meet us there. Jon was still known as 'Carless' from his aversion to owning a car and his ability to acquire climbing lifts with anyone driving north.

The chalk cliffs of the Etratat area are the geological continuation of those on the south coast of England, but the French cliffs are more featured with spectacular headlands and arches. In common with their British counterparts they are also riddled with man-made caves, although the main thrust of the Etratat caves is to link together beaches that would otherwise be inaccessible except at low tide. In climbing terms the rock at Etratat is 'rock climbing' chalk, as opposed to the softer 'ice climbing' chalk found at places like Dover. Unfortunately it is peppered with razor-sharp shattered flints which cut ropes easily and add a touch of excitement and adrenalin flow.

The eye-catching sixty-metre sea stack was first climbed back in the 1940s but the main developments took place in the 1960s when a keen group of French climbers focused on the place and put up forty or so climbs, most of them aid routes where the climbers pulled on the equipment they placed rather than the rock itself. Their climbs were recorded in a French guidebook that Carless had brought along but there appeared to have been very few climbing visits over the last thirty years.

Etratat is a bustling holiday town with an extensive shingle beach. In August it had been thronged with holidaymakers but on a bleak and drizzly Saturday in late September it all looked slightly less inviting than I remembered. To add to the problems, high tide was at 10am and most of the climbs here are tidal.

We stood uncertainly on the shingle beach. For Mike and me in particular the demands of family life meant that weekends away had become something of a rarity. There was no way we could contemplate doing nothing, but, with the rock wet and the tide in, even the ever active Morrison had to admit that the possibilities were distinctly limited.

Eastwood prodded the rock hesitantly with one finger.

'Feels nice and slimy. What's it like when it's dry?'

'I'm sure it's very nice,' I heard myself saying, whilst recalling how slimy the Dover chalk cliffs can get in anything vaguely resembling a sea mist.

A suitably lengthy coffee and croissant break was in order.

'Important to savour the delights of French cuisine,' enthused Ramsden stuffing in yet more *pain au chocolat*.

After ninety minutes five very well fed would-be climbers were back on the beach. The tide had turned now, the drizzle moderated and the rocky parts of the beach were teaming with people wielding crowbars and digging about under the rocks. We stared amazed. Whatever were these people doing? It wasn't like the average scene on the English south coast just a few miles across the channel.

'Crab-collectors,' announced Carless with the authority of an adopted Belgian living nowhere near to the sea but having a French wife. And he was right. Loads of them.

Despite our lengthy breakfast the tide was still too far in for us to reach any of the climbs. But Paul Eastwood had made a team investment of £27.00 and come prepared. To increasing interest he produced a large package of brightly coloured plastic which he proceeded to transform into a three-metre long, bright orange inflatable with 'Winnie the Pooh' on the side. The idea was that we would put the rucksacks in the inflatable and swim alongside.

Armed with this unusual approach craft, the two Pauls decided to have a go at the nearest route to the beach, which also happened to be the most difficult free-climb in the area. It takes a lot to interrupt the concentration of dedicated French crab-collectors but the sight of two pale, goose-pimpled Englishmen stripping off and plunging in alongside a bright orange Winnie the Pooh inflatable was enough to distract all but the most narrow minded specimens.

In fact, by the end of the day, our investment looked to be distinctly sound. The Pauls managed their route and Mike, Carless and I managed to climb the stack – even arriving with dry gear, having swum the fifty-metres or so to get to it. Ramsden had a particularly memorable finish to the challenging last pitch. Reaching over and twanging in his ice-axe while in extremis, he was surprised to discover that he had very nearly pierced the lunch spread of a French family who had chosen to picnic seriously close to the edge. He was even more baffled when a man approached.

'Ah, bonjour! Etes vous Mick Fowler?'

It was Mike Morrison's neighbour from Newbury who had decided to include Etratat in his weekend itinerary.

It had struck us during the day that the in situ equipment on the climbs was not the most reliable we had seen. In fact it very much had the appearance of original 1960s ironware and crumbled readily at the slightest touch. Exchanges in the bar that night confirmed our suspicions. The barman, a rotund character who prided himself on knowing everything that ever happened in Etratat, had never heard of anyone climbing here. Perhaps it was unsurprising but the cliffs were clearly not over-popular.

As the bières went down, Mike's French neighbour became obsessed with the idea of sleeping out on the cliff tops. This seemed great at the time and sometime after midnight two small tents were pitched on a flattish area nestled next to the big floodlights that illuminate the cliffs hereabouts.

In the gung-ho atmosphere of the bar it had generally been agreed that a 5am start would beat the tides and leave us with the best chance of grabbing a route or two on the Sunday. Somehow the plan didn't seem quite so appealing as my nauseatingly bleepy alarm pierced the early morning blackness. The floodlights, which attractively illuminate the cliffs in the evening, had been turned off now and I stumbled blindly away from the tent to start the day with a pee. As my eyes grew accustomed to the dark my brain focused on the fact that I had wandered to within two metres from the cliff edge. On the bright side, I could see the numerous lights of crab-collectors already in action. The tide was obviously out, the sky was clear and (perhaps most surprisingly) we had managed to get up on time.

'These crab-collectors are outrageous.' Morrison, himself a paragon of energy and enthusiasm, could not believe their dedication to duty.

There was now just the slightest hint of dawn and the beach was peppered with perhaps fifty lights. Each collector worked silently, alone or in pairs, and paid little attention to four clanking climbers carrying a bright orange inflatable boat.

The idea was that Mike, Carless and I would have a go at the Elephant's Trunk arch whilst the Pauls would walk out to the stack (only possible at dead low tide) and use the boat to get back. Stage one worked well, not surprising really as our super early start had at least ensured that we were in the right place at low tide. I tried to salvage something from not checking the tides before leaving England.

'Said the tides would be OK, didn't I?'

Discontented grumbling from heavy heads pointed out the benefit of mid-morning low tides whilst I tried to stress the benefits of starting and finishing early. I then twisted my ankle in the dark which rather lent support to the others' viewpoint.

The Elephant's Trunk looked challenging. It was remarkable that it stayed in place really. Chalk generally collapses well before weathering into such a spectacular feature. Photographic evidence showed that this arch had changed little in thirty-five years. Hopefully it would last another day.

The first twenty-metres was a steep wall split by a leaning, and in places overhanging, crack. After their success the previous day the Pauls had sniffed around here with an optimistic plan 'to tick the Trunk' quickly before the pub. The end result was two flints parting company simultaneously, resulting an uncharacteristically outrageous plummet by Paul Eastwood. In situ ironware had crumbed and he was held by a small wire nut wedged between two projecting flints. Memorable indeed, although Paul didn't seem very keen to relive the experience.

Mindful of this rebuff, Mike, Carless and I uncoiled our ropes hesitantly, very aware of the obvious difficulty, dubious rock and now the lack of in situ equipment – except, of course, the crucial wire nut which was clearly visible at ten metres. The usual sparring started:

'Carless, you live on the continent now. That classes you as a local expert. Your lead.'

'No, no. I've never been here before. Your family holiday has accustomed you to the unique feel of Etratat.'

More token excuses followed until I found myself tying onto the ropes and contemplating the weed-covered overhanging moves necessary to get started. It has to be admitted that I could feel an urge to get to grips with the wonderfully exposed soaring Trunk of chalk which pierced the early morning sky and formed such an eye-catching feature hereabouts.

The nut that held Paul looked frighteningly insecure. Cracked flints projected from either side of a shattered crack, and there, perched between them, was a 1cm block of metal. It wasn't wedged as such and pivoted gently as the sea breeze swayed the sling and karabiner hanging from it. I had hoped that it would provide something solid and secure to aim for but now I could well understand why Paul Eastwood had been rather subdued in the bar the previous evening. If it hadn't held, he, and now I, would have had a good chance of smacking into the barnacle-encrusted rock ledge at the base.

A few feet higher I hung unashamedly from a nut that I managed to jam in the back of the crack. The remains of one of the in situ pieces of ironmongery that had failed the day before stared me in the face. I fingered it cautiously. It looked to be a probable relic of the first ascent back in the 1960s. The corrosive powers of salt water are impressive in the extreme and now, in its broken state, this apparently homemade peg could be seen to be rotten to the core. I was feeling frightened. There wasn't very much in the way of protection except for these unique in situ affairs. Would they all be as weak and corroded as this one? Erring on the side of caution I took an ice screw from my harness and pounded it into the crack. The old-fashioned drive-in type screws dated from my youth and were of limited use in ice but they come into their own in soft rock like chalk. I clipped the rope in and felt a little happier. But I still moved cautiously, pulling out with difficulty onto a small sloping ledge and taking great care to attach myself securely before giving the signal for the others to climb.

It was full daylight by now and the tide was rapidly coming in. The crab collectors were concentrated into a narrow strip of foreshore, whilst the two Pauls could be seen halfway up the sea stack. Now that the tide was in it could be seen that the sea was interestingly rough. Somehow this hadn't been obvious when it was well out.

Above us the main section of the Trunk soared up for about sixty metres before abutting against the steep headwall. The wind was getting up and there was now a hint of drizzle in the air. But with the tide in and a longed for objective within our grasp, retreat was never a seriously considered option.

Shouts from the stack indicated that things were not going according to plan. It seemed that the boat had not been secured high enough and the rapidly rising tide was grating the trusty inflatable against the barnacles to such an extent that a retreat was deemed to be in order. We watched with interest as the Pauls launched themselves off towards the shore, one either side and with rucksacks perched in the boat. Twenty feet or so from the beach they appeared to opt for a sudden change of heart and turned sharp left, surging under the arch of the Trunk and disappearing from view.

'Perhaps they felt in need of a little more excitement,' commented Carless.

We peered together into the boiling cauldron on the far side. There was no sign of them and we could only assume that they had hugged the rock and pulled out somewhere out of sight.

Meanwhile the Etratat early strollers were gathering on the cliff top. Despite the dubious weather we could see at least twenty people peering over the edge. There was no escaping it – we were becoming something of a Sunday attraction. That was OK for the next pitch, a wonderfully spectacular, but not too difficult, one up the crest of the Trunk but above that the top section looked much more difficult than we had anticipated. Certainly not the sort of ground where an increasing crowd of onlookers is particularly welcome.

'What's going on down there?'

Mike was pointing to a chunky-looking inflatable which was bobbing around below us. The two men on board appeared to have erected a five-metre ladder and were clearly very interested in what we were up to.

'Coastguard?' suggested Carless.

'Perhaps they are keen to join us! Ladder's a bit short though.'

We stared downwards for a minute or so. The men were shouting something but the pounding sea combined with the language problem effectively prevented any communication. We waited expectantly, keen to see how the combination of inflatable boat, five-metre ladder and 100-metre cliff would come together.

Disappointingly the coastguards clearly came to the conclusion that there was little they could do. Hopefully they had concluded that we were safe and happy and should be left alone. But all we knew for sure was that they were soon throbbing towards the calmer waters of Etratat Bay and we were left again to soak up the splendours in silence. It was not to last long.

The upper section of the trunk-like arch gave delicate and exposed climbing. When I was two-thirds of the way up, spread-eagled on a particularly tricky section, I became aware of a new and louder throbbing sound. A helicopter. Past experience has left me in no doubt that the appearance of a helicopter almost always means bad news. Usually there has been a serious accident but sometimes it is the harbinger of an unwelcome rescue attempt. Fortunately nearly all of my experiences have fallen into the latter category. But I wondered about the Pauls, last seen being swept under the arch whilst clinging onto a child's inflatable. I recalled particularly Paul Ramsden's protestations at his weak swimming ability. There was no doubt about it, the chances were that there was a likely link between our activities and the appearance of the helicopter.

It was now close enough for me to see the pilot.

I know enough to be cautious about making arm signals in such situations. On one occasion a rescue effort was prompted at Dover because a fisherman thought that we were waving our arms around in a signal to be rescued, when, in fact, we were climbing the chalk cliffs using ice-axes – which involves swinging them so that the picks bite in the chalk. On another occasion a Dover helicopter pilot spoke to us through an ear-splitting megaphone. 'If you are safe and do not wish to be rescued put your hands above your head.' It was all very well for my partner who was safe and secure on the belay, but I was half-way up a vertical pitch and fought frantically to get a good enough placement to clip in and stick my hands in the air before a full-scale rescue was under way. I was successful on that occasion but such experiences have left me with a complex about what to do with my arms whenever a helicopter appears and I am climbing.

At least I could stand in balance here, which meant that I could drop my hands by my side and at least look as if I was safe, secure and comfortable. Unfortunately it was a rather precarious balance position and the increasing downdraught from the rotas did nothing to help my feeling of insecurity. I tried to smile inanely whilst making no movement whatsoever and hoping that the strong down-draught would not blow me off or bring about the demise of the much photographed Elephant's Trunk.

An incomprehensible megaphone announcement in French followed, before, with a deafening roar, the helicopter banked sharply and rose up over the cliff top and out of view. I was left to gibber up the rest of the pitch and contemplate the difficult top section.

The guidebook description mentioned something about a Grade IV pitch climbing horizontally across a wall to the right. Grade IV should be reasonable standard rock climbing, the sort of thing that we should find pleasant rather than challenging. But the wall to the right overhung; admittedly there was a rusty old peg five metres away but surely that couldn't be the way?

Carless and I scanned for other possibilities whilst Mike seconded the pitch. A shout from above brought our attention to the crowd, which had now increased to about fifty, and a uniformed man with a peaked hat was shouting down to us. I couldn't follow what he was saying but it didn't take much to form the impression that he wasn't very happy.

Carless shouted something back in French and a short exchange followed which was largely drowned out by the helicopter doing a quick flyover and momentarily blasting the cliff top watchers in the down-draught. I released my grip on the rock and turned to Jon.

'What's going on?' I asked.

He hesitated slightly.

'I'm not completely sure, something to do with a monument and us not climbing as fast as they would like. They don't seem to have noticed that there are three of us, they think we are just sitting here wasting their time.'

I had forgotten about Mike. The rope hadn't gone tight so presumably he hadn't been blown off by the sudden down-draught.

With the noise subsiding, contact was re-established and a rather dishevelled Morrison was soon with us.

'Bastards!' he spluttered, his eyes red and face caked in a layer of chalk dust. 'It's hard enough anyway without having to climb in a dust storm!'

But he was still smiling. It takes more than a short, sharp turmoil of dust, snow, or rain to dent the Morrison cheerfulness.

Now we were together again it was time to think about performing in front of the crowd. They had a perfect view of proceedings and, as they clearly weren't going to go away, there was little option but to overcome any shyness and move into full action mode.

The interventions by the helicopter had not changed our perception of the way ahead. The best way forward looked to be to try a ten-metre horizontal traverse to a grass gully leading back up to the crest. One or two pegs were visible but they seemed a long way apart and the ground between them overhung disturbingly. I probed tentatively, to the gasps of the audience, as rocks fell away in the void to my right. It was going to be hard and frightening. Not good ground for public performances.

'Watch me.'

I hung unashamedly, linking the rotting ironmongery with insecure movements which clearly (judging by the appreciative oohs and aahs) looked as precarious as they felt.

Hesitantly we regrouped after the traverse before Mike led up to the waiting hordes and an appreciative round of applause from all but the gendarmes and other assorted officials. The Pauls could be seen hovering on the edge of the crowd, looking rather wet and dishevelled, but doing their best to distance themselves from any behaviour that might not be gendarme-approved.

It later transpired that their retreat from the stack had not been quite as calm and collected as we had imagined. They had reached within ten-metres of the beach when, despite their best efforts, a strong current swept them swiftly under the arch of the Elephant's Trunk. At this point a volley of rocks loosened by us above them, peppered the sea. Paul Ramsden, whose swimming abilities are almost as poor as my own, was particularly unimpressed by what was assumed to be our purposeful attempt to add interest to their predicament.

Under the Trunk they were also exposed to the full force of waves surging in from either side. With a breaking swell of six-metres or so it became increasingly difficult to control a child's inflatable with a ruck-sack perched on it. A frantic effort to direct themselves towards a place where they might be able to escape the sea resulted in serious barnacle scratches and a deep gash in the side of the boat. This latter point was a particular problem in that the boat had only two compartments – floor and walls. With walls gone they were left with rucksacks perched precariously on the floor ringed by a fringe of floppy plastic. The situation had become serious but, remarkably, after a series of body scraping attempts, the Pauls, rucksacks and boat remains ended up clinging pre-cariously out of reach of the waves. It was a frightening and dangerous situation but ultimately they were able to traverse to a cave[1] which led through to the narrow strip of beach not yet covered by the incoming tide. Aware of coastguard activity and not wanting to be identified as beach

---

[1] We later discovered that this was part of a system of wartime defence passages that were tunnelled through the whole Etretat headland.

strollers cut off by the tide, they were keen to extricate themselves somehow.

Once a set of steps used to give access to this beach but rockfalls have eaten into the cliff and a fifteen-metre wall now guards access to the easier slopes above. Driving in ice screws and covering the attention-grabbing remains of the bright orange boat as best they could, they made faltering progress to just below the cliff top. At this point the helicopter returned, prompting them to avoid rescue efforts by seeking refuge in some shrubby bushes. Emerging onto the cliff top footpath, they were then pleased to note that all attention seemed to be focused on activity on the Elephant's Trunk, a hundred yards to the east. Having hidden the boat remains, they did their best to merge in with the crowd. Wet, dishevelled and bleeding from numerous barnacle scratches, they looked unlikely cliff top walkers but with attention focused elsewhere, they melted seamlessly into the throng. This ploy had worked well until crowd attention was steered in their direction by our greetings.

Meanwhile the French authorities had moved into full rescue and apprehend mode. In addition to the three gendarmes there were at least two coastguards and two firemen on the cliff top, along with several others who appeared to be involved in some way – not to mention the helicopter pilot and the lifeguards crewing the inflatable. An impressive, indeed menacing, plalanx of officialdom.

The gendarmes clearly wanted us to accompany them and, judging by the expression on Carless's face, what they had to say was not going to be to our liking.

'They say that we have damaged a National Monument.'

This was confusing news indeed.

'What monument?' enquired Mike peering around in case some sort of Nelson's Column-type structure had somehow escaped his attention.

Further exchanges between Carless and the gendarmes followed.

'The *cliff* is the monument,' he explained.

We plodded on down the cliff top path in silence.

Our interpreter, Carless, spoke up again.

'He's saying something about a fine and footing the bill for the rescue efforts.'

This didn't sound too good. Back down at the car park in Etratat a huge bulbous coastguard inflatable sat on a trailer next to a fire engine (purpose uncertain!) and police car. The gendarmes clearly thought we might do a runner and signalled that one of us should get in the police car and the others follow in Paul's car. This was all being taken terribly seriously.

At the gendarmerie passports were inspected, details taken, bags emptied and charges read. It did indeed appear that they intended a prosecution along the lines of 'wilful damage to national monument'. Frankly, if there hadn't been five gendarmes, all looking so stern and officious, I would have had trouble not laughing. After all the French public had seemed most appreciative of our efforts, we hadn't really caused any damage and how were we supposed to know that it was a national monument in the first place?

Poor Carless inevitably suffered most of the questioning, which, as far as I could understand, was focusing on what our motives might have been. Clearly they felt there must be some ulterior motive behind four Englishmen deciding to come over from middle England for the weekend just to visit the cliffs at Etratat.

Explanations along the line that 'We thought it looked a fun, adventurous place to climb' seemed to be going down badly. They looked glum and unconvinced. Their searches of our gear had uncovered items like ice screws which they obviously found interesting, but nothing really incriminating like explosives, paperwork linking us to a National Monument Destruction Society or anything like that. They did though come across Carless's guidebook to rock climbing in Northern France. One gendarme thumbed blankly through the pages, whilst others seemed to concentrate on filling in as many forms as possible.

Something in the guide clearly caught the man's attention. He called his colleagues who left their form-filling duties to peer together at the crumpled pages. Glancing across we could see that they were looking at the Etratat section. One of them turned to Carless:

'Equipé?'

Carless repeated the word several times, seeking desperately to convey the impression that any sane person would note the guidebook use of the work 'Equipé' (meaning equipment in place) and assume that the climbs here were popular classics.

The gendarmes left us together whilst they discuss the situation privately in another room. Eventually they re-appeared behaving in a totally different manner. Glum, officious looks were replaced with smiles all round, handshakes and apologies. Suddenly we were free to pose for photographs outside the gendarmerie and head for home.

'What happened?' All faces were turned to Carless.

'We are innocent English climbers misled by an irresponsible French publication,' he explained. 'They are going to write to the publishers.'

'And the rescue fees and fine?'

'Not mentioned.'

We squeezed into the car to head for Calais and home.

Mike had been uncharacteristically subdued while the gendarmes were around. Now he was back in full enthusiasm mode.

'I really fancy coming back for that line just right of the Trunk.'

The response was muted.

I sat quietly contemplating the dubious honour of being the first climber to be apprehended by the authorities for climbing chalk cliffs on both sides of the channel.

15

Disappointment on Peak 43

*The Nick Estcourt Award – early skiing efforts – a bag of gear lost –
Nepalese rubbish requirements – Tangnag tourist developments –
Peak 43 reconnoitred – Mark Twight's training methods*

In Great Britain adventurous travel of all types seems to be greatly
respected. Mountaineers are fortunate in that there are several organisa-
tions that allocate grants to expeditions intent on tackling exploratory
unclimbed objectives in the less frequented parts of the world.

The two main ones are the Mount Everest Foundation and the
British Mountaineering Council. The former was set up to administrate
the profits made by the book and film of the successful 1953 Everest
expedition, the intention being that these should be ploughed back into
primarily British and New Zealand mountaineering (the latter because of
the involvement of Ed Hillary and George Lowe in the 1953 first ascent).
The BMC administers grants on behalf of the Sports Council. Of the
smaller grant-giving bodies, there is one in particular that I have become
involved with in recent years. The Nick Estcourt Award was set up after
Nick's death in an avalanche on the West Ridge of K2 in 1978. He was
one of Britain's leading mountaineers in the 1970s and played a major
role in the important Bonington expeditions of the 1970s to Annapurna
and the South-West Face of Everest.

Somehow I was invited to be on the award panel and so now, once
a year, I enjoy sharing a meal with such illustrious company as Chris
Bonington, Doug Scott and Paul (Tut) Braithwaite. As well as enjoying
Caroline Estcourt's excellent cooking, we swap stories and decide who will
be the annual recipient of the award.

To be invited was all very flattering. Chris and Doug in particular
were iconic figures in my formative years and it felt a real honour to be
in their company. My entrance to the group was eased by the fact that
I did once spend a week climbing with Chris on the Outer Hebridean
island of Mingulay. Chris is over twenty years older than I am, and I will
always remember how impressed I was with his boyish enthusiasm and
irrepressible determination to succeed. At one point we were high on an
unclimbed crack line when Chris, who was in the lead, clearly began to

find it hard. I could see his leg shaking and sensed a level of uncertainly that would prompt a much younger man to beat a hasty retreat.

'Watch me,' came from above.

I locked the belay plate, assuming a fall or at least a precarious retreat was inevitable.

'I'm going for it.'

I was seriously impressed and can only hope that I too can maintain the same sort of drive and determination as the years tick by.

But I digress. It was at one of the Nick Estcourt Award meetings that Paul Braithwaite reminded me of an occasion in the early 1980s when he, Doug Scott, Pat Littlejohn and I were the English representatives at an Austrian ice-climbing festival. Andy Nisbet and Rab Anderson were there too, representing Scotland. We Brits seemed to make up a disproportionately large percentage of the attendees and I could only assume that Austrians were impressed by the sort of ice climbing we get up to in Scotland.

But Tut did not have climbing in mind.

'Your skiing ability! Brilliant!' he recalled.

I knew exactly what he was remembering. We had poured out of the Rudolfshütte on the first morning and been invited to ski to a series of icefalls where the action would take place. Littlejohn, Scott and Braithwaite had no problem but Nisbet, Anderson and I had encountered certain difficulties. To the amazement of the continentals we had never been on skis before.

To begin with we were on a blue run and, with a bit of side-slipping here and there, I was just about managing. But then someone ahead indicated that we should leave the piste and head down some 500 metres of 50-degree slope dotted with rock outcrops. Soon I was lying down, skis flailing, with my embarrassment only partly relieved by the sight of Nisbet and Anderson already carrying their skis.

I was still trying to stand up when a clinically efficient Austrian guide approached.

'I think it is best that I carry your skis?' he suggested.

I then joined the others and together we traipsed down the slopes to join the waiting throng.

'We will now skin up the glacier from here' explained the efficient guide who had surged down the slope with my skis on his shoulder.

I had no idea exactly how I was supposed to use the two strips of synthetic 'skin' that were passed to me.

After a fumbling attempt to attach them using the obvious hooks, my new guide friend took pity on me and, amidst great hilarity, showed me how to peel off the covering layer of plastic and stick the skins to my skis.

Rather subdued, I finally arrived at the climbing area where the others were already attacking the dauntingly steep and glinting ice cliffs.

'Now we will see what the British *are* good at,' he announced with apparent sincerity.

Seconds later Andy Nisbet fell three metres catching his crampon points in the pocket of an Italian climber's posh Gore-Tex suite and ripping it wide open.

The Littlejohn/Scott/Braithwaite trio, who all ski well, had managed to distance themselves from this behaviour but now, twenty years later, I had prompted such recollections by letting slip, on the Mount Kennedy trip, I had again donned skis and tried to skin around on the glacier.

'I've improved,' I protested, amidst general hilarity.

Doug and Tut chuckled and were clearly not convinced.

'So where are you going to demonstrate these talents this year then?' enquired Tut .

'Er ... Peak 43,' I replied.

'Lucky there's not a lot of skiing there, youth' said Doug.

The enigmatically named Peak 43, sometimes called Kyasher, towers above the Hinku Valley in the Khumbu region of Nepal. Doug had studied it closely during his ascent of nearby Kusum Kanguru in 1979, whereas I had first become aware of it through photographs that my father took when he trekked beneath it *en route* to Mera Peak in the early 1990s. Interest was then heightened by Henry Todd giving me a painted image from a different angle. This was sufficiently inspiring for me to pin on the family noticeboard where it spent some years jostling with the sponsored spell and school football fixture paperwork. The final impetus for the trip came in 2000 when word from Nepal was that the government was beginning to relax the rules on permits.

Peak 43 was unclimbed and was officially not on the permitted list. Nevertheless by dint of judicious negotiations and payment of an extra $500 we were able to secure a permit to climb Kantega, a slightly lower peak to the north, by traversing over Peak 43. A bit of lateral thinking is sometimes necessary to overcome Nepalese bureaucratic challenges! We anticipated that we might feel so tired on summitting Peak 43 that we could well have to give up on Kantega and descend immediately. But we wouldn't be too disappointed if we failed on our permitted objective in this way.

My partner on this trip was to be Paul Ramsden, who had taken part in the Etratat goings on. A stout Yorkshireman from Pudsey, Paul had moved south to Nottingham to be with his fiancée Mary, who worked in the family wine business, whilst Paul pursued a varied career ranging from a health and safety consultant to being a key part of the safety team in the latest James Bond film. The combination seemed to be a good one in that it appeared to give him an interesting work life, plenty of time off and an unlimited supply of fine wine.

Paul was very much part of our evening climbing group where we got on well together, performing at much the same standard and regularly bruised our egos on the harsh gritstone edges of the Peak District. We also had similar inspirations farther afield, and managed a couple of good new winter lines on the less frequented cliffs on the Isle of Skye. On one of these, Whispering Wall on Sgurr a'Mhadaidh, I remember him leading a particularly desperate and poorly protected pitch with a minimum of fuss. Other reports carried the same thread of solid dependability, plenty of ability and an expressive personality linked with a dry sense of humour.

Sorting out people to accompany us was more of a problem. Pat Littlejohn and Steve Sustad were keen, but that idea quickly fell by the wayside when we realised the chances of us all being attracted to the same line were too high. In the end Paul and I decided to go as a two-man team – something I had never tried before.

Peak 43 was not an expedition destined to be crowned with success. The first portent of that was when my flight failed to land at Kathmandu and returned to Dhaka in Bangladesh. Paul was already in Kathmandu getting things going in the interests of time and motion.

At least I had the telephone number of our agent in Kathmandu and soon was straining to understand difficult Nepalese accented English on a terrible line. I tried to keep it simple.

'Hello. I'm stuck in Dhaka. Hopefully I'll be with you tomorrow.'

'Yes, there was a storm, but it has cleared now. You can come.'

This was not quite the expected response. I got the impression he thought I was piloting a private jet.

I spent the night in a Dhaka hotel with a chap called Graham who had just broken up with his wife and wanted to regale me with stories of how awful she was. Then there was Ahmed and Neil who had come for the girls. Back home in Britain they were married to two sisters who were under the impression they went on keep fit holidays. Which in a way they did. They used to take these in Kenya, but someone had tipped them off that Nepal was the place. They seemed appalled at the prospect of mountaineering and only vaguely aware that Nepal has any mountains in it. It is good to travel and meet people with varied views on life.

By the time I caught up with Paul at the Lukla airstrip I was getting a bit tired of the self-inflicted hassle caused solely by my obsession with saving one day of my holiday entitlement. It was with a great sense of relief that I was greeted by his broad grin as I stepped unsteadily from the small noisy helicopter.

But at this point there was another problem. My bag, because of its weight, had been put on another helicopter and now it was becoming increasingly clear that something had gone horribly wrong. As it contained everying from sleeping bag to climbing boots it was not the sort of baggage that we could afford to lose.

A flurry of telephone calls by Dawa, our Sherpa cook from Pangboche, left a smile on his face that surely meant the problem had been resolved.

'No problem Sahib ... your bag is in Namche Bazar.'

As Namche Bazar was a day's walk in the wrong direction, I couldn't quite equate this with no problem. It seemed quite a big problem to me. But Dawa was suddenly keen to move and it seemed churlish to object to his suggestion that we went ahead with the porters whilst he stayed behind to sort out the bag.

'I'll catch up with you this evening' were his last words as we straggled across the newly tarmacked runway, passing the half-built airport terminal building, and picked our way through the extensive rubbish dump that dominates the first section of the track to the Hinku Valley.

Paul stared around, aghast.

'We have had to pay a $2000 bond to help keep Nepal nice and clean.'

It was true; we had been forced to make this payment to the authorities in Kathmandu. The idea was that if we returned to an official check with a realistic amount of rubbish, our trip would be classed as 'clean' and the $2000 returned.

Here there was so much rubbish just lying around that it looked quite feasible for anyone who was so inclined to simply leave their own rubbish in the mountains and gather up 'the required amount' on the outskirts of Lukla.

With these dark thoughts curdling in our minds we plodded in silence, passing through the rubbish dump and then an extensive area of deforestation. It was impossible not to notice the ecological devastation which is the by-product of tourism in the Solu Khumbu Valley and the rapid expansion of Lukla.

By the time night fell it was cold and snowing heavily. There was no sign of Dawa or my bag. Paul looked bleakly down the track.

'There are loads of black North Face bags like yours around down there. How do you know if Dawa found yours? In fact how do you know if we will ever see him again?'

Efforts to share one sleeping bag were not a success. Several centimetres of snow fell during the night and I quickly formed a real appreciation of the value of good sleeping bags. Paul too seemed dissatisfied and I was accused of being a poor bedfellow.

By the third night there was still no sign of Dawa or the bag and we were tiring slightly of our sleeping arrangements. The nights were long and cold and the porters appeared to be getting an increasingly distorted view of our nocturnal preferences.

Dawa and the lost bag eventually arrived on our second day at Base Camp and five days after leaving Lukla. By this time we were also in position to examine Peak 43. From here, the upper part of our chosen objective looked a very attractive line, a magnificent buttress dropping directly from the summit. Our photographs, taken by my father from a different angle, showed that the easiest approach looked to be from the eastern side which was out of sight from here. But we could see the upper part clearly. It appeared to comprise challenging mixed ground leading to an overhanging headwall with a frighteningly spectacular line of ice cutting across very steep ground to finish. There wasn't very much ice visible on the lower part; in fact, it looked as if it could be powder snow resting on very steep slabs. But such negative thoughts could easily be pushed to one side.

The next morning we excitedly made our first reconnaissance. From a vantage point an hour beyond Base Camp we could see the whole of our intended approach route. This was what we had come to do. In the last six months we had put many hours of effort into organising this. We stared in silence for a long time. It did not make pleasant viewing. I was first to speak.

'Sorry, but I'm not going across there.'

Paul too looked less than enthusiastic. I knew that his previous Himalayan trips had foundered and he was hungry for some challenging climbing. This was unlikely to be it however. Just to get to the shoulder at half-height would involve traversing beneath a distressingly active icefall and then climbing for 500 metres or so beneath a series of obviously unstable séracs. As if we needed any further disincentive, it was clear that much of the falling debris ended up in a deep lake and so would we, if we were hit by any of it. The whole of the eastern end of the lake was choked with floating debris which had clearly fallen there in the recent past.

Our surroundings were certainly impressive, if not conducive to success. Paul was staring around. Eventually he spoke with a heavy hint of sarcasm, 'Pleasant spot to swim with a rucksack on.'

I chose not to respond, my eyes being drawn to the huge vertical wall dropping sheer into the far side of the lake. The lake was perhaps a mile long by half a mile wide and had what looked to be a tidemark about sixty metres above the water level. We later discovered that in September 1999 a huge icefall had broken off into the lake, the resulting wave breaching the moraine dam and causing a massive rock and water avalanche which resulted in many fatalities and considerable devastation in the valley below. The tidemark was very real. It was clear that we weren't going to get anywhere near our objective from this side.

Our Base Camp at Tangnag was filling up with trekking parties. When George, my father, had been here in 1989 his photos showed a single shepherds' hut and the odd grazing yak. Now the grazing area had been cut into terraces which could accommodate perhaps eighty tents and there were at least twenty buildings, several of which offered food and accommodation. One owner proudly explained that he was hoping to install computers in 2002 so that trekkers could use Internet services. Keen to escape Tangnag as soon as possible, we struggled up open slopes to check out a possible left-hand start to the buttress. We had looked briefly at this before and dismissed it as far less attractive than the right-hand option. But with our original plan thwarted, the series of overhanging walls and tenuous snow ramps on this side somehow looked more promising. At least there weren't any obvious objective dangers – well, not many.

After a brief exchange, we decided we would have to make a try using this left-hand approach. Although, as I later discovered, we both felt a bit uncomfortable with this decision, at the time we chose to ignore this and set about acclimatising on a nearby 5600-metre peak which we hoped would give us an excellent view of the upper section. Perhaps this was the point at which everything would change in our favour? It didn't. From our modest summit we stared in silence at the soaring upper section of the South-East Buttress of Peak 43. This was indeed a magnificent viewpoint. The problem was what we saw was not what we had hoped for at all. The whole of the lower section looked to be unstable snow resting on steep loose slabs. These slabs were broken occasionally by rock walls. Before leaving Britain we had taken it that these would be areas of mixed climbing. Now occasional light avalanches cascaded over them, making it all too clear that they were in fact overhanging bands which stretched right across the buttress. Above this section we could see a crenellated Peruvian-style snow ridge, leading up towards a nastily unstable-looking little sérac, followed by a couple of snow-plastered towers and the final impending headwall. A line, right of the crest, looked to give superb climbing through the headwall but this was the only point that we could actually see any ice on the entire route. Through the binoculars the rest appeared to be awful snow, similar to what we had just spent ages wading through thigh-deep, but at a far steeper angle. Almost as a final twist of the knife, the descent that we had planned along the ridge towards Kantega, and then circuitously down to Tangnag, looked completely out of the question. Other than abseiling down the line of ascent, the only realistic way back to Tangnag was to descend the icefall glacier that we had already run away from. The situation was pretty clear-cut. It didn't take long to decide. The risks just looked too high and the chances of a safe ascent too slim. A wimp-out was in order. Crestfallen and despondent, we retraced our steps back down to Base Camp, where a foot of snow promptly fell in the night.

Some trips just don't go according to plan. It had been a nice holiday, albeit without adventure other than of the imagined kind. We decided to put it down to experience and concentrate our efforts in finding a really good project for 2002.

I always worked on the basis that by climbing every now and then I maintain a general level of fitness that makes specific training unnecessary. But not getting under way on Peak 43 meant that I now had two years of blubber build up around the middle and a visit to the Alps with Paul in December 2001 left me very aware that I was not exactly in peak condition. There was no way I stood a hope in hell on any new project unless I could ratchet up the fitness level somehow. Ramsden clearly sensed this too.

'I've just the book for you,' he announced when we met for a beer the following week.

'Here it is, *Extreme Alpinism – climbing light, fast and high* by Mark Twight. Look at the training chapters. Just what you need. Twenty-nine pages of tips.'

We studied it together.

'Training and Endurance' stated the heading – 'strong muscles run out of gas when limited by a sub-par cardiovascular system.'

'There you go,' said Paul. 'You just need strong muscles and a top-notch cardiovascular system. Look – read on. You have got to get onto "a structured training and brain synchronisation programme and take regular tests to determine your VO^2 max and anaerobic threshold".'

This was all sounding a bit extreme. When Paul gets his teeth into something he really applies himself 100 per cent. I looked at him questioningly but he didn't appear to be joking. In fact, he had a stern look on his face and was pointing firmly to a section headed 'The Training Cycle'.

INDIA / GARHWAL 1999 48 - 49 Arwa Tower and Arwa Spire (both unclimbed) offered enticing challenges for myself, Steve Sustad, Crag Jones and Kenton Cool. At the head of the approach glacier we studied Arwa Tower's elegant but blank North-East Face *(above)* but on reaching a high col found that the North-West Face *(right)* offered a more feasible way of climbing the peak.

50 *(inset)* Steve Sustad on one of the initial hard rock pitches on Arwa Tower.

51-52 On days 2 and 3 the hard rock gave way to mixed work with tenuous strips of snow/ice frozen to the blank rock *(this page and right)* giving lines through the rock bands to the summit ridge where we placed a fourth camp.

ARWA TOWER (continued)

53 - 55 The way to the summit was barred by a prominent gendarme *(top right)* which we avoided by abseiling down the south side to gain easier-angled mixed ground *(centre right* – with Chaukhamba in the background)*.* After some difficult pitches an entertaining chimney *(right)* led to the exposed summit. Here we celebrated our success in climbing a difficult virgin peak and studied the nearby Arwa Spire (where Crag and Kenton were at work).

ALASKA / YUKON 2000 56 - 57 Andy Cave and I made an alpine-style ascent of Mt. Kennedy's 1800-metre North Buttress. We reached the peak in Kurt Gloyer's aircraft. Gloyer (on the right in the inset) died in 2001 while assisting another team.

FRANCE 1999 58 - 60 Etratat's fine sea stack and Elephant's Trunk gave us an entertaining weekend climbing jaunt.

SICHUAN, CHINA
2002

61 - 62 Siguniang (6250m) the highest peak in the Qionglai Range was the objective of Paul Ramsden and myself. We had heard that its North Face was good objective but were astonished when we first saw the face. It offered a line to gladden the heart of any serious ice climber – a long vertical basalt dyke stuffed with ice which at several points looked very steep. Bivouac sites appeared sparse and we were unable to see the foot of the dyke. On entering the icy cwm below the face *(inset)* it was obvious that the dyke could be reached from the left. This 'Great White Dyke' was a line worth striving for, a thought we mulled over in our first tenuous bivouac below the face, both of us preparing ourselves for the challenges to come.

63 - 64 The first hard pitch (80°) in the dyke *(cover photo)* was followed by thin ice over the basalt, *(top left)* before a steep finish *(above right)*. A long pitch of solid 60° ice gained a secure stance under the left rock wall where the afternoon storms forced us to stop.

65 Next day the more defined dyke *(lower left)* culminated with two very steep pitches that gave access to the sloping terrace on the left. 66 - 68 After poor bivouac on a tiny ledge *(top inset – above the ice slope)* we regained the dyke *(right)* which was now vertical requiring hanging belays *(lower inset)*.

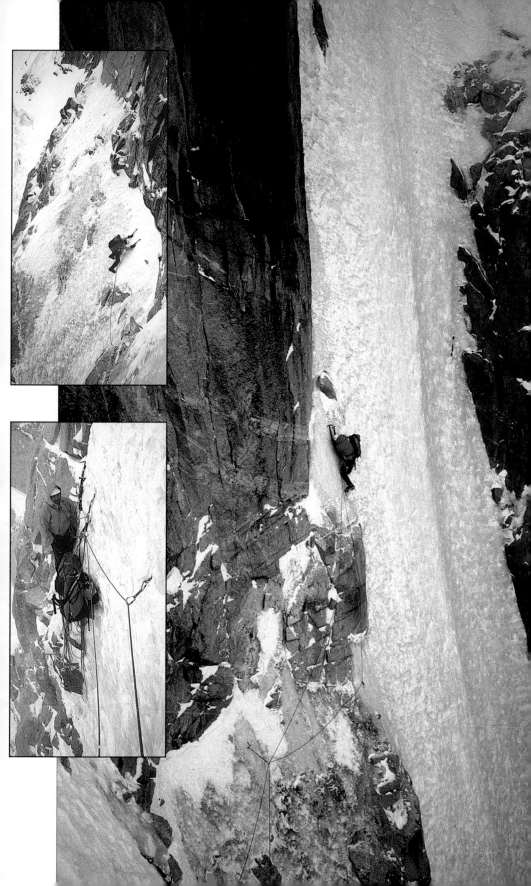

69 - 72 *(top left)* The dyke led to a steep finale when Paul *(right)* thrashed up overhanging ice in a torrent of spindrift. After another bivi *(above)* one final pitch and the 750-metre dyke merged into broken ground *(below)* with only the summit ice cliffs to deal with. 73 - 74 Summit joy *(right)* before the long North Ridge descent where Abalakov abseil anchors played a key role *(lower right)*.

'Here we are – a summary. "Foundation building – 4 to 6 weeks; Power training – 4 to 6 weeks; Cardiovascular power-endurance training and muscular-endurance training – 3 to 4 weeks; tapering and rest – 1 to 2 weeks; Peaking – 1 to 2 weeks." '

'Peaking?' I enquired. 'Does that mean you should train too – so we can peak together?'

Somehow this seemed to give the wrong impression but the intense Ramsden veneer was broken as he spluttered into his beer. Relief! He was joking after all. We looked again at the training schedules. I had never seen anything like this before. The suggestion was that after a vigorous programme of mental and physical preparation 'peaking' was probably only possible twice a year.

The suggestion was along the lines that our whole world should be focused on getting the timing just right. This didn't sit very comfortably in the usual Fowler regime of five days behind the desk and occasional climbing weekends. In fact, I have always tended to look on mountaineering as an excellent way to keep fit rather than something to get fit for.

But, joking aside, I knew that there was a grain of truth in Paul's ribbing. Passing years, family life and a sedentary job are not conducive to maintaining a high fitness level. Peak 43 had not got rid of the previous year's blubber layer and, much as I hate specifically training, I did, for the first time ever, feel the needed to do something.

And so, to my intense discomfort, I joined a Nottingham gym. For three months I did my utmost to break off from tax work and exercise my body two or three lunchtimes a week. It was awful. Feeling like a fish out of water I fiddled with controls on rowing machines, tried not to feel self-conscious on curious step-up devices and made an effort to give my all whilst running nowhere on a moving belt. I hated it, but it made me breathe heavily, so I was at least able to convince myself that it was doing some good.

I also tried some fell-running. That was much better, in that it was outdoors, but potentially demoralising in that it introduced me to numerous outrageously fit people. At one race in the Peak District I moved to say hello to the well known rock climber Ron Fawcett, but the race started before I got to him and by the time I finished he had gone home.

'It's OK. All you need is experience and willpower,' I explained to a sceptical-looking Ramsden.

Shortly before we were due to leave on our 2002 expedition to China Paul approached me looking much more positive and drew my attention to another section of Mark Twight's book.

'Look, it's OK after all. This bit is about those alpinists who have presumably peaked correctly in that they have influenced the way he approaches mountain climbing. Your name's here. Look. Talking about Spantik and Changabang.'

I could not help but smile. The only training I did for those routes was to eat copious quantities of low quality hot curry in an effort to condition myself to germ-laden food and build up some bivi blubber!

16

Modern China: the Approach to Siguniang

*Jack Tackle's project – meeting Mr Lion – bus ride to Rilong –
entering the Chang Ping Valley – Mr Ma's lodging house –
the Siguniang National Park*

Peak 43 had been a negative experience. Not only had we failed to even attempt our intended climb but our experiences of mass tourism in once peaceful and remote valleys were distinctly underwhelming. Also, despite the generous support of the British Mountaineering Council, the Mount Everest Foundation and Malden Mills, the Nepalese money-grabbing system had worked so efficiently that it had been an expensive as well as unproductive trip. Paul Ramsden and I vowed to forget the experience and move on as quickly as possible. But spending three weeks failing clearly hadn't dampened our enthusiasm for doing a route together and we moved into research mode.

One man, more than any other, was to help us in this respect. Tomatsu Nakamura from Japan is now in his late sixties and has been climbing and exploring for over forty years. He has become a devotee of Eastern Tibet and Sichuan and has made many visits to this part of the world. He wrote an article for the 2001 *American Alpine Journal* which included a spectacular photograph of a 6250-metre mountain called Siguniang. I had never heard of it before but it certainly looked impressive. Closer research revealed that the North Face was unclimbed and the mountain had only been climbed three times before, twice by Japanese sieged ascents and once by the globe-trotting American, Charlie Fowler (no relation), who made an epic solo ascent from the south in 1992. Amazingly it appeared not to have been attempted by the Chinese, whose mountaineering culture is very different from the west and focuses almost exclusively on 8000-metre peaks. Also the peak was apparently accessible after payment of a modest National Park entrance fee and no British climbers had been there before. All the necessary criteria were present to give us a big urge.

Mike Morrison was, as ever, easy to persuade and with Roger Gibbs, whom I had only met once before, on board, we were a team of four which I think both Paul and I found a better number than the two we had been on Peak 43. It wasn't that we didn't get on in Nepal but two is inevitably a limiting number and having two more able climbers in the vicinity would certainly increase security if anything should go wrong.

Mountaineers tend to be naturally very helpful people. With Siguniang decided upon a few e-mails soon resulted in a wave of interesting material. Charlie Fowler supplied heaps of background information and useful tips. Craig Luebbens, the well-known American icefall climber, had visited the winter icefalls of the area a couple of times and it was he who introduced us to the intriguingly named Mr Lion who had acted as his interpreter. It also transpired that Mr Lion was friendly with a Mr Ma who offered cheap accommodation in the road-head village of Rilong. It seemed that they both understood the strange western urge to go climbing and Mr Ma was very familiar with the whole area.

Gradually the outline of our trip was starting to come together, although it was thanks to the American mountaineer Jack Tackle that we were really able to focus our plans. Up until Jack's input we knew that the north side of the mountain was unclimbed and we had managed to track down some photographs in a Japanese magazine which showed a bare granite wall with an array of drooling ice streaks. Unfortunately, it was not clear from the photo whether the streaks stretched all the way to the bottom of the face. And as it was taken in 1992, there was no telling what impact global warming might have had over the intervening ten years. I couldn't help but think back to my experience with Simon Yates on Siula Chico in Peru in 1998. There the snow and ice had receded so much over thirteen years that the face had changed completely and become very dangerous.

Jack Tackle must be almost as old as I am. He visited Siguniang back in 1981 as his first mountaineering trip outside the USA. At that time the mountain was unclimbed and an American team of luminaries, including Jim Donini and Kim Schmitz, chose to try a line on the right side of the North Face. They ground to a halt at about half-height but not before Jack had noticed something exciting a bit farther left.

I first met Jack at the Banff Mountain Film Festival in Canada in 2000 after our Mount Kennedy climb earlier that year. He was particularly known for his many fine first ascents in Alaska. We had of course considered attempting the Tackle/Roberts line on Kennedy but decided against it because of the intensity of the spindrift avalanches. It wasn't until I met him at Banff that I realised that we obviously share similar urges in the mountaineering field. Not only had he been to Siguniang but he had also been on the South Buttress of Taulliraju in Peru, the line I climbed with Chris Watts back in 1982, just one year after Jack was on Siguniang.

We seemed to get on well and loosely arranged to think about climbing together on a 'project' that he had in mind for 2002. He wouldn't say what this project was but I felt pretty confident that I would think it worthwhile.

But time passed, Jack was struck down by an incapacitating virus, and after the dismal failure of Peak 43, Paul and I were keen to try something else together. So I ended up contacting Jack to quiz him about the face of Siguniang that he had been on twenty-one years earlier. The response was interesting:

'My project. How do you know about it? What have I said?'

Presumably he felt that, after one too many beers at Banff, he had mistakenly spilled the beans. But no, it was a genuine, if amazing, coincidence. Out of all the unclimbed faces in the world we had focused on the same one! But he sounded too excited. What did he know that we didn't?

That had to wait until an Alpine Club lecture day in Sheffield in March 2002, just a month before we were due to leave.

Jack was speaking about his Alaskan routes but had kindly brought over some photos of the north side of Siguniang. They were much more detailed than anything we had seen before and showed a series of smooth, ice-streaked granite walls cleft by a huge vertical fault line which was choked with something white. Whether or not this was ice or powder snow would make a big difference. Jack hadn't been close enough to know but the look in his eyes gave away what he thought. And it was one of the most eye-catching lines I had ever seen in the big mountains – a sort of mega version of the Dru Couloir at Chamonix squeezed between towering Yosemite-style shields of granite. A sérac barrier crowning the face looked as if it could cause a few problems but what can one do but err on the optimistic side? Perhaps the intervening twenty-one years would have seen the ice cliffs melt back a bit but preserved nice soft white ice in the fault line?

Chengdu airport, in Sichuan, was a surprise. Polished marble floors and a thoroughly modern feel made it much more akin to plush western airports than we had expected. But our immediate challenge was to find Mr Lion, our interpreter. We had telephoned ahead from Beijing and arranged to meet him at the airport, but we had not thought to get a description. Hopefully it would be difficult for him to miss four travel-weary, heavily laden western climbers amongst a plane full of soberly dressed Chinese people.

We need not have feared. Within the crowd was a young man of twenty or so, possibly younger. He sported a fashionable North Face fleece, bright yellow reflective sunglasses and a back-to-front Nike base-ball cap. His mannerisms and accent were strongly American, although he had never actually been outside China. Everything had been learned from the Internet and American acquaintances.

'Howdy, Mick. Welcome to Chengdu,' he drawled.

I knew that he had been running an outdoor gear business in Chengdu and somehow was expecting a much older person. But Mr Lion was young, active and streetwise. He was in near non-stop conversation on his £400 top-of-the-range mobile phone and I must admit my first impression was of a successful young drug dealer rather than the level-headed, reliable interpreter we were after. This initial impression was reinforced by a sign over his recently closed retail premises which read 'Welcome to the home of the English junkies' and his mention in passing that he had considered taking a part share in a huge partially completed office block in central Chengdu.

But initial impressions can be very wrong. Mr Lion turned out to be witty, jovial, easy to get on with and generally invaluable to a climbing team whose knowledge of Chinese was non-existent and Chinese culture scarcely less so. We never actually got to know his name beyond Lion but it didn't seem to matter really.

Potentially difficult purchases, such as gas cylinders, were made with disarming ease, his gorgeous girlfriend assisted with otherwise challenging supermarket purchases and to top it all he insisted on treating us to a meal. This was nothing like any meal I have ever had in a Chinese restaurant in Britain. It consisted of numerous small plates overflowing with largely unidentifiable, but apparently edible, objects. One dish looked to be full of something like human eyeballs. Like so many things in China, we never did get to the bottom of what these were but they were curiously textured and burst memorably when chewed.

It is six hours by bus from Chengdu to the village of Rilong. None of us was actually sick but it was a close thing. Chengdu is near to the edge of huge depression known as the Sichuan basin. The road soon left the densely populated areas of the plain and rose up through narrow, steep-sided, lushly vegetated valleys. Here is the natural habitat of the Giant Panda and the Wolong Panda Reserve where efforts are being made to increase the numbers of this endangered animal. It seemed to us that the density of the vegetation and steepness of the valley sides made it extremely difficult for humans to venture away from the road and disrupt the Pandas in their natural habitat. But for whatever reason numbers have dwindled and the Panda Reserve presumably generates good income from tourists keen to ogle them. Paul caught a glimpse of a Panda's backside in a cage as we zoomed past en route to Rilong.

Low down in the valley the flatter areas were occupied by attractive smallholdings which were immaculately maintained with regular neat rows of vegetables and plenty of people tending them. But the 155-mile approach road from Chengdu to Rilong rises relentlessly to the Balang Pass at an altitude of 4467 metres. Vegetation thinned and soon we were well above the tree line with a sprinkling of snow on the ground. The pass is a magnificent viewpoint and I could not help but think that in somewhere like Switzerland there would be a restaurant, chairlift and a full range of gaudy souvenirs on offer. Here though there was one small scruffy building, a toilet, at which our bus driver for some reason decided not to stop. Hence our first photos of the Siguniang range, which opened before us with alarming suddenness, were blurred by the jolting of the bus. But what a view it was. First a few spiky peaks were visible, then bigger, more spectacular ones, one of which I recognised as the perfectly symmetrical Celestial Peak, first climbed by the Americans in 1983. At this point things were getting sufficiently spectacular for me to nudge Paul, who was snoozing gently. He awoke just in time to see an outrageously spectacular snow-covered peak creep into view – Siguniang. A full 500 metres higher than anything else in the vicinity, its impact was immediate and startling. We *had* to climb it!

Endless hairpin bends took us down to the settlement of Rilong where we were greeted by extensive building works and a huge blue motorway style sign saying 'Siguniang', complete with a large arrow pointing up the Chang Ping Valley towards the mountain. An explanation is required but at least there was no doubt that we had come to the right place!

Up until about 1999 it was a challenging journey on unmetalled roads to reach this point but in China government-backed projects can change things remarkably quickly. In the late 1990s the Siguniang area was designated an AAAA-rated tourist attraction. Whether they liked it or not, Chinese holidaymakers were to be directed here. Prisoners were brought in to concrete the road and projections drawn up advising startled locals to expect one million visitors a year by 2005. Though China is a far less restricted society than it used to be, it is still very much the norm for employees to allow their work union (effectively the Communist Party) to organise their holidays for them. We were told that it is possible for individuals to organise their own holidays but the cost is prohibitive and so the vast majority go with the company. The result is that those behind the development of Rilong (i.e. the Communist Party) know that their projections will be achieved and so feel no need to hold back from building the entire infrastructure before the first tourist arrives. The end result is like taking a beautiful unspoilt Lake District valley, removing all planning restrictions and then within the space of a year or two, clearing the locals off the prime sites and building a selection of huge concrete hotels. The scheme was in full flow with several enormous neon light-flashing hotels (complete with life-sized decorative stone lions) nearing completion. There were also plans for a road up the Chang Ping Valley towards Siguniang and a chairlift up a nearby mountain. All this where just five years ago there was nothing but a small village.

Bearing in mind that Rilong was very much a devout Buddhist village prior to the Chinese takeover in 1950 and that its monastery was gutted in Chairman Mao's Cultural Revolution in the 1970s, it is perhaps unsurprising that there is much bad feeling between the indigenous locals and the Chinese. In fact we were told that just before we arrived the Chinese officials got so sick of their posh cars being vandalised that they replaced them with more basic vehicles.

Squeezed in between the towering hotels and busy building sites is the delightfully simple and friendly accommodation offered by Mr Ma and his family. We had no hesitation in choosing this but could not resist the temptation to have a closer look at some of the more glitzy offerings. The completed hotels that we looked in were standard, smart, quality establishments but the tourist offerings on display were something new to my experience. Under glass-topped display cabinets were rows of what initially looked like polished tortoise shells. It was only on close inspection that we realised that they were in fact human skull tops, sliced off just above the eye sockets and then decorated round the base with coloured gems. If these didn't appeal another cabinet displayed flutes made out of human leg bones. Somehow I didn't think that my children or UK customs officials would appreciate such gifts, even though I had a general family directive to return with presents of local interest.

Mr Ma not only ran an excellent lodging house, he also owned several horses that he was prepared to rent to us at about half the price that Chinese tourists had to pay. His premises were right opposite the entrance of the National Park and the track leading up the Chang Ping Valley towards Siguniang. From his balcony we could see an imposing entrance checkpoint, complete with gate across the road and roof observation platform. It appeared that access to the Siguniang National Park was very strictly controlled and we could only hope that we passed all the entrance criteria.

No one we had come across since leaving Chengdu spoke a word of English and without Mr Lion's communication help we would have found life very difficult. Even sign language just didn't seem to work; it seemed that the underlying cultural differences were such that only the most straightforward and obvious signals were understood.

'You have to pay him 40 RMB,' drawled Lion, pointing towards the green-suited officer operating the entrance gate.

I duly obliged and our party of five horses, Lion, Mr Ma and about five hangers on passed through into the Park.

'Forty RMB? That's less than £4.' Paul sounded concerned rather than overjoyed at such a low entrance fee. China is cheap compared to Britain but, even so, less than £4 for four of us to spend over two weeks in the

Park did seem remarkably good value. I decided to quiz Lion about this. His explanation was initially baffling.

'Ah yes, Mr Ma does not like you to pay more money than you have to. He has only paid an entry fee for one day.' Lion was looking uncomfortable now. 'I think it might cause problems later. They might come and look for us.'

This was all getting very strange and like so many things in China the whole picture didn't add up too well. If Lion had been concerned why hadn't he intervened at the gate? And surely the intimidating security officials didn't really think that four of us and five heavily laden horses were only going in for one day? And what were they going to make of it when the horses returned unladen? It all seemed very odd but there was little we could do about it now and anyway our eyes were soon drawn to the spectacular sight of Siguniang which was beginning to totally dominate the skyline.

After a mile or so the motorable road ended at the charred remains of the Buddhist monastery which we were told the monks had been forced to burn down in the early 1970s. Beyond this we transferred on to an amazing duckboard track through the forest. It soon became clear that the Chinese authorities like duckboards; little side spurs shot off in various directions leading to viewing platforms and picnic areas. After an hour or so the duckboards ended and a shiny sign indicated that we had arrived at 'Withered Trees Beach', a shingly riverside beach with, unsurprisingly, some rather withered trees. This point seemed to mark the end of the road for the average Chinese tourist so, to add interest, a couple of camels had been brought in. Their exact significance was mystifying but they were very friendly and one put its tongue in my ear as I posed for 'look at me on holiday' shots.

Difficult as it was to leave such attractions behind, we splashed bravely onwards up muddy tracks through the dense forest without duckboards. Dirty boots became inevitable and clearly we had passed the furthest point reached by all but the most adventurous tourists.

Of great concern to Lion was the fact that we also seemed to be close to the farthest point that he could get a usable signal on his mobile telephone. I have no idea why, or how he funded the cost, but the amount of time he spent on one of his two mobile telephones was remarkable. Mobiles are great but I do have reservations about their use in mountain wilderness areas. I must admit to enjoying the sense of freedom of being out of contact with the wider world and stories of climbers blocking rescue lines with unnecessary calls are frequently heard. But mobile telephones in the mountains can lead to some hilarious and memorable calls. One in particular I remember extremely well. Nicki had arranged a

New Year dinner at our place and just as everyone had got round the table to eat the telephone rang with a rather subdued sounding Simon Fenwick on the line. Simon is an Essex character with a hard East End wide-boy-type image, so it caused immense hilarity as it became clear that he was lost halfway up Buachaille Etive Mor in Glen Coe.

'Have you got the latest guidebook?' he asked.'My old one's not very clear.'

And so a memorable exchange took place with me, sitting at a food and wine laden table with guidebook in one hand, offering advice on how Simon, stuck in the dark in a Scottish blizzard, might overcome a steep snow-plastered wall about 750 metres up the Buachaille. Unfortunately for Simon the combination of darkness and being clagged in meant that my efforts to read out helpful chunks of the guidebook were of little use – other than to provide a focal point of merriment for those round the table whose unhelpful interruptions increased in direct proportion to the amount of alcohol consumed.

'It's wild up here and you're not being very helpful,' announced Simon, to roars of laughter.

Finally the call ended with a whole host of unrepeatable suggestions about what he should do next.

At about 3am Simon rang again.

'Had to abseil off but we're down now. Didn't want you to have a sleepless night worrying about us.'

He was left in no doubt that our party had not been caused too much stress by his predicament!

But I digress. Lion presumably did not want to use his telephone for such purposes. What he did want to use it for was not at all clear. We quizzed him a lot about this and why he had two mobiles with him at all times but, as with so many things in China, a comprehensible answer was not forthcoming. Plenty of other uncertainties fell into this category. At one point on the walk in Mr Ma rummaged around in a hole under some tree roots and withdrew a rotting piece of ornate yellow silk which he seemed to be saying dated back to the Chang dynasty. Presumably it had been rescued from the monastery but quite why this apparently priceless garment was kept stuffed into a dank hole was never clear to me. Lion too professed himself suitably mystified on this one too.

After several hours of squelching through mud, squeezing between trees and admiring spectacular unclimbed and unnamed peaks on the far side of the valley, the track emerged suddenly into flat open pastures where a collection of yaks showed absolutely no interest whatsoever in us. Paul gesticulated wildly up to our right. Our intended objective, the North Face of Siguniang, could be glimpsed for the first time. And, despite the clouds, it could be seen to be disturbingly steep.

'Looks exciting,' was the general thrust of his exclamations.

The horses left promptly for Rilong and suddenly we had to fend for ourselves. First task was to ferry loads up the debris of an enormous avalanche to an idyllic Base Camp at just under 4000 metres. Then came the least popular part of any high-altitude trip, acclimatising. True to form the weather was indifferent but, after four days lying down at up to 5100 metres listening to snow drum against the tent, we pronounced ourselves ready for action.

Back at Base Camp though Lion was not looking his normal laid back self.

'The men from the Company. They've been,' he announced miserably.

He made it sound as if some sort of Mafia-style gang had ransacked the place but a quick glance around showed the tents were still standing and everything seemed in order. Also, bearing in mind the silliness at the entrance gate, a visit from the Park personnel was not exactly unexpected. It transpired that a fee had been calculated based on a floor space of two square metres per tent and the total charge would be in the region of 720 RMB, about £60. After debating the pros and cons we left Lion 750 RMB and settled down to focus on what we had come to do.

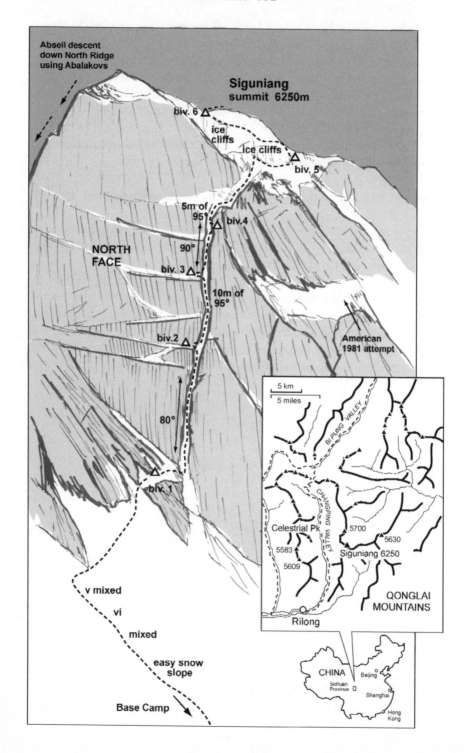

Abseil descent
down North Ridge
using Abalakovs

Siguniang
summit 6250m

biv. 6

ice
cliffs

ice cliffs

biv. 5

5m of
95°

biv.4

90°

**NORTH
FACE**

biv. 3

10m of
95°

biv.2

American
1981 attempt

80°

biv. 1

v mixed

vi

mixed

easy snow
slope

Base Camp

5 km

5 miles

BI PUNG VALLEY

CHANGPING VALLEY

Celestrial Pk

5700

5630

5583

Siguniang 6250

5609

**QONGLAI
MOUNTAINS**

Rilong

CHINA

Sichuan
Province

Beijing

Shanghai

Hong
Kong

17

Siguniang's Great White Dyke

Careful inspection – a sequence of poor bivouacs – Ramsden's stoicism –
steep ice climbing at altitude – breathtaking summit views – a descent on Abalakovs –
Golden Pitons and Piolets D'Or – The Kiss of the Destivelle.

Breaks in the cloud on our acclimatisation jaunts had provided us
with superb views of Siguniang's North Face. Paul and I had been a bit
concerned that conditions might have changed since Jack Tackle took his
photos back in 1981 but we need not have feared – the all important white
streak was intact and looked to provide a suitably tantalising line. We
spent endless hours staring at it through Paul's binoculars.

Ice or powder snow? It was still impossible to tell but it would make
a big difference. In at least one place the ground was overhanging. Overhanging ice would require big arms (over to Paul!) whereas overhanging
powder snow would be interesting. We would have to wait and see.

Paul is a good culinary-type chap, who always does the cooking at
home. As such, he likes his food, so it was only natural for him to take
the lead in sorting out what to take with us. After half an hour or so I
was called to comment on the end product which Paul had proudly laid
out for inspection.

'What do you think?'

I am usually the one arguing to cut down and live on one's reserves
but this time such thoughts were clearly unnecessary. With a cereal bar
for breakfast, two boiled sweets each per day and a small packet of 3
minute noodles for the evening we were not exactly going to get fat.

'It's very light,' Paul enthused.

It struck me that our bodies might well be too by the time we'd
finished. Lucky I could afford to use up some reserves.

Mike was suffering from a recurring stomach bug so he and Roger
decided to explore the Upper Changping Valley, whilst Paul and I strained
awkwardly up the small glacier beneath the face. However much you cut
down, sacks somehow never feel light when starting out. Jack Tackle had
recalled that the approach looked dead easy but things seemed to have
changed somewhat.

'Perhaps he is just very good,' I gibbered, whilst teetering insecurely up smooth rock slabs where Jack had assured us we would find easy snow slopes.

The slabs gave way to an ice slope and suddenly it was time to find somewhere to spend the night. Comfortable options were not obvious, in fact they seemed non-existent. Paul looked forlornly at the steepness surrounding us. Nothing was less than 50 degrees.

'Well? This is your department.'

Reputations are funny things. We had done most of our climbing together in the English Peak District and, despite our efforts on Peak 43, had never actually climbed a multi-day route together. Paul had nevertheless formed the view that I was an expert at miraculously unearthing luxury ledges in inhospitable terrain. In fact I am not. I just have a lot of experience of spending the night in uncomfortable positions.

There was nothing for it but to snuggle up to the base of a rock buttress and start cutting a ledge of some sort. Paul looked shocked at my inability to come up with a better solution. The end result was a snaking four metres long, thirty centimetres wide ledge that we tried our best to lie on nose to tail.

'This is a crap bivi,' the call-a-spade-a-spade Yorkshireman noted.

However, by dint of pushing balled socks into the bivi bag fabric and larks-footing them into ice screws, we did manage to secure ourselves in a vaguely comfortable manner. But the endless tide of spindrift somehow found its way into my sleeping bag and by morning uncomfortable balls of ice had begun to form within the insulation. But bivouacs can be a lot worse and we were at last under way.

The first ice dyke pitch was mine. After an hour or so I realised that Paul was shouting up to me.

'What do you think? It looks even steeper above.'

He was obviously not impressed with my efforts. To be honest, neither was I. Initially it had seemed as if the ice would be soft and twangy – ideal for secure placements. Gradually though it thinned and became brittle. Large plates broke away and the angle increased. Projecting bits of rock, which looked potentially helpful from below, turned out to be rotten basalt which did not take protection well. Suddenly my rucksack seemed ludicrously heavy. Placing a dodgy ice screw I extricated myself from the straps, left it for Paul to sort out later, and applied myself to the problem. Paul's comments were unsurprising. I was very slow – and I knew it.

'Ice might be better higher up.'

I did my best to sound positive whilst feeling anything but. The last section to the belay was memorable. The thick-looking ice in the centre was too sugary to take screws and that at the edge was too thin. Nervously

I edged up rightwards very aware of my insecure position and the potential for a big fall as my last decent screw was at least ten metres below. I needed a runner. The ice appeared a trifle thicker up to the right so hanging on the axe with my left hand and leaving the right axe placed as high as possible I reached up to place the screw. It bottomed halfway in but it had to do so placing a wire runner over it I clipped in the rope. With this slight extra reassurance I moved up onto the edge of the dyke where, to my great relief, a hidden block provided an excellent belay.

From there things looked slightly better. For a start I wasn't breathing so heavily and could assess the situation more rationally. Secondly, it did seem that the next section, although at least as steep, might actually have better ice that might well take decent screws.

First though, Paul had to get himself and two sacks up to the stance. This required a phenomenal effort and led to such unusually heavy breathing that it was decided I should lead on whilst he recovered. Starting fresh with no sack made a big difference. It almost felt unethical. But by late afternoon (amazing where the time goes when you're enjoying yourself) the first really steep section was behind us and it was time to start thinking about where to spend the night.

From a distance it had looked as if there should be reasonable ledges at convenient intervals on the left side. Close up, things didn't look so encouraging. All ledge lines on the left sloped outwards at about 50 degrees and had a thin covering of powder snow. It was difficult enough to find a place to stand comfortably let alone spend the night. The smooth monolithic granite on the right offered even less in the way of luxurious opportunities.

Eventually I found a vertical corner where I was able to place a good nut and stand in balance. By now a storm had developed, spindrift obscured everything and Paul was obliged to take my word about the belay being good. We stood there for a few minutes, waiting for a break in the weather. I was tired and cold and slumped regularly onto the nut.

'Tent over the head?'

It took me a moment to register what Paul was suggesting. I had been optimistically waiting for a lull that would enable us to get into the tent and use it as a double bivouac sack. I had never before used it as a large bag over the head, although I had read about Joe Tasker and Dick Renshaw spending a night like this on the North Face of the Dent Blanche back in the 1970s. It all sounded very unpleasant and I was not keen to emulate their experiences. But it had to be admitted that the weather was particularly grim and any attempt to get into the tent fabric from the top was inevitably destined to end with the tent and everything else full of spindrift.

'Could be as unpleasant as your Taweche bivouac.'

It was nice of Ramsden to remind me of the most uncomfortable night of my life when Littlejohn and I had spent our night in the ice tube. Spindrift had poured in all night, we never managed to get into our sleeping bags and the 'one on top of the other' position was not exactly very comfortable. Surely this couldn't be that bad? Or perhaps it could.

I stood there miserably, making negative noises about the difficulties of belaying securely with a bag over one's head. But I knew that I was tired and cooling down rapidly. We had to do something quickly and, in the conditions, I was bleakly aware that I couldn't offer a better suggestion.

Wrapping a large nut in the tent fabric, Paul larks-footed it into our solitary belay and clipped himself into the sling on the inside of the tent.

'Different world in here,' he announced cheerfully.

I looked dubiously through the gloom at the tent fabric wondering why I apparently enjoy mountaineering so much. The tent was well used and I feared that any serious strain on the already experienced fabric could have unfortunate results.

'Are you getting in or what?' came from somewhere deep within.

It was dark outside now and the urgency in Paul's voice brought home to me the fact that I was moving lethargically. It was time to double check the safety of the arrangement and make a move.

He was right. It *was* a different world inside. A world where we hung like a bunch of bananas from a single sling whilst the fabric flapped against our faces and the entrance zips flailed disconcerting around our ankles. Extreme care was required, as anything we dropped would disappear straight out the bottom of the tent. As if to prove the point, my sleeping mat had miraculously disappeared by the time I came to search for it.

'Crap bivouac this,' was the Yorkshire adjudication.

Conversation drifted as we intermittently dozed. We had been unable to get our sleeping bags out and had opted for hanging/standing in our climbing clothes, supplemented by down jackets. Nevertheless, despite –20°C outside, we did not feel worryingly cold. What I mean of course is that it was bloody freezing but, remarkably, frostbite was not a major concern. Good stuff this modern gear.

So much in alpine-style mountaineering is down to the mental side of things. It is easy to get demoralised when the weather is nasty and retreat comes easily to those whose will to continue is not strong. In comfortable surroundings my view is clear-cut – it's obvious, isn't it? – you just carry on up unless there are good reasons to go down. I recalled Doug Scott's description of a bivouac on Denali when he hinted at the possibility of descent to Dougal Haston who said, 'Are you frostbitten yet?' Scott said he wasn't and as such concluded, as Haston already had, that there was no reason not to carry on.

In the thick of foul conditions it is sometimes more difficult to think so clearly. These days, with better clothing and equipment, the range of options is greater. Frankly, it is unrealistic to expect to climb non-stop for a week or so and not suffer any bad weather at all. The key to success is balancing the pros and cons of staying put (bad news unless the bivi is comfortable and you have plenty of food), pushing on (could be rash if there's nothing welcoming to aim for) and retreating (may be sensible but certainly won't get you up).

Here our situation was unpleasant and uncomfortable but our gear was (relatively) dry, we were safe and we had plenty of food and gas. There was no real reason to go down. Nevertheless the night was excruciatingly uncomfortable, the ground ahead looked distinctly uncompromising and the regular roaring sound of spindrift avalanches was a constant reminder that our nice ice line was not a good place to be in bad weather. I was desperate for a drink but it was impossible to light the stove and melt snow in the confines of the flapping fabric. How was Paul feeling I wondered? This was our first really nasty bivouac together. I thought back to the tone of his comments as I had dithered on the first ice streak pitch. Had he underestimated the difficulty of the pitch? Was my slowness such that he was close to suggesting retreat? Most importantly, what did he think now we had passed the thin section and were faced with steeper, albeit thicker, ice?

At some point I became aware that it was getting light outside and Paul was lifting the zip section to peer out the bottom. The steady swish of spindrift on fabric gave me a good idea of what it was like. He made no comment. I lifted my side and we peered around together. It was a grey, bleak and uninspiring day with very little in the way of visibility. Perhaps there was slightly less spindrift than the night before but there wasn't much else to comment positively about. Paul was the first to speak. It was exactly the sort of moment when the morale of the party hangs in the balance.

'How about we move up a few pitches and see how it goes? We might at least find a better bivi site.'

Those few words made such a difference. Paul was, of course, completely right. Somehow I found him making positive noises and me agreeing much more of a boost than the other way round. There is something wonderfully refreshing about a realisation that two minds are thinking the same. Suddenly the day seemed much brighter. Onwards and upwards it was. Actually it wasn't upwards because the day had to start with a fifty-metre diagonal abseil to get back on line. This was rather time-consuming and it was two hours after we had packed the tent away before we were back on the ice streak and level with our bivouac spot.

The weather in this part of the world is nothing if not varied. After a couple of hours of 'full' conditions the sky brightened, the sun came out (everywhere except in the deep frozen confines of our chosen line!) and thoughts of simply moving up to a better bivi spot were abandoned. We would make as much progress as we could.

The parting clouds revealed spectacular scenery. We were climbing this mega version of the Dru Couloir – a great ice dyke with Yosemite-style granite walls on either side. Above us the ice steepened to vertical, capped by an apparently overhanging mixed section. It all looked very impressive but also disturbing. And, although we didn't need one now, I noted a total absence of good bivouac sites.

Back down in Base Camp it had seemed a good idea to cut down the weight and bring only six ice screws. Now, faced with using two at each belay, that only left two for each sixty-metre pitch. Somehow that didn't seem very many – but Paul was up to the challenge.

'Abalakovs,' he announced.

I was aware of the test reports showing how strong Abalakov threads can be but somewhat to my embarrassment I had never actually used one. This despite promises to myself after descending Taweche entirely by using a very memorable retrievable ice screw technique. Vitali Abalakov was a well known Russian climber who died when his bathroom water heater exploded, but before that had come up with the bright idea of using two ice screw holes (angled inwards by 45 degrees to eventually join up) to make his eponymous thread. They are used mainly for abseil anchors but Paul's plan was to use them as runners to supplement our meagre collection of ice screws. And he was a star at it. I hung back on the belays and marvelled as he used three or four Abalakovs for protection as he progressed steadily up the near vertical ice which choked this section of the fault line. At the top of this section of the dyke there was an overhanging band of basalt, visible from afar.

When I joined Paul it was clear that this would be a crucial section. There looked to be slightly more ice in the right bounding corner and I headed up in that direction, pausing before the difficulties to clip into a screw, recover my breathing and take a picture of Paul on his impressive hanging belay on two ice screws. Above the ice became thin, and rotten basalt protruded liberally. Further good protection looked unlikely. I edged my way upwards, trying to conserve energy, distributing my weight as evenly as possible so as to avoid weighting individual points of contact (crampons and axes) more than necessary. Although slightly overhanging for about five metres there looked to be ice placements nearly all the way. As soon as I was committed though I found that the ice was unusually hard, transparent and only a centimetre or two thick. The potential for a memorable fall increased. Rests were not possible. This was not the place to risk clipping into dodgy placements. Tying off the odd piece of projecting rock as quickly as I could, I fought hard to get the balance right between going for it and worrying so much about protection that I would run out of energy. By the time I could look over the top of the pitch the balance between control and panic was getting fine. With a final burst of adrenaline I flopped out onto hard 60-degree ice, placed a screw and hung gasping before recovering sufficiently to assess my new surroundings. Above the seemingly never ending steep ice continued, whilst up and out to my left was an icy horizontal line that looked as if it might offer a bivouac possibility.

'Searching' for a bivi site is, of course, a relative term. Altitude and difficult ground resulted in such slow progress that we could only sensibly 'search' the immediate area we happened to be in when dusk was upon us. And there was little on offer. Paul led a pitch out leftwards to a slight prow but there was little of note there and another night of sitting/hanging passed uneventfully but wearingly.

'That was a crap bivi Fowler. More steep ice today!'

It was getting to the stage where it would somehow have felt wrong if the day had not started with this blunt pronouncement – in a way it was curiously reassuring.

It was morning again and Paul's summary was indeed correct. There was yet more steep ice ahead. Usually I like ice climbing but the repetitive and exhausting movements at this altitude were beginning to take their toll. It was all becoming a bit like hard work. Paul later summarised it:

> We settled into a routine of climbing in spurts until lack of oxygen and cramping forearms brought us to a panting halt. The exposure became truly head-spinning ... Halfway up one pitch I became concerned that my lungs might burst from my desperate effort to suck in more oxygen. Steep climbing at altitude really hurts.[1]

We worked steadily upwards via pitches of extremely steep but solid ice, reaching the steepest pitch of the day in late afternoon. The weather, which had been threatening for some time, turned to snow and Paul was forced to thrash purposefully upwards through a shielding curtain of heavy spindrift. One advantage was that the couloir was so steep that the main force of the spindrift was falling behind him – helpful in a way but also serving to emphasise the size of the snow cornice that crowned the

[1] 'The North Face of Siguniang', *Alpine Journal* 2003, pp 28-31

pitch. I huddled inside my Gore-Tex jacket whilst the occasional exertion-packed grunt filtered down from above. Suddenly the rope went so tight I sensed he might be off. The visibility was such that I couldn't see if he was hanging anywhere ... but there was no sound of cursing so, after a few minutes, there seemed nothing for it but to start climbing.

The technique that we had settled into over the previous three days involved the leader climbing the steepest pitches without his pack whilst the second followed wearing his and manhandling the leader's whenever it got stuck. Leading was more mentally wearing but seconding involved greater exertion, especially when the going got really steep. And so when I reached the overhang it was little surprise to find myself gasping uncontrollably and gulping in huge lungfulls of spindrift. With strength failing, I clipped into a less than perfect placement. Twice the ice failed and twice I dangled free, marvelling that my heart could beat so fast. Paul had mastered this with precise judgement and stubborn determination:

> The pillar had consisted of soft rotten ice with a fragile crust. Ice screws could be pulled straight out by hand. I was repeatedly engulfed in spindrift. My lungs pumped like bellows and my forearms burnt with real pain. Then, in a white blur, it was over and the angle eased back to classic fifty degree alpine ice slopes.

It was a superb lead and a vital one, which pulled us out of the main dyke section and put us in sight of the summit séracs. Here the ground beside the dyke was more broken and the bivi possibilities were slightly better. There was at least a chance of getting the poles in our little tent – not that this should be read as implying any degree of comfort. We attempted to build up a platform of sorts with loose blocks. To begin with this looked to be working well with a good two-thirds of the tent floor on the ledge. Once we were inside though Paul's end collapsed which meant that his head was some two feet lower than his feet. As I was the other way round this made things more comfortable for me but apparently not so for him. Fortunately my end was so narrow that his turning round wasn't really an option so, to ease his predicament, I promised to stretch my legs (and kick him in the face) only when it was absolutely necessary.

'Can you get a brew on?'

This muffled request came from somewhere below me and seemed not unreasonable. One of the difficulties with the bivis we had experienced so far was that we had not managed to use the stove anywhere near as much as we would have liked. The end result was severe dehydration and all our snack-type foods, that didn't need cooking, consumed already. Only noodles remained ... the prospect of which did not exactly cause the taste buds to over salivate.

Usually we hang the stove from the centre point of the tent. Here the angle of the tent was such that it hung dangerously against the sidewall. Deciding to opt for an easy solution to the problem ('Typical,' I hear my wife say), I lit the stove, wedged my cup between the windshield and the fabric, and got out my Harry Potter book.

I really did feel quite comfortable, indeed cosy. The temperature inside my sleeping bag was just right, there were no bits of rock sticking uncomfortably into me and for the first time on the climb I was bivouacing without half hanging from my harness. I contrasted the situation to the four star hotels I sometimes end up staying in during tax office work – overheated rooms, noisy guests, windows that don't open properly and not even a decent view. I concluded that this accommodation was not at all bad.

Before long disgruntled noises coming from the other end suggested that the undisputed stove and cooking expert of the team was less than impressed with my efforts. It was the globules of molten plastic landing on his sleeping bag that seemed to cause the most distress but the tent filling with foul, acrid smoke didn't go down well either. I had to admit that all was not quite as one might expect at home but, as I pointed out, the end result was remarkably little damage to his sleeping bag, the tent fabric intact and the snow melted. With the only real casualty being my mug, I argued that the main aim of the exercise had been achieved and the effort should be judged a success. But I was dismissed and amidst much squirming, Paul took over stage two of the cooking – noodle production. Meanwhile I returned to the magical happenings at Hogwarts, content that my children would be pleased that I was keeping up.

Our inability to understand a word of written Chinese prompted a few surprises on the food front. Though Paul applied himself magnificently, vindaloo noodles are not to be recommended as high-altitude bivouac food. Maybe it was his inverted position that caused the problems but he seemed to have some difficulty digesting these and complained of his worst night yet. He did though manage an 850ml pee in our calibrated pee bottle – a trip record, which he assured me, was easier to achieve whilst semi-inverted. For my part, I felt relatively comfortable but flapping tent fabric, swishing spindrift and a partner who kept moaning about me kicking him in the face were not exactly conducive to a good night's sleep. I could only manage 650ml.

'Another crap bivouac,' came the jolly wake-up call.

Only one more pitch of ice streak remained, a fact that I felt grateful for as I struggled to overcome early morning lethargy laced with strongly flavoured curry burps.

Above us now was the line of ice cliffs marking the lower edge of the summit icefields. At Base Camp the binoculars had revealed an easy-looking line of weakness but now, as so often happens, things didn't look quite so straightforward. Firstly the line of weakness turned out to be a slanting vertical section on a series of overhanging ice walls. (The fact that it caught the sun when the rest of the wall was in shade had given us a completely false impression.) And secondly the sérac ice itself was truly awful, dinner plating in large uncontrollable sections. Paul set off with gusto but soon ground to a halt.

'It's a nightmare! Are you going to have a look?'

I wasn't, I had great faith in his ability and the problems were all too apparent. Outflanking the ice cliffs on the right was quickly agreed as the best option. But all this was taking time. After abseiling out of the séracs and traversing laboriously rightwards, it was dark again by the time we were struggling up the easier-angled, but iron-hard, sérac ice bounding the right edge of the cliffs.

Paul is an Alaskan veteran who has partaken in the currently fashionable idea of climbing non-stop until you either drop or reach the top. Moreover his faith in my inability to fashion comfortable bivouacs had clearly had an effect and, being a bold young man, he suggested surging on into the night. But I was feeling middle-aged, cold and tired. In true traditionalist form I lectured forth on the dangers of combining exhaustion, darkness and nowhere particular to head for. I won – not so much by reasoned argument but by the fact that the brewing storm suddenly broke with a vengeance, the shallow couloir we had to cross became a torrent of spindrift and further progress was clearly impossible.

The problems with bum-ledge bivouacs in bad weather are numerous, a notable one being that, however careful you are, spindrift rapidly accumulates between the bivi bag and the slope and pushes you off the ledge. Those bits and pieces that inevitably end up at the bottom of the bag then pull the fabric tight against the head for maximum discomfort. The higher the head the greater the pressure on it. A helmet is invaluable in such situations. Here though it was not just the discomfort that was a problem. We were getting increasingly worried about the strength of the tent seams and daren't let anything drop down into the bottom. So to ease the pressure, our boots ended up hanging inside at face level – a face full of snow-packed cleats for a pillow adding memorably to the discomfort level. Despite the fact that we managed to get into our sleeping bags I voted this as the worst night yet on a climb of notably bad nights. Paul still felt that inhaling acrid fumes, having molten plastic dripped on him, vindaloo noodles to eat and being kicked all night whilst being semi-inverted was slightly worse. Either way the weather was such that using the stove was out of the question, so nothing to eat or drink. The night's pee record was only 300ml.

But we were only fifty metres from easy ground and dawn brought shards of blue sky and no precipitation. The way across the exit couloir was open again. We kicked hard to bash blunt crampons into steely blue ice and make toe-screaming progress.

And then suddenly the angle kicked back and our concern changed from the force of the spindrift to the stability of the slope. But luck was with us. Ice cliffs provided secure belays and the cloud burned off to reveal a glorious day. A lot of panting, a short corniced ridge and then we were there – the culmination of all that planning and effort! Siguniang is more than 500 metres higher than any other peak in the immediate area.

The sky was clear and the view vast. Range upon range of untouched snow-covered mountains stretched into the distance. Potential unlimited. Much satisfaction. I sat down, suddenly feeling very tired.

The plan now was to descend the unclimbed North Ridge. Mountaineering textbooks advise against descending unknown terrain and this has to be sound advice. But a traverse (up one route and down another – especially if the descent route is also a new climb) appeals to a mountaineering mind and the North Ridge did look particularly fine. Thankfully the clear weather at least allowed us to locate the top of it. If it had been misty I fear that much summit snowfield wandering would have occurred. As it was, we were soon engrossed in a very different sort of terrain to that we had become accustomed to. The ridge clearly caught the prevailing wind and was decorated with spectacular fragile snow formations. Fortunately, much of it was very steep with the result that we could abseil right through these formations rather than having to try and traverse over them. This had been our reserve objective if the ice streak had gone all wrong, but it would have been a nightmare to ascend.

After six abseils down these baroque encrustations it was time for our next bivouac. It was easy to cut into snow and fashion a gloriously comfortable platform for the tent. Somehow though I felt curiously cold during our evening of non-stop brewing. Our little tent seemed not to be providing quite the degree of protection that I like. Closer inspection revealed that the fabric around the floor seams was now so thin that the wind was blowing straight through! I had to agree with Paul's increasingly persistent comments that it was past its best. I think it fair to say that we too were feeling past ours, as Paul later wrote:

> Mick had convinced me that it would be more rewarding as well as more aesthetic to descend this yet unclimbed ridge that bound our ascent face on the left. Its razor sharp but not quite vertical angle made abseiling difficult. The 1500 metres of descent took two days to get down with giant snow mushrooms and some loose rock thrown in for good measure. Much of the rack

swallowed up and the endless Abalakov anchors required us to shorten one of the ropes considerably ...

At least the halfway bivi was good, even palatial. The tent *almost* fitted the ledge.

Eight days of noodles and not much else made for a lethargic final day of abseiling and a slow return to Base Camp. It also led to a record weight loss and the Ramsden body breaking a personal best by not defecating for twelve days.

Mike and Roger were already at Base Camp. Mike's illness had persisted with the result that their efforts were restricted to exploring and Roger soloing a peak at the head of the valley. It was great to meet fellow humans and feast our eyes on the sight of green grass again.

Wallowing in satisfaction, whilst enjoying a beer at Mr Ma's, I had time to contemplate further. It had been a memorable climb up one of the most stunning features I have ever seen in the big mountains. And we both sensed strongly that all those other mountains visible from the summit had their fair share of secrets waiting to be explored.

There is more to do than one can fit into a lifetime.

POSTSCRIPT

Some time after our return I received an e-mail from the American magazine *Climbing*.

'You and Paul have won our 2002 Mountaineering Golden Piton award for your route on Siguniang.'

It seemed that this was a new American award for the 'most significant mountaineering achievement of the year', something of a US version of the French Piolet D'Or award. This was a strange sensation. An award for going on holiday – excellent! In fact both Paul and I had tended to dismiss such things as meaningless journalism divorced from mainstream mountaineering. Why should we want an award when we climb because we enjoy it and because it is our hobby? But then it's very flattering to be told you have won an award, even one that you didn't realize existed. It changes your view about such things.

'Awards are an excellent idea, great for raising the profile of mountaineering.' I explained to Paul who readily offered wholehearted agreement. But life was to get even more award-laden.

An e-mail from France explained that we had been nominated for the Piolet D'Or award. This award was dreamt up back in 1991 by the magazine *Montagnes* in conjunction with the Groupe de Haute Montagne the French elite group of active alpinists. By 2003 the award had become well known throughout mountaineering circles but I had never really paid that much attention to it and had the impression that the sort of routes that I did weren't Golden Ice-Axe-type contenders. But fashions change. The e-mail continued:

'The presentation will be in Paris and we will arrange accommodation for you and your girls.'

'Perhaps the girls are all part of the award,' suggested Paul.

Reading between the lines it didn't seem that we had a hope in hell of winning but Nicki, who is not overly troubled by political correctitude, was very flattered to be referred to as a 'girl' and it would be churlish to decline an invitation to spend three days with our 'girls' in Paris. I had never been before and with such summits as the Eiffel Tower on offer it just had to be done.

'Hang on – what's this here?'

Paul was pointing to a passage further on in the e-mail.

'Send your DVD for your presentation to the judges.'

'DVD!!'

We collapsed laughing together. It was all we could do to take as many one-handed still photographs as we could. The thought of trying to produce movie film whilst belaying in a spindrift-laden couloir filled us with horror. But what was expected from us in Paris? Would a modest slide presentation appear hopelessly unprofessional and outdated?

Manu at *Montagnes* had helpfully e-mailed details of the other short-listed teams and we looked down them with interest.

'Richard Cross and Jules Cartwright on Ama Dablam.'

'Amazing ascent – eleven days out in pure alpine-style. Think they might be DVD boys?' asked Paul.

I thought back to Changabang and remembered going so far as to leave the tent behind on day eleven. Any movie camera would have gone well before that.

'Can't imagine it – but look, Dean Potter's going to be in with even more of a problem.'

Dean Potter, from the United States, was nominated for a trilogy of wild solos in Patagonia. The possibility of a self-filmed DVD looked slim indeed. We couldn't help but sympathise with his predicament.

'You will give a twenty-minute presentation to the judges,' continued the e-mail.

Discussing how a solo climber with no support might do this kept us occupied for some time.

And so, in February, the nominated teams arrived in Paris.

At the last moment we were told that time constraints were such that everyone should limit themselves to ten slides. Whilst Jean Christopher Lafaille and Alberto Inurrategi, the favourites, started with a mega professional DVD on their lung-bursting *aller-retour* on Annapurna the rest of us held slides up to the dim lights trying to choose ten that best summed up our respective climbs. The covers of both the press release literature and *Montagnes* featured the Annapurna climb and the clear impression was that the outcome had already been decided. Nevertheless each team hyped their climb for fifteen minutes or so, underwent some questioning by the judging panel, and then retired to await the outcome.

The afternoon blended into evening via a rather pleasant champagne reception and by the time the gathering audience moved in to an imposing 700-seater, three-tier, auditorium, Paul and I were getting quite keen on the concept of climbing awards.

To our amazement the place was full. Holding up slides to dim light bulbs behind the scenes seemed a million miles away now. This was clearly organised as a big do and Paul, his wife Mary, Nicki and I settled down discreetly a few rows from the front.

All nominees were required to appear in turn on stage and answer some questions about their climb. A microphone was thrust into my hand.

'Told you it would be more stressful than the climb,' whispered Paul.

Soon we were struggling vainly to give interesting answers to haltingly interpreted questions such as: 'Who lost the most weight?'

My answer that 'Paul did but he had more to start with' doubtless gave the audience a deep insight into the finer detail of the Siguniang climb.

We fidgeted nervously. It's amazing how aware you become of your hands in such situations. For near on half an hour Paul and I stood trying not to pick our noses or scratch our privates whilst in the glare of the spotlights in front of 700 people.

Eventually the moment came. Catherine Destivelle, darling of the French outdoor public, came to the stage and Paul Braithwaite, chair of the judges, stood forward to announce the winner.

'The award this year goes to … Mick Fowler and Paul Ramsden … for their climb on Siguniang.'

And so we got a Golden Ice-Axe and a kiss from Catherine.

Then we all went out and were refused entry to the Buddha Bar because of improper dress. It wouldn't happen after the Oscars. There's hope for climbing yet!

Climbing Record

Symbols used: * new climb, *w first winter ascent, *f first free ascent of a previously aided line, *wt first ascents on Dover cliffs using winter techniques and equipment, # alpine-style ascent of route in the greater ranges. (*Editor's Note:* This is an abridged list with many British rock and ice first ascents left out).

1964/69 Harrisons Rocks visits and mountain walks with George Fowler (father) including: Snowdon Horseshoe (1965), Scafell Pike via Skew Gill and Curved Ridge, Buachaille Etive Mor (1966), Lords Rake, Scafell w (1967); Pinnacle Ridge, Sgurr nan Gillean (1968). Austrian Alpine Club course: Wildspitze, Zuckerhütl etc (1969).

1970/71 Early rock and alpine climbs (George Fowler): Western Gully, Dinas Mot, Ordinary Route, Idwal Slabs. Bishorn, Rimpfischhorn (1970) – our first unguided 4000m peaks – GF having been guided on the Allalinhorn in 1950. Lagginhorn, Weissmies (1971).

1972 YHA Pen-y-Pass climbing course – Munich Climb (led by Bill Harrison). Little Chamonix and Soapgut (early leads with George Fowler) having seconded Soapgut on the YHA course. Mont Blanc de Cheilon, Mt. Velan (George Fowler).

1973 YHA Pen-y-Pass climbing course: The Mole, Cenotaph Corner (with Bill Harrison and Pete Macdonald). Corvus, Ardus and Fisher's Folly – first VS lead (George Fowler).

1974 S.W. Corner, Harrison's Rocks – first 6a (*tr*). Cenotaph Corner – first extreme lead – and Vector (John Miller). Dent Blanche, Zinal Rothorn (George Fowler).

1975 Numerous extremes in Lakes and Wales. First visits to Peak and Devon (Moonraker – Mike Morrison and John Stevenson).

1976 Hate (solo – 6a) Bowles Rocks. First winter visit to Scotland: Crowberry Gully w (Mike Morrison, John Stevenson, Geraldine Taylor). Prayer Mat, Blackchurch (believed, wrongly, to be first new route). Cecchinel/Nominé, Mont Blanc (Howard Crumpton). Linden* Curbar (Mike Morrison, John Stevenson).

1977 The Curtain, Ben Nevis (Phill Thomas). Stairway to Heaven* Blaven and Titan's Wall*f Ben Nevis (Phill Thomas). Eckpfeiler variations* Mont Blanc (Phill Thomas).

1978 Cascade*w Craig Rheadr (Phill Thomas) first new winter route in Wales. Ludwig* and Paddington* (Mike Morrison), The Missionary (Phill Thomas) * and Heart of Gold* (Stevie Haston / Phill Thomas), Craig Gogarth. Dent d'Herens, North Face (Mike Morrison). Attempt on Eigerwand (Mike Morrison).

1979 Central Icefall*w Craig Rheadr, Silver Machine*w (Chris Griffiths) and Jubilee Climb*w (Mike Morrison), Clogwyn Du'r Arddu. Shield Direct*w Ben Nevis (Victor Saunders). Spreadeagle* Cl. Du'r Arddu (Phill Thomas). Breakaway* N. Devon (Mike Morrison), Depth Charge• Berry Head (Arnis Strapcans). Walker Spur (Phill Thomas).

1980 Stone Bridge* Pembroke (Brian Wyvill). Crowley's Crack* Beachy Head (Mike Morrison, Brian Wyvill) – first rock climb on chalk. Eigerwand (Mike Morrison).

1981 Sheet Whitening*w Applecross (Mark Lynden, Simon Fenwick). Stone*f Sron Ulladale, Isle of Harris (Andy Meyers). Dry Ice *wt Dover – first 'winter techniques' route on chalk cliffs. Matterhorn North Face (Mike Morrison).

1982 Death Trap* South Stack, Anglesey (Alan Baker). Caveman* Berry Head (Andy Meyers). Monster Crack* Beachy Head (Chris Watts, Mike Morrison). Taulliraju South Face*# *Peru.* (Chris Watts).

1983 Fly Direct*w Creagh Meaghaidh (Victor Saunders). Albino* Beachy Head (Lois Cole). Western Gully* Kilimanjaro (Caradoc Jones).

1984 Great Overhanging Gully*w Applecross (Phil Butler). Helmet Boiler* Gogarth (Victor Saunders). Bojohagur attempt, *Pakistan* (Chris Watts) – first visit to Himalaya.

1985 Colonial Virgin*w Central Wales (Bruce Craig). Illegal Alien* Cornwall (Bruce Craig). Dru Couloir (Caradoc Jones).

1986 Icicle Factory*w Skye (Victor Saunders). Cumbrian, Eskdale (Victor Saunders). Ushba West Face* Caucasus, *CIS* (Victor Saunders).

1987 West Central Gully*w Ben Eighe (Mike Morrison). Old Harry* Swanage Chalk (Mark Lynden, Chris Newcombe). Golden Pillar of Spantik*# *Pakistan* (Victor Saunders).

1988 Against All Odds*w Glencoe (Chris Watts). Big John* St Johns Head, Hoy (Jon Lincoln). Delone North Face (solo) Altai Range, *Siberia*.

1989 Houdini*wt Dover (Mark Lynden). Clo Mhor Crack* Cape Wrath (Chris Watts). Attempt on Cerro Kishtwar# *India* (Mike Morrison).

1990 Sunday Sport* Beachy Head (Frank Ramsay, Steve Sustad). Ak-su North-West Ridge, *Kyrgyzstan*# (Chris Watts).

1991 Tubular Bells*w Achnashellach (Dave Wills). Reffell Route* *Gibralter* (Duncan Tunstall). Hunza Pk*# Bublimoting and Ultar S. Ridge attempt *Pakistan* (Caradoc Jones).

1992 The Spindle* and other stacks, Shetland (Caradoc Jones, Andy Nisbet, Chris Watts).

1993 Some Like it Hot*wt Dover (Caradoc Jones). Liver Bird* Mingulay (Chris Bonington). Cerro Kishtwar NW Face/N Buttress*# *India* (Steve Sustad).

1994 Triple Echo*w Applecross (Steve Sustad).

1995 Exiguous Gully*w Skye (Andy Cave). The Urge* Cornwall (Mike Morrison). Taweche North-East Pillar*# *Nepal* (Pat Littlejohn).

1996 The Main Course* Skye (Steve Sustad), Beriberi* Hoy (Caradoc Jones).

1997 Changabang N Face*# *India* (Steve Sustad, with Andy Cave and Brendan Murphy on descent when Murphy was swept away in an avalanche).

1998 Cima Ovest, Cassin Route (Mike Morrison). Siula Chico, W. Face attempt *Peru* (Simon Yates).

1999 Whispering Wall* Skye (Paul Ramsden). Arwa Tower, North-West Face* *India* (Steve Sustad). Codfather* Lofoten Islands, *Norway* (Mark Garthwaite).

2000 Storr Gully*w Skye (Paul Ramsden). Mount Kennedy, North Buttress #* Yukon, *Canada* (Andy Cave).

2001 Peak 43 attempt, Nepal (Paul Ramsden).

2002 Foul Cave Route* Bempton, Yorkshire (Andy Cave). Siguniang North Face*# Sichuan, *China* (Paul Ramsden).

2003 Mount Grosvenor attempt#, Daxue Shan, *China* (Andy Cave).

2004 Wild Whoop Gully*w Skye (Peta Watts). Devil's Appendix w Cwm Idwal, Wales.

2005 Route 68 Direct*w Clogwyn D'ur Arddu, Wales (Paul Ramsden). Gemini w Ben Nevis (Chris Watts).

INDEX

HIMALAYA ALPINE-STYLE

The most challenging routes on the highest peaks

Andy Fanshawe and Stephen Venables

Lightweight attempts on Himalayan peaks have always been evident from Longstaff, the Schlaginweits and Kellas etc prior to WW1, Bauer, Roche, Smythe and Shipton in the interwar years and the growing confidence in the fifty post-war years, starting with the dazzling Broad Peak ascent in 1958 and gathering pace as equipment, clothing and food improved. This magnificent large-format book gives an informed overview of this evolving scene describing forty of the finest climbs of this ilk. The book has become a bible for innovative mountaineers, playing a large part in the growth of alpine-style activity in recent years. Winner of the Grand Prize at Banff.

290 x 280mm   hardback/jacketed   200 colour photos 50 maps and diagrams
Baton Wicks 1-898573-39-5   £30   The Mountaineers (US) 0-89886-456-9

SHISHA PANGMA

The alpine-style first ascent of the South-West Face

Doug Scott and Alex MacIntyre

The ascent of the greatest face of a superb 8027m peak was a stunning demonstration of what was possible. This edition has been improved by the addition of colour photographs (showing the complexities of the summits) and tables of ascentionists. This was one of the first expeditions allowed into Tibet after the Chinese takeover and the book describes the social, cultural and religious impact of the occupation. First winner of the Boardman/Tasker Literary Award (two winners that year the other being *Living High*).

230 x 150mm   tpbk(f)   18 colour photos   58 b/w photos   6 maps and diagrams
Baton Wicks 1-898573-36-0   £12.99   The Mountaineers (US) 0-89886-723-1 $19.95

CONQUISTADORS OF THE USELESS

by Lionel Terray

Terray's classic is valuable as it describes first ascents of all types: the heavyweight Annapurna and Makalu ascents (1950/1954); FitzRoy (1952) with its use of snow holes; various Andean climbs in the alpine-style idiom; Jannu and Mount Huntington (1962/1964), both of which displayed a hybrid expedition/alpine-style approach.

230 x 150mm   tpbk   69 b/w photos   8 maps and diagrams
Baton Wicks (UK) 1-898573-38-7   £10.99   The Mountaineers (US) 0-89886-778-9